Royal Statistical Society Lecture Note Series

SERIES EDITORS

JOHN B. COPAS   RICHARD L. SMITH

Royal Statistical Society Lecture Note Series

Interpreting Crime Statistics

Edited by

MONICA A. WALKER

Research Fellow, Centre for Criminological and Legal Research
University of Sheffield

CLARENDON PRESS • OXFORD
1995

Oxford University Press, Walton Street, Oxford OX2 6DP

Oxford   New York
Athens   Auckland   Bangkok   Bombay
Calcutta   Cape Town   Dar es Salaam   Delhi
Florence   Hong Kong   Istanbul   Karachi
Kuala Lumpur   Madras   Madrid   Melbourne
Mexico City   Nairobi   Paris   Singapore
Taipei   Tokyo   Toronto
and associated companies in
Berlin   Ibadan

Oxford is a trade mark by Oxford University Press

Published in the United States
by Oxford University Press Inc., New York

A catalogue record for this book is available from the British Library

Library of Congress Cataloging in Publication Data
Interpreting crime statistics / edited by Monica A. Walker.
(Royal Statistical Society lecture notes series)
1. Criminal statistics – Great Britain. 2. Criminal justice,
Administration of – Great Britain – Statistical services. I. Walker,
Monica A. II. Series.
HV6946. I57 1995   364.941–dc20   94–32492
ISBN 0 19 852306 8

Typeset by EXPO Holdings, Malaysia

Printed in Great Britain by
Biddles Ltd,
Guildford & King's Lynn

Preface

The purpose of this monograph is to explore the statistics that are published (or are easily accessible) relating to certain aspects of crime, criminals, and the criminal justice system in England and Wales. The bases of the statistics are described, together with problems of their interpretation, and what can (or cannot) be inferred from them. Besides this, certain specific topics are investigated.

Overall, it is expected that the volume will be of interest to all those involved in aspects of the criminal justice system such as the police, the courts, sentencing, the Probation Service and the prisons. It should also be of particular value to criminologists, sociologists, teachers and students of criminology, and research workers in this field.

The volume illustrates the need for clarity as to the meaning and limitations of statistical data and the statistical techniques involved, and the importance of understanding the processes which give rise to the final tabulations. Although the topics discussed are all related to 'crime' in this country there are undoubtedly analogous problems in other areas where published statistics are used, such as employment, education, and medicine, and also in the criminal statistics produced in other countries.

I wish to thank my colleague, Tony Jefferson, and the series editor, John Copas for their advice and support. I am greatly indebted to Lilian Bloodworth for her secretarial assistance. I also wish to thank all the contributors for their collaboration in this project.

Sheffield   M. A. W
May 1994

Contents

Contributors

Natalie Aye Maung is a Senior Research Officer at the Home Office Research and Planning Unit. Prior to this, she worked for Social and Community Planning Research, an independent survey research organization.

Keith Bottomley is Professor of Criminology and Director of the Centre for Criminology and Criminal Justice at the University of Hull. He is the author or co-author of several books on criminology and criminal justice including *Decisions in the Penal Process* (Martin Robertson, 1973), *Criminology in Focus* (Martin Robertson, 1979), *Understanding Crime Rates* (Gower, 1981), *Crime and Punishment: Interpreting the Data* (Open University, 1986) and *From Custody to Community: Throughcare for Young Offenders* (Avebury, 1992).

Clive Coleman is a Lecturer in Criminology in the Centre for Criminology and Criminal Justice at the University of Hull. He is the co-author of *Understanding Crime Rates* (Gower, 1981) and *The Impact of PACE* (University of Hull, 1991).

John Copas is Professor of Statistics at the University of Warwick and has published extensively in both theoretical and applied statistics. His work on the methodology of risk assessment includes several papers on a theory of shrinkage of statistical predictors, for which he has been awarded the Royal Statistical Society's Guy Silver Medal. He has collaborated widely on applications of statistics to criminology.

John Ditchfield is a Principal Research Officer in the Home Office Research and Planning Unit. He has been chiefly concerned with prisons and has researched and written about the prison disciplinary and grievance systems as well as the way in which control is maintained in establishments. More recently, he has been involved with the redevelopment of the reconviction prediction score (RPS) which is described in Chapter 7.

Marian FitzGerald is currently a Principal Research Officer in the Home Office Research and Planning Unit where she has special responsibility for work on 'race relations'/'race' equality issues generally, and for criminal justice research related to this. She previously worked as a freelance researcher. Her publications have covered 'race' and politics, 'race relations' policies in local government and racial harassment as well as 'race' and criminal justice issues.

Carol Hedderman is a Principal Research Officer in the Home Office Research and Planning Unit. Her current projects include an examination of remanding and sentencing decisions in relation to women offenders, and the assessment and treatment of mentally disordered offenders.

Jean Hine is Research and Information Officer with Derbyshire Probation Service. She has worked in Research and Information in the Probation Service since 1974, during which time she has regularly been involved with both the production and the use of probation statistics. She has been a member of the Home Office Statistics Working Group and has recently worked with the Home Office in developing a new offence classification system. She has a particular interest in community service orders and undertook a major national study of community service orders for the Home Office in 1988–90.

Rod Morgan is Professor of Criminal Justice and Dean of Law at the University of Bristol. He was an assessor to Lord Justice Woolf's Inquiry into the Strangeways riot in 1990. He has written widely on many aspects of criminal justice and has most recently co-edited *The Oxford Handbook of Criminology* (OUP, 1994) and *The Politics of Sentencing Reform* (OUP, 1994).

Monica Walker is a Research Fellow at the Centre for Criminological and Legal Research in the University of Sheffield. She was formerly a lecturer in statistics in the University of London. She has assisted in many research projects and was author of a volume entitled '*Crime*' in a Series of Reviews of United Kingdom Statistical Sources, (Pergamon, 1981).

Philip White is a statistician in the Home Office Research and Statistics Department. His current responsibilities include the statistics of homicide, but he works with a range of police statistics, including firearms offences. He has for some years been involved in the design and conduct of statistical enquiries, including social surveys, and was part of the team responsible for the 1991 census.

Abbreviations

ADP	Average daily population in prison
BCS	British Crime Survey
CJA	Criminal Justice Act
CPS	Crown Prosecution Service
CS	*Criminal Statistics*
CS,ST	*Criminal Statistics, Supplementary Tables*
CSO	Community service order
HMCIP	Her Majesty's Chief Inspector of Prisons
HOSB	Home Office Statistical Bulletin
LCD	Lord Chancellor's Department
LFS	Labour Force Survey
LRC	Local Review Committee
NACRO	National Association for the Care and Rehabilitation of Offenders
NFA	No further action
OPCS	Office of Population, Censuses and Surveys
PACE	Police and Criminal Evidence Act, 1984
PS	*Prison Statistics*
ROR	Risk of reconvinction
RPS	Reconviction prediction score
TDA/	Taking and driving away/
TWOC	Taking a vehicle without the owner's consent

Note   *Criminal Statistics England and Wales, Probation Statistics* and *Prison Statistics*, published annually by the Home Office, are referred to in the text by the date of the statistics included, rather than the year of publication.

Home Office Statistical Bulletins (HOSB) are referred to by number/date. These can be obtained from the Research and Statistics Department, Home Office, 50 Queen Anne's Gate, London SW1H 9AT.

Queries regarding Home Office statistics and further information available should be addressed to the same department.

1 Introduction

MONICA WALKER

The purpose of this monograph is to provide a starting point for anyone who wishes to understand the statistics of certain aspects of the criminal justice system in England and Wales. There has been a great expansion in the amount of statistical material published in the last ten years or so, but it is surprising to find that it is often quite difficult to understand exactly what the tables mean, to find out exactly what one wants to know, and to interpret the changes over the years (for example). The volume is divided into two parts: Chapters 2 to 7 each discuss a different aspect of the published statistics, while Chapters 8 to 12 are devoted to selected topics.

In Chapters 2 and 3 I have examined the basis of the two main types of data published in the Home Office annual publication *Criminal Statistics* – the recorded offences, and the outcome of court proceedings. We are here concerned with problems of interpretation rather than the substantive meaning of the statistics. Some years ago I investigated the sources of criminal statistics, giving details of where the statistics came from, who filled in the relevant forms, what information was available, how the statistics were affected by legislation, and problems of interpreting the tables (Walker, 1981; see also Walker 1983). Some of this material is still relevant but much more information is now collected and published. Besides this, much more is known about the processes leading up to the final tables, and there is greater awareness of the factors affecting them.

In Chapter 2 the way the offences are classified and counted is described; it is now widely realized that only a small proportion of the crimes that occur are recorded, but nevertheless the figures are widely publicized, and usually taken at their face value. Data obtained from the British Crime Survey (Mayhew *et al.*, 1992) shows that only about a third of certain offences are recorded by the police. These offences, which are those with personal or household victims, make up about half of all notifiable offences; information on other offences is more difficult to obtain.

In Chapter 3 cautions, prosecutions and offenders are discussed. The tables on court proceedings are shown to be quite difficult to interpret, and it should be realized that they say more about the *end point* of the proceedings than the processes leading up to them, which cannot easily be summarized. (Pleas, and their outcome, for example, are not discussed in detail.) The information on *offenders*, those cautioned or convicted, is discussed only briefly here. It should be borne in mind, here and throughout the volume, that convictions are obtained for only a small proportion of recorded offences – and an even smaller proportion of all those that occur. Barclay (1993), has estimated that only about 2 per cent of those offences included in the British Crime Survey result in a conviction.

In Chapter 4 Keith Bottomley and Clive Coleman describe the role of the police in the recording of crime and also present and discuss the statistics now available as a result of PACE. Jean Hine, in Chapter 5, examines and discusses the statistics of the Probation Service, with particular reference to community penalties, while Rod Morgan, in Chapter 6, carries out a detailed study of the many facets of prison statistics. Finally, in this section, John Ditchfield provides a review of the development of parole, and describes the use of scores for selection for parole.

In the second part of the volume selected topics are discussed. In Chapter 8 the statistics of homicide are described by Philip White. This is a topic of general interest in this country and, partly on account of the relatively small numbers involved, the Home Office is able to collect and analyse the data in considerable detail, covering the outcome of court proceedings (where these take place), and details of the offences which are not normally available for other offences. It would probably not be feasible to collect and publish so much detail about all other offences, but this would be of considerable interest, if it could be undertaken.

Chapters 9 and 10 deal with gender and race, by Carol Hedderman and Marian FitzGerald respectively. The importance of these topics is illustrated by the fact that the Criminal Justice Act, 1991 spelt out (in section 95) that data should be published that would assist in avoiding discrimination on the grounds of race or sex. The statistics alone cannot show if there is discrimination, but this should help to bring about an increased awareness of the problem and the need for research in this area. These chapters examine some of the statistics available, and the problems of interpreting them. They also give references which should be useful as a guide to further research.

Prediction methods have been used in criminal justice in relation to parole in the United States since about 1928. There have been many developments since then, and in Chapter 11 John Copas reviews these and discusses in detail the statistical models available and the assumptions underlying them. He examines survival models which have been developed to enable more accurate predictions of offending behaviour during the licence period on parole. He also describes the derivation of a prediction equation to assist the Probation Service in the preparation of reports.

In the final chapter Natalie Aye Maung discusses the methodology underlying the British Crime Survey. This survey has become an important source of information about the numbers of offences with personal or household victims, attitudes to crime, and other related matters. She describes the sampling methods used and the problems of questionnaire design in the context of victim surveys. This will be particularly useful for anyone wishing to undertake this type of survey. The survey has been of value in showing the extent of the under-recording of crime, as described in Chapter 2. However, it has to be remembered that the survey results are also subject to various types of error, and trends in the numbers of offences may also be subject to influences that cannot be easily measured, such as a greater awareness of being victimized.

It was decided not to attempt to include in this monograph detailed international comparisons. The complexities of the statistics of other countries are no doubt as great as those of this country, and are often based on different criminal justice systems. In Chapter 6 Rod Morgan discusses some of the difficulties of making these comparisons in relation to incarceration rates. Even homicide statistics (Chapter 8) are probably not comparable, owing to problems of definition.

One problem with this type of monograph is that the statistics quoted are out of date even before it is published. However this is not so important in the present context, as the aim is to explore the underlying problems of interpretation rather than the substantive meaning. On-going legislation makes it impossible to be up to date. Each contributor has referred to the latest statistics available at the time of writing.

It should be remembered throughout that each 'statistic'–the record of every person or event – is the end point of a process depending on observations, perceptions, judgements, decisions, conventions, policy, rules, laws, and actions. This gives them, inevitably, a subjective dimension, and renders them relative to time and place. However, while not as objective and absolute as some would wish, the tabulations do give a starting point for investigating what is happening in society, in relation to this important area. There has been awareness of the problems of interpreting criminal statistics for many years. Morrison, for example, published an article (followed by a discussion) in 1897. It is to be hoped we now have a greater understanding of the problems.

Research on every topic covered here (and many others) is frequently published, and it has not been feasible, or appropriate, to refer to this research exhaustively. Those interested should refer to Home Office Statistical Bulletins, research studies published by the Home Office Research and Planning Unit, and journals such as the *Criminal Law Review, The British Journal of Criminology*, and *The Howard Journal*.

REFERENCES

Barclay, G. (1993). *Digest 2: Information on the Criminal Justice System in England and Wales*. Home Office Research and Statistics Department, London.

Mayhew, P., Aye Maung, N., and Mirlees-Black, C. (1992). *The 1991 British Crime Survey*. Home Office Research Study 132, HMSO, London.

Morrison W.D. (1897) The interpretation of criminal statistics. *Journal of the Royal Statistical Society*, LX, 1–24.

Walker, M. A. (1981). *Reviews of United Kingdom Statistical Sources Vol. XV: Crime*. Pergamon, Oxford.

Walker, M. A. (1983). Some problems in interpreting statistics relating to crime. *Journal of the Royal Statistical Society*, **146**, 281–93.

2 Statistics of offences

MONICA WALKER

INTRODUCTION

There are two main sources of data on offences committed in England and Wales. The most detailed are those recorded by the police and published regularly by the Home Office: half-yearly in Statistical Bulletins (HOSB), annually in *Criminal Statistics* and in the *Digest of Information on the Criminal Justice System* (e.g. Barclay 1993). These give the numbers of what are called 'notifiable offences' of about 70 types, summarized in eight offence groups.

Secondly, there are surveys of the general public and in particular the British Crime Survey (BCS). This gives statistics based on the reports by individual victims of certain offences committed against them. It has been estimated that under half of these offences are recorded by the police. The police statistics thus under-estimate the amount of crime committed. Using the BCS figures it is now possible to assess whether some of the increases in recorded crime are in fact actual increases or due to changes in reporting or recording.

Annual reports by certain government bodies, such as the Board of Inland Revenue, H. M. Customs and Excise, and the Health and Safety Executive give details of offences recorded by them and how they are dealt with. Also British Transport Police record the number of offences committed on British Rail property. For all these offences only the numbers prosecuted are recorded in Home Office *Criminal Statistics*.

However, there is a considerable amount of crime that does not get included in published statistics. Many studies have shown that there is a vast amount of crime carried out which is not recorded for various reasons. Within 'property crime', theft from the workplace, for example, is thought to be rife, and sometimes condoned by the employers in that it would not be feasible, or acceptable to the workers, to monitor or discipline these offences (see Mars 1982). The defrauding of insurance companies by making false claims is considerable and it has been estimated that credit card fraud alone accounted for £165 million pounds in 1992 (the *Observer*, 11 April 1993). Business fraud is also carried out on a large scale, with a few well-known cases running to millions of pounds. Frequently offences of fraud are only known about some time after their occurrence, and the detection and prosecution of the offenders is complex (see Levi 1993 for example). The victims are often members of the general public who are cheated of their dividends or pension rights and may not even be aware of it.

This chapter concentrates on recorded notifiable offences, focusing on how these data are defined and collected, together with some comparisons with the BCS and trends since 1981. Offences which are not notifiable will be briefly discussed, and also the very large number of motoring offences. The statistics prior to 1971 are not comparable for various reasons, and will not be described in detail. However, *Crime in England and Wales* (McClintock and Avison 1968) gives an overview of crime statistics since 1900, and discusses in detail crime statistics for 1955 to 1965; N. Walker (1988) also gives a useful historical survey. Walker (1981) is a source book of crime statistics, although some of this material has now been superseded.

CLASSES OF OFFENCES

Notifiable offences

The Home Office publishes annually in *Criminal Statistics* and half-yearly in Statistical Bulletins (e.g. HOSB 3/93 for 1992 statistics) the number of so-called 'notifiable offences' recorded by the police in England and Wales. This has risen fairly steadily from 1.7 million in 1971 to 5.1 million in 1991. Adjustments for the size of the resident population produces only minor changes in the rate of increase. In 1971, for example, the number per 1000 population was 3.4, and in 1991 it was 10.0, a factor of 2.9 compared with a factor of 3.0 in the actual numbers. Adjustments for changes in the age structure of the population have also been shown to make little difference but, in any case, such figures can only be based on the ages of *known* offenders, which may differ from those of actual offenders. The method of counting the offences is described below.

Those offences which are defined as 'notifiable' are listed in an appendix to *Criminal Statistics* and are mainly indictable, that is, they can be or have to be tried by a judge and jury. A few notifiable offences are now summary, and can only be tried in the magistrates' courts. In particular all criminal damage is notifiable, although if the value is less than a specified amount (see p. 19) it is generally treated as a summary offence. The only offences relating to motor vehicles which are notifiable are 'causing death by reckless driving',[1] 'theft from a motor vehicle', and 'theft or unauthorized taking of a motor vehicle'. There are about 70 notifiable offences (numbered between 1 and 99) and these are classified into eight main groups as follows (the figures in brackets refer to the percentage in each group in 1991): violence against the person (4 per cent), sexual offences (0.7 per cent), burglary (23 per cent), robbery (0.9 percent), theft and handling (52 per cent), fraud and forgery (3 per cent), criminal damage (16 per cent), and 'other' (0.7 per cent). The distributions for 1971, 1981, and 1991 are given in Table 2.1. The specific offences in each group are listed in an appendix to *Criminal Statistics*, where changes over recent years in legislation, definitions, and methods of counting offences are also given. These changes mean, in particular, that the 1971 figures are not strictly comparable with later years.

Non-notifiable offences

Offences which are not notifiable fall into two groups: motoring offences (which may be summary or indictable) and 'other summary offences'. 'Other summary offences'

---

[1] Now 'dangerous', see p. 7 and p.21.

Table 2.1. Distribution of notifiable offences in 1971, 1981, and 1991

| | 1971 | | 1981 | | 1991 | |
	000s	%	000s	%	000s	%
Violence	47	2.8	100	3.4	190	3.6
Sex	24	1.4	19	0.7	29	0.6
Burglary	452	27.1	718	24.2	1 219	23.1
Robbery	8	0.5	20	0.7	45	0.9
Theft	1 004	60.3	1 603	54.1	2 761	52.3
Fraud	100	6.0	107	3.6	175	3.3
Damage	27	1.6	387	13.0	821	15.6
Other	6	0.4	9	0.3	35	0.7
Total	1 666	100.0	2 964	100.0	5 276	100.0

Note: There were some changes in the counting rules in 1980, and there were other changes which make the figures for 1971 not comparable with later figures (see text and *CS 1980*, Appendix). In particular, the 1971 figures for damage excludes offences of value £100 and under, which are included for 1981 and 1991.

are almost entirely dealt with in the magistrates' courts. A record of the numbers of these offences is not made by the police and can only be estimated from the tables giving the numbers of people cautioned or convicted of them (described in Chapter 3). These give the number of offenders but not the numbers of offences, and there may be more than one offence per offender.

In 1991, 450 000 persons were convicted of summary non-motoring offences and 100 000 were cautioned. For comparison, 340 000 persons were convicted of indictable offences and 180 000 cautioned.

Motoring offences

There were over 8 million offences related to motoring dealt with by the police in 1991. Some of these resulted in prosecutions and for others written warnings, etc. were issued. Details are given in 'Motoring Offences' (e.g. HOSB 34/93) and the related supplementary tables, which give the results of court proceedings for each offence. The method of counting these is different from those above and is described below (p. 20).

Standard list offences

These consist of all notifiable offences, plus certain summary offences, such as assault on a constable and motoring offences tried in the Crown Court (see Appendix 4, *Criminal Statistics 1991* for list of offences). All criminal damage is included (even if of low value) but drink driving and speeding are excluded. So although 'standard list' offences are, in general, regarded as 'serious' this is not necessarily the case; and some offences which are serious are excluded.

This group is the basis of the Offenders' Index (see Chapter 3) and is used mainly for research purposes; the reasons for the offences included are mainly historical and have been left unchanged to maintain continuity.

LEGISLATION

Offences are defined as such in accordance with either common or statute law, and are classified by standards laid down by the Home Office. Common law offences (which include murder and robbery) have been accepted by precedent, according to decisions of judges in courts of law, often in earlier centuries.

Statute law is continually changing. That on personal crimes refers back to the Offences against the Person Act, 1861. The Theft Act, 1968, redefined and reclassified a large number of offences against property, some of which were anachronistic (e.g. theft by a servant). Offences which could or had to be tried in the higher courts (formerly the Assizes and Quarter Sessions, which were replaced by the Crown Court in 1972) were all called indictable and are the basis of the current list of notifiable offences. McClintock and Avison (1968) sheds light on the earlier classification. The appendices to Walker (1981) give details of changes in legislation, classification, etc. up to and including 1977.

The Criminal Law Act, 1977 introduced many changes regarding the classification of offences. As a result, offences were then reclassified as being indictable only, summary, or triable-either-way. The latter are tried in the magistrates' courts unless the magistrate declines jurisdiction or the defendant elects for Crown Court trial. *Criminal Statistics 1992* Appendix 4 identifies triable-either-way offences in the list of indictable offences. These changes in definition caused several discontinuities in the statistics and *Criminal Statistics* has incorporated several adjustments into its tables of offences. The result is that statistics up to and including 1977 are not strictly comparable with the later ones.

There have been several other changes in the law which, while important in themselves, have not greatly affected the statistics. Two examples are those relating to homosexual offences and abortion (the first is classified in the sex offences group and the second as an 'offence against the person'). There have also been changes in motoring offences, such as that from 'dangerous driving' to 'reckless driving' in the Criminal Law Act, 1977 (the latter being harder to prove). This has now been changed back (Road Traffic Act, 1991). 'Causing death by dangerous driving' was an offence first defined in 1956; it had previously been incorporated with manslaughter, but it was thought not to be acceptable for 'respectable' people, with no criminal intent, to be convicted of manslaughter. It has tended to receive lesser penalties (see p. 134).

Since 1981 the two major pieces of relevant legislation affecting these statistics have been the Criminal Justice Act, 1982 and the Criminal Justice Act, 1988. Under the 1982 Act, from the beginning of 1983 'gross indecency with a child' and 'trafficking in controlled drugs' became notifiable, the former classified under 'sex offences' and the latter included in 'other offences'. Other sections of these Acts referred to venue of trial and sentencing, and are discussed in Chapter 3. The Race

Relations Acts (1965, 1968 and 1976) introduced offences of racial discrimination. The Criminal Justice Act, 1991 has not affected the classification of offences.

THE RECORDING, CLASSIFICATION, AND COUNTING OF OFFENCES

Recording

When a notifiable offence is reported to the police, they will classify it and record it on a 'crime report form' although more often, these days, details are entered on a computer straight away. They will record details of the offence such as time, place, circumstances, value of property stolen, degree of injury, and so on; also some details of the victim (if any) and of possible suspects. Most of this material is for internal use by the local police. Monthly returns are made to the Home Office, giving the total number of offences in each offence group, and the value of property stolen. Offences involving firearms are reported individually, as are all homicides. The classification made at that time is not generally changed as a result of other information or as a result of court proceedings except for homicide (see Chapter 8 below). In court proceedings the charge (which may not be the same as the offence first recorded) for which a person is proceeded against can be reduced but not increased, so there may be a tendency for the police initially to record a more serious offence than the case warrants. Besides this, the offence for which a person is dealt with in the magistrates' courts, and for which he is committed to the Crown Court for trial, may have a different (less serious) classification when it is finally dealt with there (see Chapter 3). The figures for court proceedings may give an indication of the change in classification (e.g. from robbery to theft).

If an offence is later found not to have occurred at all – for example if an article recorded as stolen has been found – it will be written off as 'no crime'. (However, the 'victim' may not trouble to tell the police, in which case it would stand as a recorded offence.) The number 'no crimed' in each category is also recorded, and finally substracted from the total in the current year. An offence is recorded as 'cleared up' if, roughly speaking, there is a suspect (see Chapter 4 below). The numbers and proportions cleared up are listed in *Criminal Statistics* for each offence type.

Classification

The reduction of charges in the courts is one of the reasons why the number of offences of a particular type cleared up may bear little resemblance to the number of persons cautioned for or convicted of this offence (see Chapter 3). The only offences dealt with differently, in respect of police recording methods, are those classified as homicide (see Chapter 8). The number finally classified as homicide as the result of court proceedings is given in *Criminal Statistics* and this is about 86 per cent of the number originally recorded as homicide. Some of the incidents are found not to have been offences at all (being accidents, for example) and it seems likely that this would also apply to other incidents listed as offences (which are not 'corrected back' as a result of court proceedings).

Counting rules

If an incident occurs with several criminal elements, the problem arises as to how many offences to count and classify. Prior to 1979 the 'Instructions for the Preparation of Statistics Relating to Crime' issued by the Home Office left a certain amount of discretion to the police. Some forces would count every element, some picked out the most serious elements, while some would count just one, judged to be the most serious. Some forces may have been influenced by whether or not there was a suspect, for if there is a suspect for an offence, this offence is regarded as 'cleared up' and therefore the proportion of offences cleared up would be increased if every element was counted. As the 'clear-up rate' is sometimes used as an indication of police efficiency, this was one way of increasing it, just as omission to record an offence sometimes may occur if there is no possibility of finding a suspect.

In 1980 the Home Office produced a new set of 'Requirements of the Police' regarding the recording of offences and these were 'to improve the consistency of recording multiple, continuous, and repeated offences' (footnote to Table 2.12 *Criminal Statistics 1989* and elsewhere). In the main, just one offence is to be recorded per incident, and this is the most serious, except for offences of violence, when the number of *victims* is recorded. Threats, attempts, and 'aiding and abetting' an offence, count as the offence, except for homicide, where threats and attempts are treated separately. If several offences were reported under the same circumstances, as part of a series, these are called 'a continuous offence' or a repeated offence and counted as just one. The guidelines are detailed, and the result may be complex as the following example shows:

A group of three men with knives might attack another group of five men at a bus-stop, injuring two of them, robbing all of them of ready cash and stealing all their credit cards which are passed on and used to buy goods.

Extract from Lewis (1992)

The Home Office (personal communication) have supplied the following advice on counting this incident:

The rule for robbery is applied, as stated in the counting rules: an offence is counted for each person injured but only one of these is counted as robbery and the rest as the appropriate offence of violence against the person. In this case, we probably have two woundings (either classifications 5 or 8, depending on severity), and one robbery, in which case one robbery and one wounding should be counted.

In addition to this, we have the subsequent offence of obtaining property by deception (classification 53), which covers the use of the credit cards. We would normally only advise the counting of such offences if they took place in a police force area other than that of the robbery (otherwise they would be considered a continuation of the theft). If this is the case, the rule is one offence for each owner of goods fraudulently bought who reports the incident. We do not know how many did so, but we might assume that there is some common pattern in the use of the cards, in which case one continuous offence is counted.

So, in summary, we have one offence of robbery, one of wounding, and maybe one or more offences of obtaining property by deception.

There were reductions in 1980 in the number of some offences which might be attributed to these changes. 'Going equipped for stealing etc.' is an offence almost always cleared up, by definition, but often associated with an actual burglary. The number was reduced from 5010 (1979) to 4257 (1980). This offence was formerly included in the 'burglary' group, but is now included with 'other offences'. There were also reductions in the numbers of 'thefts by an employee' – perhaps due to the repetition of similar offences which would now be counted as only one. This was also the case for the offence of 'handling stolen goods' which probably previously included some offences which occurred at the same time as a theft offence. 'Fraud and forgery' had the largest reduction in numbers, presumably due to the 'continuous offence' rule, several offences occurring as a result of theft of a cheque book or credit card now being counted as one (there was a reduction from 118 000 in 1979 to 105 000 in 1980). All these reductions were soon overtaken by increases in subsequent years.

The counting rules spelt out by the Home Office requirements are to some extent arbitrary even though there is now more consistency between forces. Firstly, assessment of the 'most serious' offence in the incident is not entirely objective. Officially an offence A is more serious than an offence B if the maximum sentence available for A exceeds that for B, and this is determined by the maximum lengths of imprisonment available. These are listed by the Home Office, but several offences have the same maxima so the decision which to record may depend on the judgement of the police at the time of recording.

Another result is that violent offences, where the number of victims is counted, are over-represented compared with offences of theft where there may be several 'victims' but the offence is counted as one. An alternative approach might be to count the number of charges it would be possible to bring of each offence type in the incident. This would surely be a more meaningful number than that currently used, which results in the total number of offences being a mixture of the number of incidents (for offences where one offence per incident is counted) and the number of victims (for violent offences).

In the next section some of the results of victim surveys will be reviewed. These have their own problems of interpretation, but have shed considerable light on the limitations of the police statistics. Following this, each main offence group will be examined separately.

VICTIM SURVEYS

The General Household Survey, conducted in England and Wales by OPCS at intervals commencing in 1972, included a question on burglary with loss, and estimated that (an average of four surveys) about twice as many burglaries and thefts in dwellings had occurred as were recorded by the police. However, while the recorded burglaries had increased between 1971 and 1980, the numbers estimated by the survey had remained fairly constant (see *Criminal Statistics 1980* p. 29). There appeared to be two reasons for the discrepancy: more householders had *reported* the offence to the police, and the proportion of those which were *recorded* by the police had also increased, so the recorded increase was in fact misleading. It was surprising to find that only about two-thirds of victims *reported* the offence to the police and also that the police only *recorded* about three-quarters of the burglaries reported to them. A possible reason was that while some householders thought a burglary or attempted burglary had taken place, the police perceived and recorded the incident as one of criminal damage, or theft in a dwelling, or even did not record the event at all.

The British Crime Survey (BCS) of over 10 000 of the general population in England and Wales was first carried out in 1982 and has been repeated in 1984, 1988, and 1992, and will continue biennially. The number of people who had been victims of personal and household offences in the preceding year was estimated and it was found that there was a vast amount of under-recording of those offences included in the survey. In 1991, only 50 per cent of these offences were reported to the police and about 60 per cent of these were recorded by police, so about 30 per cent of all offences which had occurred were recorded with considerable variation between offence types (see Table 2.2). The respondents were also asked why they did *not* report offences to the police. The main reasons were that the offence was too trivial (55 per cent), or the police could not do anything (25 per cent), or the victim dealt with it privately (12 per cent) (1991 figures). It was found that more serious offences were more likely to be reported. Chapter 12 gives a discussion of the technical problems involved in victim surveys. As with all surveys, it has to be realized that the non-response rate (in this case about 23 per cent) means that the figures have an unknown error (as well as a sampling error) and there are also possible errors due to the fallibility of people's memories, and perhaps unwillingness or inability to reply accurately. These factors themselves may change over time.

The comparisons between successive surveys indicated that there have been increases in the numbers of offences covered by the survey, but the increases have not been as large as those recorded by the police. Whereas the latter showed an increase of 100 per cent between 1981 and 1991, the BCS found an increase of only 50 per cent.

Many of the offences included fall into one of three groups: acquisitive crime, vandalism, and violence, for the purposes of comparison with police statistics. For all groups there was an increase in the proportion of offences recorded, but this was particularly the case for vandalism, which the BCS recorded as fairly constant but Home Office figures showed had doubled.

These victim surveys have been concerned with personal and household offences but there have been a few surveys of other types of crime. For example, Burrows *et al.* (1993) carried out a survey of arson in schools, while Johnston *et al.* (1991) reported on a survey of crime on industrial estates.

Variation between areas

While national figures, both those from police statistics and from the British Crime Survey, are of considerable interest, it is important to realize that there is a great deal of variation between police force areas.

Table 2.2. A comparison of the British Crime Survey and notifiable offences recorded by the police (in 000s)

	1981[a] BCS	1991 Police	1991[a] BCS	1991 % reported of number reported	1991 % recorded of all reported	1991 % recorded BCS crimes	% change 81–91 Police	% change 81–91 BCS
Comparable with recorded offences								
Acquisitive crime	3 153	2 264	6 174	60	62	37	95	96
Vandalism	2 715	410	2 730	27	56	15	105	1
Violence	670	198	809	48	51	24	93	21
Total	6 538	2 872	9 713	50	60	30	96	49
Vandalism	2 715	410	2 730	27	56	15	105	1
Burglary: attempts and no loss	376	145	660	53	41	22	96	76
Burglary: with loss	374	480	705	92	74	68	74	88
Theft from motor vehicle	1 287	769	2 400	53	61	32	128	86
Theft of motor vehicle	286	481	517	99	94	93	68	81
Attempted thefts of and from vehicles	180	123	890	41	34	14	336	395
Bicycle theft	216	225	564	69	58	40	78	161
Wounding	507	157	626	48	53	25	86	23
Robbery	163	41	183	47	48	22	123	13
Theft from the person	434	41	439	35	27	9	19	1
Other BCS Offences								
Other household theft	1 518	–	1 838	29	–	–	–	21
Common assault	1 402	–	1 757	26	–	–	–	25
Other personal theft	1 588	–	1 744	38	–	–	–	10
All BCS Offences	11 045	–	15 052	43	–	–	–	36

[a] Figures estimated from the survey.
Notes: Acquisitive crimes include burglary, thefts of and from vehicles (including attempts), bicycle thefts, theft from the person. Vandalism is to household property and vehicles. Violence includes wounding and robbery.
Police figures have been adjusted to improve comparability with the BCS. The main adjustments needed are: to exclude offences against victims aged under 16, and vandalism against public property; and to add offences recorded only by the British Transport Police (which are excluded from police figures). Police figures for 'burglary' comprise burglary in a dwelling only. Police figures of thefts of and from motor vehicles exclude 'nil value' incidents; these are shown as 'attempted thefts of and from vehicles'. Some adjustment is also made to exclude incidents involving commercial vehicles.
Source: Mayhew *et al.* (1993) Tables A2.1, A2.4.

Numbers of offences and rates per 100 000 population are given in *Criminal Statistics* for each of the 43 police force areas. Clear-up rates are also given. The figures refer to where the offences are committed, so whereas they may give an indication of the amount of work for the police in the area, they do not necessarily give an indication of the criminality of the resident population on account of daily and seasonal variations in numbers due to work, holidays, and tourists. This would particularly affect the Metropolitan Police District which includes all of Greater London (plus some small outlying areas), but excludes the 'City of London'. It should be noted that national figures are over-weighted with those of London and other large metropolitan cities. The interpretation of the variations may not be straightforward. Mayhew *et al.* (1993:3) have pointed out:

Crime Surveys have (also) shown that police statistics can mislead when used to make comparisons across different areas. Farrington and Dowds (1988), for instance, demonstrated that levels of crime in Nottinghamshire were actually only slightly higher than in adjacent counties, and that its very high recorded crime rate could be largely attributed to distinctive recording practices on the part of the Nottinghamshire police.

The BCS has shown how crime rates vary between different types of housing. Relationships which may exist between crime rates and various socio-economic variables of small areas may well be masked in analyses of national figures by the existence of variations between areas in some of the key variables. Detailed studies need to be undertaken to examine these.

In the following sections each offence group will be discussed and more detailed comparisons with the BCS will be made where this is possible. Table 2.2 and Table 4.1 summarize some of the findings.

VIOLENCE AGAINST THE PERSON

If an incident involves violence (or threat of violence), the number of victims determines the number of offences recorded regardless of the number of attackers. (Robbery, which is also violent, is in a group of its own). This group makes up only 3.6 per cent of all notifiable offences but contains the most serious. While this percentage has hardly changed since 1981, the total number has increased greatly, being about 100 000 in 1981 and 190 000 in 1991 (a 90 per cent increase). The Home Office classifies seven of the 15 items as 'more serious' offences, and, in 1991, these made up 16 000 (or 8 per cent of the group). The main items are 'wounding or other act endangering life' (59 per cent), threat or conspiracy to murder (30 per cent), homicide (5 per cent), attempted murder (4 per cent), and causing death by dangerous driving (3 per cent) (see Table 8.2 p. 132 below). The number in this more serious group was 6300 in 1981, so it has more than doubled over the period. While homicide has increased by only 30 per cent (from 449 to 725), threat or conspiracy to murder has increased from 620 to 4712, a factor of eight. This is likely to reflect police recording practice rather than an increase in murder plots.

Homicide offences, which include murder and manslaughter (and a very small number of infanticides) are discussed in detail in Chapter 8. The reasons for the court deciding there was 'no offence' are not always clear. 'Self-defence' and 'accident' together are estimated to account for nearly half these cases. For offences other than homicide, the numbers are based on the initial classification of the offence by the police when it is recorded; these figures may therefore also exaggerate the number of offences of a particular type, or there may not be an offence at all. An incident regarded as a 'wounding' offence, for example, may have occurred in self-defence or be accidental. There is also a problem where the intention of the possible offender may define the offence. There are three types of wounding offences. The most serious is classified under section 18 of the Offences against the Person Act, 1861, which involves 'intent to commit grievous bodily harm' (GBH) and is indictable only. This clearly requires an assessment of the state of mind of the suspect which may be difficult to make. Next in this group are the triable-either-way offences under section 20 (which does not require the element of intent but results in GBH) and under section 47 which involves 'actual bodily harm'. These are called 'other wounding etc.' The lesser offence of 'common assault', became a summary offence under CJA, 1988 and is no longer notifiable. This involves a lesser degree of injury.

The fact that the police tend to record a more serious offence than may be warranted is illustrated by the fact the average number of 'attempted murders' recorded and cleared up was 433, whereas the average number of persons cautioned or convicted of this offence was only 65 (1989–91), and the number acquitted averaged 19. The difference (of nearly 350) may be due to a suspect being convicted for several such offences or the charge being reduced to a wounding offence (which seems more likely), or the trial may have been discontinued for some reason.

An offence with even greater disparity between recorded offences and convictions is 'threat or conspiracy to murder' with about 4000 offences recorded and about 3000 cleared up. Finally about 590 were cautioned or convicted of this offence and 600 acquitted of this and all lesser offences. These two outcomes account for less than 1200 offenders (but possibly more offences). It would be interesting to know the justification for the classification as such of the 1000 offences *not* cleared up, and, of those cleared up, the number of cases not proceeded with, and the final classification of the remaining offences.

The British Crime Survey estimated that 809 000 people were victims of violent offences in 1991, compared to a figure of 198 000 comparable offences in the Home Office tables. Thus, four times as many offences occurred as were recorded by the police. It was estimated that 48 per cent of the offences were reported to the police, 51 per cent of which were recorded by the police, so that only 24 per cent of all BCS crimes were recorded. It was found that there was an increase of 21 per cent from 1981, far smaller than the 90 per cent increase in Home Office figures. This appears to be due to an increase in the reporting of the offence to the police, perhaps due to a lower tolerance of violent behaviour.

SEXUAL OFFENCES

The total number of offences recorded in this group has increased fairly steadily from 19 000 in 1981 to 29 000 in 1991, but the increase is slightly less than that of other offence groups. These made up 1 per cent of all offences in both years. The offence with the largest number is 'indecent assault of a female' (54 per cent of group) which increased from 11 000 in 1981 to 16 000 in 1991. The most serious is rape, making up 14 per cent of the group. This offence is indictable only, and has increased from about 1000 in 1981 to about 4000 in 1991.

'Gross indecency with a child' was added in 1981, and in 1991 there were just over 1000 offences recorded.

The British Crime Survey estimated that there were 60 000 sex offences (against women) in 1987 or 29 per 10 000 women, increasing from 15 per 10 000 in 1981. The total number of rapes and 'indecent assaults on a female' recorded by the police was about 12 000 in 1981 and 16 000 in 1987, a somewhat smaller increase. However, the number of offences reported either to the police or to interviewers in the survey will depend on many factors, and in particular how sympathetic the recipient of the information is expected to be. The police have improved the procedures in this respect and this may account for the increase in the police statistics. It may also be the case that respondents in the survey are becoming less inhibited in talking about these matters, and that survey methods are improving. However, Mayhew *et al.* (1993:5) state that sexual offences are very likely to be under-estimated in the surveys.

On average over the three years 1989–91 the number of recorded rapes per year was about 3000 and the number cleared up about 2200 (the clear-up rate being about 75 per cent). However, the average number of persons 'convicted or cautioned' was only about 500, with about 400 acquitted. The remaining cases may have been withdrawn for various reasons or the charge may have reduced to 'indecent assault of a female' (see Chapter 9 and Grace *et al.* 1993 for a detailed study of rape cases).

The actual number of rapes will almost certainly remain an unknown quantity, and the definition of rape may also change as people's perception of the offence changes.

BURGLARY

Burglary offences made up 23 per cent of all notifiable offences in 1991 and have increased from 718 000 in 1981 to 1 219 000 in 1991, an increase of 70 per cent. Burglary occurs when a person enters a building 'as a trespasser' and attempts to steal or injure somebody. It should be distinguished from 'theft in a dwelling' which is classified as theft. This group has four items: burglary in a dwelling; burglary other than in a dwelling; and for both items whether or not the offence is 'aggravated', which means whether an offensive weapon was being carried at the time of the burglary. If the burglary is aggravated or there is violence or threat of violence the offence is indictable only. Just over half (51 per cent) (in 1991) were 'burglary in a dwelling', and about 0.3 per cent of those were 'aggravated'. The 1988 British Crime Survey estimated that only about two-thirds of burglaries in a dwelling were reported to the police, only two-thirds of these were recorded by them, so finally only 41 per cent of these offences were recorded by the police. However, Table 2.2 shows (for the 1992 survey) that there was a big difference between cases where there were only attempts, or no loss, and those with loss, the latter having a much higher reporting and recording rate.

Burglary in a building other than a dwelling made up 49 per cent of burglaries in 1991, the increase in the offence being slightly less than burglary in a dwelling. This offence was, of course, not included in the BCS, which excluded businesses (see Johnston *et al.* 1991). Altogether the number of aggravated burglaries has nearly trebled since 1981, but remains only a small percentage.

In a quarter of recorded offences of burglary (including attempts) the value of property stolen was recorded as 'nil' and this proportion has remained fairly constant. Over the years 1989 to 1991, the average value (excluding offences where 'nil' was recorded), was just under £1000, for non-aggravated cases (dwelling and non-dwelling), but just under £4000 for the small number of aggravated burglaries, with considerable variation. In both cases less than 7 per cent of the property was recovered, compared with 10 per cent in 1981.

The report of the Association of British Insurers 1993 gives figures which also indicate an increase in burglary. They report that the losses incurred from household crime increased from £105 million in 1981 to £591 million in 1991 and £749 million in 1992.

ROBBERY

Robbery makes up about 8.8 per cent of notifiable offences. The definition is as follows:

A person is guilty of robbery if he steals, and immediately before or at the time of doing so, and in order to do so, he uses force on any person or puts or seeks to put any person in fear of being then and there subjected to force.

There were 45 000 robberies recorded in 1991: 19 per cent were offences 'of nil value' and the average value of what was stolen was £1300. (Credit cards are regarded as being of no value, only of potential value. However, see comment on p. 4 above.) The total amount stolen was £48 million (average value £1300) of which only 8 per cent was recovered. (Offences described as 'bank robberies' are strictly speaking 'burglaries', if there was no evidence of violence against a person, or fear of violence being involved.) The number of offences in 1981 was about 20 000 so the number has more than doubled in ten years, but is still considerably less than burglary.

This offence is indictable only, so adults who are prosecuted can only be tried in the Crown Court. The data on court proceedings suggest that some of these cases were not robberies but 'theft from the person' perhaps, or assault. Of 5080 committed for trial only 4730 were finally dealt with for this offence (three year averages). The distinction between robbery and 'theft from the person' may be fine one, as can be readily seen if one considers a case of handbag snatching in the street.

The 1992 BCS found that 47 per cent of robberies were reported to the police and 48 per cent of those were recorded by them, so overall only 22 per cent of those committed were recorded. This offence has one of the lowest clear-up rates (23 per cent) so the actual proportion for which there is a suspect may be as low as 5 per cent.

THEFT AND HANDLING STOLEN GOODS

This group contained 2 760 000 offences in 1991 and made up over half (52 per cent) of all notifiable offences and, together with burglary (23 per cent), which usually involves theft or attempted theft, these property offences made up three-quarters of all recorded offences, or nearly 4 million. There has been a 72 per cent increase in the group in the ten years from 1981 (when 1 600 000 were recorded) and this is largely accounted for by offences related to cars. The largest item was 'theft from a vehicle', about a third of all in the group, and this more than doubled over the period. A fifth (20 per cent) in both years were 'theft or unauthorized taking of a motor vehicle'. Theft *from* cars increased from 380 000 to 910 000 (an increase of about 140 per cent) and theft or unauthorized taking of cars (TWOC) from 330 000 to 580 000 (an increase of about 75 per cent). The number of vehicles licenced increased from 19.3 million in 1981 to 24.5 million in 1991, an increase of only 25 per cent, so proportionately more cars are stolen or stolen from.

'Theft from shops' makes up about 10 per cent of the group, with about 280 000 offences, and this has fluctuated slightly (but hardly increased) over the years since 1981. Variation in the frequency of this offence has been ascribed to the way cases are dealt with by the stores rather than to the actual amount of shoplifting (see Farrington and Burrows 1993). (This offence is usually only reported when the offender is known, so the clear-up rate is much higher than for other theft offences. An increase in the amount of shoplifting can therefore increase the clear-up rate.)

'Theft by an employee' makes up less than 1 per cent of the offences in the group. It is undoubtedly a very small proportion of such offences as take place; many employers evidently prefer to ignore such offences, or else deal with them privately (Martin 1962; Mars 1982; Johnston et al. 1991). 'Theft from the person of another' makes up less than 1.5 per cent of the offences (that is, about 35 000).

Criminal Statistics 1991 showed that overall about 7 per cent of the recorded offences in the theft group had 'value of property stolen' as nil; many of these would be attempts, but again they include theft of credit cards (of potential value only). Apart from theft of a car, the highest average value of thefts were those by an employee (nearly £2000). The average value for theft from shops was £76. There seems to be considerable variation from year to year in the value of 'other thefts'. The method of recording several offences committed in the same circumstances as only one, a 'continuous offence', would under-estimate the actual number of thefts if there were several victims. The 1992 British Crime Survey found that in 1991 only 35 per cent of victims reported the offence to the police, but the reporting rate varies considerably with the type of offence, especially because theft of cars is almost always reported and recorded for insurance purposes. The police only recorded less than one-third of the offences of theft from the person reported to them, so that overall only 9 per cent were recorded. The BCS, of course, estimates the number of *victims* as the survey method cannot always distinguish whether the offence was part of one 'continuous offence'.

FRAUD AND FORGERY

This group makes up about 3 per cent of all recorded offences, about 175 000 in 1991. A very considerable amount of fraud undoubtedly takes place unbeknown to the victim. In some cases estimates have been made; for example, insurance companies recently estimated (TV report, December 1993) that they were cheated of £900 000 a year from false claims.

Besides this, owing to the counting rules for continuous offences, one stolen cheque book or credit card may result in a larger number of offences being carried out but these would be counted as only one offence. Credit card fraud may result in loss by either an individual or a bank – and thence by the general public through increased interest rates, etc.

Computer frauds involve complexities relating to accounting that are only gradually being revealed to the inexpert general public. Some of these frauds involve large sums of money, but there are probably many that involve smaller sums that are not recognized as such.

A large-scale business fraud in which the magnitude of the fraud is enormous may result in the number of victims (investors and pensioners, for example) being uncountable. Clearly this presents problems of 'counting' but to count it as just one offence seems inappropriate. There were 53 offences of 'fraud by company director, etc.' in 1990 and 134 000 'other fraud' recorded by the police. No figures for the value of the frauds are given in *Criminal Statistics* to compare with those of theft or burglary, this often being impossible to assess (see Levi 1993).

Social Security fraud statistics (which are included in *Criminal Statistics* with 'other fraud') are, in the main, only available for the numbers 'authorized to be prosecuted'. These decreased from about 19 000 (1980–2) to about 8000 (1990–1). The reason for the decrease can be ascribed to a change in policy regarding decision to prosecute rather than a real decline in the number of frauds (personal communication, Benefits Agency).

Forgery of a drug prescription is included in this group; on average there are about 1000 such offences. This offence might perhaps more appropriately be included with drug offences.

CRIMINAL DAMAGE

These offences make up 16 per cent of all notifiable offences, totalling 821 000 in 1991, but only 387 000 in 1981 (an increase of 112 per cent). The most serious offences in the group are arson, which is indictable only, and criminal damage endangering life. Arson increased from 15 000 in 1981 to nearly 30 000 in 1991, and just one such offence can result in millions of pounds worth of damage (see Burrows *et al.*

1993). Criminal damage endangering life increased from 68 to 246 offences. The largest component of the group is simply 'other criminal damage'. There have been some changes in recording practice. From 1969 to 1971 offences of value not exceeding £100 were excluded from the tables. From 1972 onwards the numbers are given both including and excluding damage of value £20 and under. About 200 000 (or a quarter of all these offences in 1991) were of value under £20, the number having increased slightly since 1981 (it might have been expected to decrease on account of inflation). Offences of value over £20 have nearly tripled in the ten-year period.

The reporting rate of criminal damage, particularly when it is of little value, is undoubtedly very low. The 1992 British Crime Survey (which calls the offence vandalism) found only 27 per cent of victims reported the offence to the police. The police recorded 56 per cent of these, so overall only 15 per cent of offences occurring were recorded by the police. There was little change in the amount of vandalism since 1981, according to the British Crime Surveys, so the increase in the number of offences recorded by the police was ascribed mainly to increases in reporting by the victim.

These offences are all notifiable, regardless of the value of the damage. Whether or not they are summary offences depends on this value. In 1977 it became a summary offence if of value less than £200. This was raised to £400 in 1984, £2000 in 1988, and £5000 in October 1992.

OTHER NOTIFIABLE OFFENCES

The 33 000 offences in this group make up less than 1 per cent of all notifiable offences. The largest and most serious is 'trafficking in controlled drugs', which has only been recorded since 1983 (as a result of the CJA, 1982). It has increased from about 5000 to about 11 000 since then. These drug offences come to light almost entirely as the result of pro-active policing, and the increase in numbers may reflect this, rather than an actual increase in the amount of trafficking. This offence may well be the largest component of the 'dark figure' of unknown offences (although fraud offences may be a large component). The list of drug-related offences which are triable-either-way is somewhat longer than that for notifiable offences, and includes simply 'having possession of a controlled drug' which is not notifiable (see Appendices 2 and 3, *Criminal Statistics 1990*).

'Going equipped for stealing etc.' (with nearly 10 000 offences) is also included; as previously indicated this used to be grouped with burglary (prior to 1982).

SUMMARY OFFENCES WHICH ARE NOT NOTIFIABLE (EXCLUDING MOTORING)

The main information regarding the numbers of these offences can be obtained from tables of those cautioned or convicted. These relate to offenders and not offences but knowledge of the offence usually implies knowledge of the offender (although each offender may have been guilty of several offences of the same kind, or of others which were less serious, on one occasion). The numbers dealt with depend considerably on positive activity on the part of the police (for example in picking up drunks or prostitutes), policing agencies (such as TV licence inspectors), or local authorities (relating to Education Acts, licensing laws, etc.).

The numbers of offenders for each offence are very often gender-related, and this will be discussed in more detail in Chapters 3 and 9. About 410 000 males and 140 000 females were convicted or cautioned for summary offences in 1991. Excluding criminal damage of low value and unauthorized taking of a motor vehicle (which are summary[2] but also notifiable) the main offences were those related to drunkenness (90 000), motor vehicle licences (97 000) and TV licence evasion (126 000).

The total number of males convicted or cautioned for summary offences in 1981 was about the same as in 1991 (400 000), while for females there was a dramatic increase from 80 000 in 1981 to 140 000 in 1991. This increase was almost entirely due to convictions for TV licence evasion. It is not known whether there was a real increase in this offence, but there have now been developments in technology resulting in more checks by the TV licence authority (the Post Office) which could account for the increase.

Offences of drunkenness are dealt with in detail in a Home Office Statistical Bulletin (e.g. HOSB 20/93). Simple drunkenness is distinguished from 'drunkenness with aggravation' (which means disorderly conduct). The numbers have decreased from 98 000 convicted or cautioned in 1981 to 75 000 in 1991.

OFFENCES RELATED TO MOTOR VEHICLES (OTHER THAN THEFT)

These offences are dealt with entirely differently in the statistics from other offences, and in much more detail. The actual number of offences of each type (of which there are about 25) are given in a Home Office Statistical Bulletin (e.g. 34/93 for 1991 offences) and supplementary tables (mainly concerned with the outcome of court proceedings and other penalties). The numbers of each offence type are sent directly to the Home Office by the police, together with how they are dealt with.

The total number of *offences* increased from 6 900 000 in 1981 to 8 400 000 in 1991. The most common group of offences in 1991 was 'obstruction, waiting and parking offences' with 57 per cent (nearly 5 000 000) and next was 'licence, insurance and record keeping offences' with 15 per cent (about 1 200 000).

As mentioned above, the number of vehicles licensed has increased from 19.3 million in 1981 to 24.5 million in 1991. The offences recorded *per vehicle* has hardly changed, being 0.35 in 1981 and 0.34 in 1991. The total numbers of *persons* involved is not given, except for offences dealt with by the courts. An increasing number of offences are dealt with by fixed penalties, etc. (see Chapter 3), so comparisons of persons convicted in court with earlier years are not useful. The total number of *incidents* involving motoring offences is not given.

---

[2] Aggravated taking became triable-either-way in 1992.

The most serious offence is 'causing death by reckless driving' ('dangerous' since 1 April 1992) which is indictable only and also notifiable. Another group is triable-either-way but not notifiable. These are 'reckless driving' and fraud, forgery, etc. associated with vehicle or drivers' records. In 1991 just over 11 000 people were convicted of these offences. Most of the offences are summary, and 713 000 persons were convicted of them in 1991.

SUMMARY AND DISCUSSION

There were over 5 million offences recorded in 1991 compared with about 3 million in 1981. In looking at these statistics there are three main features to be borne in mind. First, these refer to the specific groups of offences called 'notifiable', not all of which are serious (in particular, minor criminal damage). Secondly, because of the method of counting, the figures refer to the number of *incidents* rather than the number of offences involved (except for the 4 per cent of violent offences). Thirdly, there are many offences which occur which are not recorded by the police. The BCS has estimated that where the victim was an individual or household there were 3.4 times as many offences occurring as were recorded in 1991. In 1981 there were 4.5 times as many offences estimated by BCS as were recorded by the police. Thus it appears that more victims are reporting the crimes to the police, so the increase in police statistics can be partly ascribed to this factor. However, the victim surveys have also shown an increase over the period of about 50 per cent since 1981 compared with about 100 per cent for the police statistics of comparable crimes. Offences against businesses and institutions are not included in these surveys, nor are the many offences of which the victim is unaware, such as fraud, and victimless offences such as drugs offences. Businesses, especially shops, are undoubtedly victims of many offences which are unrecorded, and the recording of drugs offences is largely determined by the amount of pro-active policing.

The number of recorded motoring offences is very large (about 8 million), and these differ from notifiable offences in that every element of an incident is counted, which is dealt with by prosecution or by other means. Many of these are minor offences. In contrast, the number of summary non-motoring offences can only be estimated from the number of offenders dealt with by caution or conviction.

A more meaningful measure of the number of notifiable offences would be to count and classify initially every offence occurring in an incident that could be charged, rather than only the most serious. While this would produce larger numbers, the figures could be published in parallel with those using the current method. They would relate more directly to the BCS figures.

A reclassification of recorded offences according to the result of court proceedings where these take place ('correcting back') would give an altogether more meaningful set of figures. This is now carried out for homicide offences. Without correcting back the seriousness of the offences recorded tends to be over-estimated, as exemplified by the reduction in the numbers of offences of 'conspiracy to murder' (see p.14).

Variations in the crime rates between different police force areas is considerable, and this is also true of clear-up rates. As a result, any overall analysis of national figures in relation to demographic and socio-economic variables may be misleading, and relationships that do exist on an area basis may be obscured.

In view of the difficulties explained here of interpreting police statistics in England and Wales, comparison with recorded crime rates of other countries with different classification and recording practices are not very meaningful. Two large-scale international victim surveys using telephone interviews have been carried out (van Dijk *et al.*, 1990; van Dijk *et al.*, 1993). Standardized questions have given an indication of the amount and variation of crime in different countries (mainly in Europe). The results show also that there are large variations in the rates of reporting offences to the police and this shows that police recorded figures cannot be compared in a meaningful way. This seems to be a way forward for estimating differences in some crimes, but the response rates tended to be fairly low, and there may be cultural differences which need to be explored.

Acknowledgement

I wish to thank Tony Bottoms and also Chris Lewis and his colleagues at the Home Office Research and Statistics Department for their comments on a draft of this chapter.

REFERENCES

Barclay, G. (1993). *Digest 2: Information on the Criminal Justice System in England and Wales.* Home Office Research and Statistics Department, Home Office, London.

Bottomley, A. K. and Pease, K. (1986). *Crime and Punishment: Interpreting the Data.* Open University Press, Milton Keynes.

Burrows, J., Shapland, J., and Wiles, P. (1993). *Arson in Schools: A Report to the Arson Prevention Bureau.* Arson Prevention Bureau, London.

van Dijk, J. J. M. and Mayhew, P. (1993). Criminal victimisation in the industrialised world: key findings of the 1989 and 1992 International Crime Surveys. In *Understanding Crime: Experiences of Crime and Crime control* (ed. A. A. del Frate, U. Zvekic and van J. J. M. van Dijk). UNICRI, Rome.

van Djik, J. J. M., Mayhew, P., and Killias, M. (1990). *Experiences of Crime across the World: Key Findings of the 1989 International Crime Survey.* Kluwer, Deventer, Netherlands.

Farrington, D. P. and Dowds, E. A. (1988). Disentangling criminal behaviour and police reaction. In *Reaction to Crime: The Public, the Police, Courts and Prisons* (ed. D. P. Farrington and J. Gunn). John Wiley, Chichester.

Farrington, D. P. and Burrows, J. (1993). Did shoplifting really decrease? *British Journal of Criminology* **33**, 57–69.

Grace, S., Lloyd, C., and Smith, L. C. F. (1993). *Rape: from Recording to Conviction.* Home Office Research and Planning Unit, Paper No. 71. HMSO, London.

Johnston, V., Leek, M., Shapland, J., and Wiles, P. (1991). *Crime and other Problems on Industrial Estates.* Faculty of Law, Sheffield. (For a shortened version, under the same title, see Crime Prevention Unit paper 54, Home Office (1994) London).

Levi, M. (1993). The investigation, prosecution and trial of serious fraud. *Royal Commission of Criminal Justice.* HMSO, London.

Lewis, C. (1992). Crime statistics: their use and misuse. *Social Trends* **22**, 13–23, Central Statistical Office, Home Office, London.

Mars, G. (1982). *Cheats at Work, an Anthropology of Workplace crime*. Allen and Unwin, London.

Martin, J. P. (1962). *Offenders as Employees*. Macmillan, London.

Mayhew, P., Aye Maung, N., and Mirrlees-Black, C. (1993). *The 1992 British Crime Survey*. Home Office Research Study, No. 132, HMSO, London.

McClintock, F. H. and Avison, N. H. (1968). *Crime in England and Wales*. Heinemann, London.

Office of Population, Censuses and Surveys (1993). *General Household Survey*. HMSO, London.

Walker, M. A. (1981). *Crime: Reviews of United Kingdom Statistical Sources*, Vol. XV. Pergamon Press, Oxford.

Walker, M. A. (1992). Do we need a clear-up rate? *Policing and Society* **2**, 293–306.

Walker, N. (1988). Crime and penal measures. In *British Social Trends since 1900* (ed. A. H. Halsey). Macmillan, London.

3 Criminal justice and offenders

MONICA WALKER

INTRODUCTION

There are a series of processes by which a suspect may become an offender, or alternatively may be released from the criminal justice system. In summary, the suspect may be arrested or summonsed by the police, after which he may be released with 'no further action', he may be given a caution, or charged and prosecuted. If he is prosecuted, the case may be discontinued, without trial. Otherwise he will be either tried in the magistrates' courts, or committed for trial to the Crown Court. If he is to be tried in the magistrates' courts the case may be withdrawn or the case dismissed (and the defendant acquitted); or the defendant will be either sentenced, or committed to the Crown Court for sentence. If he is committed for trial in the Crown Court he will be either acquitted, or convicted and sentenced (unless the case is discontinued for some reason). He may later appeal against conviction and/or sentence. At each stage he will be remanded either on bail or in custody. Barclay (1993) and Bottomley and Pease (1986) give good detailed accounts of the processes involved (see also Figure 10.1 below).

The police are mainly responsible for the early stages in the procedures, in particular whether to take no further action (NFA), caution, or submit the case to the Crown Prosecution Service (CPS). The CPS was instituted in 1986, and decides whether to continue with the prosecution or to discontinue court proceedings, if it is felt that the evidence was insufficient or that to proceed would not be in the public interest. Prosecutions may also be initiated by other law enforcement agencies, local authorities and private individuals.

The statistics available at each stage will be described; in the main these are published by the Home Office, either in *Criminal Statistics, England and Wales* (*CS*, annual) or in the accompanying Supplementary Tables (*CS, ST*). Fuller details are given there than can be described here, in particular those for police force areas and Petty Sessional Divisions. The Magistrates' Association together with the Home Office and Justices' Clerks Society also produces fairly detailed tables on sentencing in relation to some offences. This enables comparisons between courts within areas to be made, as well as comparisons between areas and with the whole country. The Home Office also publishes series of Statistical Bulletins (HOSB), giving details of particular aspects of court proceedings. Many of their tables are broken down by age group and sex; and where overall figures are given it should be remembered that males tend to be over-represented. Overall trends in numbers of offenders or types of sentences are always difficult to interpret as they may be due to many factors. Changes in policy or legislation affecting the statistics will be pointed out, where appropriate, but the reasons for some trends can often only be conjectured.

Offences are either 'summary', and normally tried in the magistrates' courts, or 'indictable only' which can (for adults) only be tried in the Crown Court, or are tri-able-either-way. The latter two groups are generally referred to as 'indictable' (see Chapter 2 and *CS 1992*, App. 4). The tables given in the chapter on court proceedings in *Criminal Statistics* are person-based and not offence-based; one person can be dealt with for several offences but is counted only once. Besides this, one person may be dealt with several times over one year. So the total number recorded in court proceedings tables does not refer to the number of *different* people.

The tables give cross-sections of the numbers of offenders at different stages of the criminal justice process. They cannot give an understanding of the processes leading up to the final outcome.

Data on offenders are dealt with only briefly here. Chapter 9 discusses differences between males and females while Chapter 10 discusses the problems of looking at ethnic differences. Tarling (1993) gives a comprehensive examination of data on offenders.

Before proceeding to a more detailed discussion, it needs to be stressed that national statistics on offence and offender rates and sentences mask very considerable variation between areas. Relationships between these variables may also vary, and caution is needed before drawing any overall conclusions without a detailed examination of the factors involved.

SOURCES OF DATA

The main sources of data used as a basis for *Criminal Statistics* are the police and the courts. Besides this some annual reports prepared by each police force give details of offences and offenders in the area. The information published is variable, but often includes results of 'stop and search', motoring offences, and arrests. Reports by clerks to the justices are also sometimes available, and give details of proceedings in individual courts.

The police complete a return for each person cautioned or dealt with in the criminal courts and these forms are returned to the Home Office at approximately monthly intervals. Some courts have now computerized this material and tapes are sent directly to the Home Office. If someone is formally cautioned for several offences, each one is recorded, together with the sex and actual age, apart from those aged 21 and over, and cautioned for certain summary offences.

If proceedings in court are commenced, a form is filled in (or data entered on tape) for each defendant in relation to the final appearance in the magistrates' court; another is used for Crown Court appearances, if relevant. Each offence initially charged in the court is recorded, and also the final offence, which may be different, together with the outcome.

Information regarding remand is also recorded. A suspect may be summonsed or arrested and if arrested he may be remanded on bail by the police or remanded in custody until his first appearance in the magistrates' courts. The remand status during magistrates' court adjournments, or on committal, is also recorded. (Data is not available from Crown Court proceedings because of the poor quality.)

The date of the final appearance in each court is recorded and this determines the year for which the defendant is recorded in the tables, and also the age of the defendant. If the sentence is deferred to a later date, that date is the relevant one.

Data from police force areas relate to the areas where the offence was committed and not where the suspect lives (with the possible exception of juveniles).

Since there is inevitably a time interval between committal to the Crown Court and the completion of proceedings there, Crown Court tables do not refer to exactly the same defendants as those committed for trial in the preceding or the current year. Besides this, those listed as having been committed for a particular offence type in the magistrates' courts' tables may have the classification changed when charged in the Crown Court, possibly as a result of decisions by the CPS. Classification problems are described in the following section.

Data on time intervals between successive stages of the proceedings at magistrates' courts are collected directly from the courts and published in Home Office Statistical Bulletins. Administration of both the magistrates' courts (since April 1993) and the Crown Court are carried out by the Lord Chancellor's Department (LCD), and computerized systems are being developed for the magistrates' courts (MAS) and the Crown Court (CREST). The LCD publishes an annual report entitled *Judicial Statistics* which includes data regarding numbers of cases dealt with by the Crown Court and the Court of Appeal (Criminal Division).

OUTCOME OF POLICE DECISIONS REGARDING SUMMONSES, ARRESTS, AND CAUTIONS BY THE POLICE

No further action

The numbers arrested and released with 'no further action' (NFA) are not collected by the Home Office. The Metropolitan Police (i.e. in London) give the figures for juveniles in their annual report. In 1990, for example, just under 25 000 aged 10–16 were arrested, and of these 14 per cent had NFA, 48 per cent were cautioned, and the rest (9400 or 38 per cent) were prosecuted (see also Farrington 1992). There appears to be a general trend towards diversion from the criminal justice system, especially for juveniles. This may well account for the apparent decrease in the numbers of juvenile offenders, and this is discussed below.

Cautions

The police may give an 'instant' or 'internal' caution to an offender (in which case a return is not made to the Home Office) or a formal caution, when the individual is officially recorded as an offender, since a caution can only be given if the offence is admitted. In some cases the Crown Prosecution Service may recommend a caution where the police had expected a prosecution. (Sometimes however, it appears that if the suspect does *not* admit the offence, but the case for prosecution is very weak, the CPS or the police may decide to discontinue the case.)

The proportion of offenders (those convicted or cautioned) who were cautioned is called the 'cautioning rate', and this has increased steadily from 19 per cent (for all offenders and all indictable offences) in 1981 to 35 per cent in 1991. A rapid increase since 1986 may be due to Home Office Circulars (14/85, also 15/90) which encouraged the greater use of cautioning. There were, in fact, several changes in about 1986, and there was an overall reduction in the number of offenders. Legislation and other factors which may have caused this will be discussed below. (There was not a corresponding decline in the number of recorded offences.)

Cautioning rates are higher for females than males, higher for the younger age groups, and higher for indictable than for summary offences (*CS 1991*, Table 5.2). Summary motoring offences are excluded because they would receive a 'written warning' and not a caution.

For males, 90 per cent of offenders aged 10–13, 70 per cent of those aged 14–16, 25 per cent of those aged 17–20 and 18 per cent of offenders aged 21 or over were cautioned for indictable offences (1991 figures). The corresponding figures for females were 97 per cent, 87 per cent, 45 per cent, and 39 per cent. Comparisons between males and females and between age groups are not straightforward because the offences involved differ. However, it does appear that, within each indictable offence group (except drugs), a greater proportion of females are cautioned.

For summary offences, the picture is slightly different. For the three youngest age groups females again have higher cautioning rates than males. However, for those aged 21 and over the rate for males is 16 per cent, and that for females only 6 per cent. This is entirely due to over 87 000 women in 1991 (or nearly three-quarters of those convicted) being convicted under the Wireless Telegraphy Acts, that is, they failed to have a TV Licence (compared with 48 000 males). This offence is dealt with by the Post Office, and hardly any were cautioned by the police, although some may have been cautioned by the Post Office. This illustrates the danger of using overall figures (for all ages and all offences) in making comparisons.

Comparisons even for specific offences may themselves be misleading. If a person is cautioned for several offences, he is listed according to the 'principal offence'. In this context this is the one with the highest possible sentence. Summary offences are automatically less serious than indictable so would be excluded if occurring at the same time. Before 1980 cautions for the principal indictable *and* principal summary offence were recorded.

Arrests, summonses and remands

The Home Office gives some information on action by the police before the first court appearance (*CS 1991*, Table 8.1ff). For those proceeded against for indictable offenses, 14 per cent were summonsed, 71 per cent were arrested and bailed, and 15 per cent were arrested and held in custody. In 1981 the corresponding figures were 22 per cent, 64 per cent, and 15 per cent, so a lower proportion are now summonsed, and more are arrested and bailed.

For summary offences (excluding motoring) the trend is the other way – more are being summonsed (the percentage increasing from 33 per cent in 1981 to 72 per cent in 1991) and fewer arrested. Only 4 per cent were arrested and held in custody in 1991. However, these differences may be due to the poor quality of the data from some forces.

For summary motoring offences there was again a decrease in the percentage summonsed (from 99 per cent to 87 per cent). Only 1 per cent were arrested and held in custody. The numbers proceeded against for summary motoring offences have decreased considerably over ten years (from 1 281 000 to 920 000). The reason for this is that an increasing number of these offences are being dealt with by other means, such as fixed penalties.

THE CONSTRUCTION OF TABLES OF COURT PROCEEDINGS IN *CRIMINAL STATISTICS*

If a defendant is charged in the magistrates' courts with just one offence and is acquitted or convicted of this offence (or the case is discontinued) or he is committed for trial, he is allocated, in the tables, to that offence. If the charge is reduced – for example, a charge of burglary is reduced to one of theft – and he is convicted of the lesser offence he is allocated to this offence. An offence is regarded as less serious than another if it is a component of it, or if the maximum penalty available is lower.

The principal offence rule

If a person is dealt with for several offences the 'principal offence' is selected for tabulation. This is the offence for which he is given the most severe penalty. Committal to the Crown Court for sentence counts as the least severe sentence except for compensation and some rarely used orders. If a person is acquitted of all offences he is allocated to the most serious offence charged. Thus if someone is charged with burglary and is acquitted of this and all lesser offences he is listed against burglary (the number of offences of which he is acquitted is not available). If he was acquitted of burglary, say, but convicted of any lesser offences (such as criminal damage or theft) he would be listed against the most serious of the latter.

Indictable offences are always regarded as more serious than summary, so that if, for example, a defendant is convicted of theft as well as drunkenness (or soliciting) only the theft will be counted in the tables. Consequently the numbers published as convicted of summary offences are, to an unknown extent, lower than the actual values. (Before 1980 a person could be listed twice for one court appearance, against the most serious indictable offence *and* against the most serious summary offence.)

In the Crown Court a similar ruling applies. Thus a person may be listed as proceeded against for robbery in the magistrates' court, and (since this offence is indictable only) committed for trial for robbery. However he may be listed against theft from the person in the Crown Court tables if the charge was reduced there. Another example is the charge of rape, which is sometimes reduced to 'indecent assault of a female' in the Crown Court. This is discussed in detail in Chapter 9. Homicide is the only offence where details are given (in *CS*) of changes in charges during court proceedings – from murder to manslaughter, for example.

The ordering of the sentences according to their severity is determined by the Home Office and available in their 'Requirements of the Police'. It is, broadly speaking and omitting some of the refinements, as follows:

(1)	Unsuspended imprisonment	Aged 21 or over
(2)	Young offender institution	Aged 15 to 20
(3)	Partially suspended imprisonment	Aged 21 or over
(4)	Fully suspended imprisonment	Aged 21 or over
(5)	Community service order	All aged 16 or over
(6)	Attendance centre order	Aged 10 to 20
(7)	Supervision order	Aged 10 to 16
(8)	Probation order	Aged 17 and over
(9)	Fine	All
(10)	Conditional discharge	All
(11)	Absolute discharge	All

(Note: Following the implementation of the Criminal Justice Act, 1991 in October 1992, (3) was abolished; (7) became available for 17 year olds; (8) became available for those aged 16 and over. Also a combination order was introduced for those aged 16 and over.)

While probably everyone would agree that the first and last items are the most and least severe penalties, respectively, research has shown that magistrates vary in their opinions on the matter, as do some solicitors, offenders, and the general public. In particular whether or not a fine is regarded as more severe than a probation order by the offender must surely depend on the size of the fine, relative to the offender's financial circumstances, while some might prefer any size of fine to a probation order.

Even a conditional discharge is sometimes regarded as more onerous than a fine, as a breach of the condition (commission of offence within a specified period) may result in a more severe penalty for the next offence than would another offence following a fine. In 1991 10 per cent of conditional discharges were breached and 18 per cent of these (1700) received an immediate prison sentence as result (*CS 1991*, Table 7.28).

TABLES OF COURT PROCEEDINGS: GENERAL INTERPRETATION

Tables of proceedings in the magistrates' courts (*CS, ST* Vol. 1) and in the Crown Court (*CS, ST* Vol. 2) are constructed in such a way that their interpretation is not straightforward and it is not always possible to find the information required. Data in the first table (Vol. 1) is for all ages, and for males and females separately. Each row represents a different offence and the number in the first column in headed 'persons proceeded against'. This is the number of defendants for whom proceedings were *completed* in the court, in relation to that offence, and is not the number actually initially proceeded against for that offence, which is not available. It cannot be used as a base for calculating, say, the proportions convicted of any particular offence of those charged with this offence, because the number *initially* proceeded against will have been higher if the charge was reduced from this offence and some offenders convicted of a lesser offence; or it will be lower if more serious charges had been reduced *to* this offence. Since a charge can be reduced in court, but not increased, the initial charge will tend, if anything, to be too high. The number in the first column of the table is, in fact, simply the total of all the numbers in the next six columns. This comment pertains to the row 'all indictable offences' and also to 'all summary offences'. However, in the final row ('all offences') the number given is actually the total number proceeded against in the magistrates' courts.

Interpretation of Crown Court tables (*CS, ST* Vol. 2) is less complex. However, these tables cannot be directly linked to magistrates' courts tables, partly because the offence classification may change and partly because of the time interval between the two hearings.

It should be noted that tables on court proceedings (*CS* and *CS, ST*) give the number of persons dealt with during a year, not the number of *different* persons. Males are more likely to be repeat offenders (Phillpotts and Lancucki 1979) so the ratio of *different* male to female offenders is likely to be less. This is evidenced by the difference in the ratio of males to females of those who have been convicted of any offence from the Offenders' Index (see p. 7 above and Chapter 9) and the overall ratio for indictable offences in one year. But, besides this, if a suspect is charged with a second offence shortly after a first charge, the court may deal with both offences at the same time. The defendant would appear in the tables just once, and would give a lower count than if the offences had been dealt with at two different court hearings.

DISCONTINUANCES

A case for which proceedings are commenced may be discontinued for various reasons and these reasons are listed for all indictable offences and all summary offences in *Criminal Statistics*. In 1991 4 per cent of indictable cases were discontinued after proceedings commenced. The main reason is section 23(3) of the Prosecution of Offences Act, 1985 – not enough evidence to proceed (71 per cent). Besides this, 28 per cent were 'adjourned *sine die*', for about 1 per cent the defendant died, and a very small number had a mental hospital order without conviction (see *CS, ST* Vol. 1, Tables 1.1(a)–1.1 (e)). Fourteen per cent had the charge withdrawn after the trial of the case had commenced (*CS 1991*, Table 6.2). The stage at which proceedings are discontinued can affect the numbers recorded in the court proceedings tables of *Criminal Statistics*.

The Crown Prosecution Service which was established in 1986 has been instrumental in increasing the efficiency of court proceedings. After submission of prosecution papers by the police to the CPS, each case is reviewed to see if prosecution should take place, to recommend a caution, or to decide to discontinue the case. The annual report of the CPS 1991–1992 states that there was discontinuation 'for about one in ten of all cases received, an increase of 15 per cent over the last year'. For a review of its work, see Fowles (1993).

The CPS believes more cases will be discontinued as more weak cases are weeded out before court proceedings begin. Cases which have been requested for trial in the Crown Court (by the magistrate or defendant) may also be discontinued (Magistrates' Courts Act (MCA), 1980 s6) if there is deemed to be insufficient evidence when the magistrate reviews the evidence. The aim of the CPS is to review the cases sufficiently early to prevent unnecessary court appearances.

The category of 'charge withdrawn' has until recently been amalgamated with 'charge dismissed' for calculations of the acquittal rate in *Criminal Statistics*. This is misleading, because 'charge withdrawn' means that at a late stage the defendant was not tried because there was not sufficient evidence for trial, or that the victim did not wish the case to proceed (for example, in a case of domestic violence), or that an essential witness had died or new evidence had come to light, or it may be because the defendant was later going to be tried in the Crown Court, on another charge. 'Charge dismissed' means that this is a verdict reached by a magistrate and is thus closer to an 'acquittal'. (*CS 1991*, Table 6.2 gives a breakdown for all indictable offences and *CS, ST 1992* Vol. 1 for each offence type).

MODE OF TRIAL

In 1991 about 434 000 persons aged 17 and over were proceeded against in the magistrates' courts for indictable offences (with 426 000 in 1981) and almost 100 000 (about a quarter) were tried in the Crown Court in 1991 (compared with 79 000 in 1981).

For those aged 17 or over,[1] if a defendant is proceeded against for a triable-either-way offence, the magistrate may decline jurisdiction, usually on the basis of the case being sufficiently serious or complex to be tried in the Crown Court and warranting a severe sentence. If the magistrate accepts jurisdiction, the defendant may himself elect for trial in the Crown Court, perhaps because he thinks he has a greater chance of acquittal (which, on the face of it, appears to be true). Of these 100 000 defendants tried in the Crown Court in 1991, 81 000 (81 per cent) were for triable-either-way offences. For about two-thirds of the latter the magistrates had declined jurisdiction (CPS Report, 1991–1992).

However, insofar as the decision by the magistrates is based on the expectation of the offender receiving a more severe sentence than the magistrate can give, it is misconceived. Less than half of the triable-either-way cases dealt with in the Crown Court received a sentence of immediate custody, and between a quarter and one-third of

---

[1] After the implementation of the CJA 1991 in October 1992, this age group was 18 or over.

these sentences were for six months or less (sentences which were available to the magistrates). (This also applies to those committed for sentence.) From an administrative point of view, it would speed up cases, and cost less, if fewer cases were committed for trial (and sentence). Whether this is in the interests of justice or the defendant (and the legal fraternity) is not clear. See Riley and Vennard (1988) and Hedderman and Moxon (1992) for research on this topic.

Criminal Statistics 1991, (Table 6.5) shows that the percentage committed for trial ranges from about 40 per cent of sex and burglary offences to 12 per cent for motoring offences. A higher proportion of males were committed than females (21 per cent compared with 15 per cent) and the proportion is higher for males for every offence group except drugs (males 25 per cent, females 33 per cent).

ACQUITTALS

Magistrates' courts

It has been pointed out that cases may be discontinued at different stages of the court proceedings. Some cases which are very weak may be discontinued before proceedings commence, whilst others may proceed to court but then be withdrawn. Before 1991, the statistical picture was confused by counting cases withdrawn together with those dismissed.

In 1991 'withdrawn or dismissed' was broken down into the two groups, for all offences together, while in 1992 this is the case for each offence type, and a clearer picture emerges. Those 'dismissed' are in fact tried by the magistrate and acquitted. The numbers that are acquitted can be compared with those found guilty to obtain an overall acquittal rate. However, the numbers pleading not guilty to all or some offences with which they are charged is not published. This would be useful to investigate trends and variation between areas and to give a clearer picture of what happens. It is shown (*CS 1991*, Table 6.2) that 67 000 were withdrawn before trial, only 19 000 were acquitted, and 402 000 were convicted, giving an acquittal rate of 4.5 per cent. The overall proportion of defendants where the charge was withdrawn increased from 3 per cent in 1981 to 14 per cent in 1991. This is probably because the CPS is weeding out more cases at this stage. Details of the numbers pleading not guilty are not given. However HOSB (8/93), for example, shows that about three-quarters of defendants tried in the magistrates' courts for indictable offences pleaded guilty. (Of all those proceeded against in the magistrates' courts 51 per cent pleaded guilty, a decrease from a figure of 65 per cent in 1983 (see *CS*, Table 6.3).)

For summary offences, only the 'withdrawn or dismissed' category is available, and the proportion in this category (excluding motoring offences) was 20 per cent in 1991. Again, the numbers who pleaded 'not guilty' to all charges would enable a more meaningful 'acquittal rate' to be calculated.

The Crown Prosecution Service report gives rather different figures, and does not distinguish between summary and indictable offences in the magistrates' courts. The total number of defendants is considerably fewer (1 069 000, compared with over

1 400 000 in *CS*) The CPS figures exclude some motoring offences and non-police prosecutions, such as TV licence evasion and revenue offences. The dismissal rate is given as 2.6 per cent which is lower than any of the Home Office figures.[2]

The Crown Court

Of those committed for trial in the Crown Court in 1991, 19 per cent were acquitted (or not tried), a similar figure to 1981 (Barclay 1993, p. 38). The CPS Report (p. 27) gives a rather different acquittal rate, namely 8.9 per cent. The reason for the difference between this figure and that of the Home Office is not clear. The report also shows that of those pleading not guilty to all charges (about 41 per cent of all defendants) about 46 per cent were acquitted, while of those acquitted 74 per cent were acquitted after trial by jury and 26 per cent after direction by the judge.

However, the CPS statistics exclude those cases where the CPS decides not to proceed and offers no evidence. The court (judge) will usually order a formal verdict of 'not guilty' or that the case should be on file, not to be proceeded with without the leave of the court.

Judicial Statistics also gives some statistics relating to pleas and, in particular, gives numbers for each Crown Court circuit. In 1992, in 69 per cent of cases there was a guilty plea. This varied from 49 per cent in London to 83 per cent in the north-eastern circuit, and differences between areas were consistent over many years. The percentages of those pleading not guilty to all charges did not vary very much, and averaged 56 per cent. The overall percentage of defendants acquitted on all counts was 16 per cent, perhaps not too dissimilar to the Home Office figure of 19 per cent.

Judicial Statistics also gives a breakdown of acquittals according to whether they were discharged by the judge, directed by the judge, or based on a jury verdict; figures are given for each Crown Court circuit.

REMAND DECISIONS BETWEEN COURT APPEARANCES

The proportions remanded by the magistrates during adjournments were 61 per cent for indictable offences, 7 per cent for summary motoring and 14 per cent for other summary offences (*CS 1991*, Table 8.4). Of particular interest is the type of remand (bail or custody) or no remand, in relation to the outcome of proceedings, which is given in *CS 1991*, (Table 8.6) for all defendants and all offences.

The outcome may be acquittal, conviction, committal for sentence, or committal for trial, and each of the last three may result in custody. 'Acquittal' figures would be more meaningful if those not tried were listed separately. Some of the percentages given in the table are not easy to interpret. For example, the overall percentage 'acquitted' is based on all appearing in the magistrates' courts (including committals), rather than just those tried there, which could be misleading. It is interesting to note that of 16 900 remanded in custody and sentenced by the magistrates, 12 900, or over

---

[2] These discrepancies are being investigated.

three-quarters, received a non-custodial sentence. This does not necessarily mean the custodial remand was not justified, as the magistrates may have thought this remand was sufficient punishment to have given the offender a 'taste of custody'. Of those bailed, and sentenced by the magistrate, 95 per cent received a non-custodial sentence, and of those not remanded at all, over 99 per cent. (These figures refer to all offences, including summary.)

The percentages remanded by the magistrate for trial in the Crown Court who were remanded in custody is given (*CS*, *ST*, Vol. 1) in relation to the offence. Also, the outcome of proceedings for all offences together in the Crown Court is given in relation to remand status on committal from the magistrates' court (*CS 1991*, Table 8.9) but not during Crown Court adjournments, which is not available. Twenty per cent of those sentenced in the Crown Court had been remanded in custody by the magistrates, although as many as a quarter received a non-custodial sentence, compared with nearly two-thirds of those bailed. Some of the percentages in the table are misleading. For example, the overall proportion of persons who were acquitted in the Crown Court in this table (*CS 1991*, Table 8.9) is given as 17.8 per cent. This could be misinterpreted, as it is based on the numbers tried *and* sentenced in the Crown Court. The percentages need to be calculated separately from the numbers given of those tried in the Crown Court.

OFFENDERS

The number of suspects and offenders dealt with by the criminal justice system, the offences listed in relation to them, and the outcome of court proceedings, represent only a partial picture of the offender population. These are, of course, 'known offenders', the ones that got caught and were dealt with, and the overall decrease in their numbers since 1981 is in contrast to the increase in the number of offences recorded by the police. The notifiable offences recorded by the police increased from 2 964 000 in 1981 to 5 276 000 in 1991, while the clear-up rate decreased over the period from 38 per cent to 29 per cent and the number of offenders (cautioned or convicted) of indictable offences (a slightly narrower group of offences) decreased from 568 000 to 518 000. There is no reason to suppose that these offenders are representative of all offenders in the community, in respect of gender, age, or race.

It is beyond the scope of this chapter to give more than an overview of offender characteristics and their offence patterns (see Chapters 9 and 10 for examination of gender and ethnic differences). Tarling (1993) has carried out both a detailed examination of the statistics of 'official' offenders and a review of self-reported offending. He has also investigated 'criminal careers' using complex statistical models.

Criminal Statistics gives the numbers of those cautioned or convicted in the courts in four age groups: 10–13, 14–16, 17–20, and 21 and over. 'Age' here refers to the date at which the person was cautioned or convicted of indictable offences. The numbers are given for each age from 10 to 20, and thereafter in six age groups, and also the rate per 10 000 in the relevant population (see Table 3.1).

The number of *first* offenders each year, in each age group would be of considerable interest. (This information is given on court forms.) It would enable one to find out, for example, whether an increase in the numbers convicted was due to more (different) people being convicted during the year or more convictions by the same people, and the ages at which offending behaviour commences.

The Offenders' Index (see p. 7 and p. 37) has enabled some analyses to be carried out regarding the number of offences of those convicted of standard list offences.

In Table 3.1, 1971 figures are given only so that a rough comparison can be made with later years, because changes due to legislation (e.g. the Criminal Law Act, 1977; see also *CS 1981*, Appendix 1) mean the interpretation is not straightforward. Comparisons between 1981 and 1991 are more meaningful and show increases in the offender rates for males aged 17–29, and for females aged 14–29 but decreases for other age groups. The reduction in the offender rates for males aged 10–16 and females aged 10–13 is probably partly due to an increase in diversion from the criminal justice system and, for males, the reclassification of some summary offences (see next section).

There were two other main events during this period which probably account for the reduction in the overall offender rate. These were the Police and Criminal Evidence Act (PACE), 1984 and the introduction of the Crown Prosecution Service (in 1986). The former tightened up procedures resulting from arrest by the police, and also required evidence for the prosecution to be made available to the defence. The latter (CPS) resulted in a weeding out of weak cases, resulting in an increase in the proportion of cases withdrawn before trial, and a higher proportion not proceeding for trial (see Fowles 1993).

The distribution of offences of all the offenders is given in Table 3.2. The following discussion illustrates the need to investigate all the factors affecting the offences, in interpreting the tables. Figures for 1971 are again only of general interest, as reasons for the changes are too complex to be discussed here. The most notable difference in 1991

Table 3.1. Offenders (convicted or cautioned) per 10 000 population (indictable offences)

Age group	1971 Male	1971 Female	1981 Male	1981 Female	1991 Male	1991 Female
10–13	324	60	299	89	182	54
14–16	656	112	748	156	638	197
17–20	585	67	705	97	768	136
21–24			404	68	459	84
25–29			315	52	301	60
30–39	98	19	154 〕 130	33 〕 26	149 〕 130	34 〕 25
40–49			94	25	74	17
50–59			47	18	39	11
60+			18	8	12	4
All	179	29	226	42	198	40

Sources: Based on *CS 1981*, Table 5.18, Table 5.19; *CS 1991*, Table 5.23, 5.22.

Table 3.2. Distribution of offences of all offenders convicted or cautioned

	1971		1981		1985		1991	
	000s	%	000s	%	000s	%	000s	%
Violence	29	7	56	10	56	10	66	13
Sex	11	3	10	2	9	2	9	2
Burglary	78	19	85	15	80	14	59	11
Robbery	3	1	4	1	5	1	5	1
Theft	247	59	312	55	325	55	242	47
Fraud	18	4	27	5	28	5	27	5
Criminal damage	27	6	14	2	15	2	14	3
Drugs	–	–	16	3	23	4	45	9
Other	5	1	14	3	20	3	38	7
Motoring	2	0	28	5	29	5	11	2
All indictable	417	100	568	100	589	100	518	100
Summary	419[b]		480		488		553	
Summary motoring[a]	1 054		1 640		1 466		713	
Total (convicted or sentenced)	1 890		2 688		2 544		1784	

Source: *Criminal Statistics 1971, 1991* (Tables 45.11, 7.4).
[a] Summary motoring offences do not receive a caution, but only a written warning.
[b] Estimate from *CS 1971*, Fig 5.1.

(compared with 1981, 1985) is the drop in theft offenders (discussed below). Apart from this there has been a considerable decline in burglary offenders (from 85 000 to 59 000) and an increase in drugs offenders (from 16 000 to 45 000). There was also a decrease in indictable motoring offenders (from 28 000 to 11 000).

An important factor affecting the number of persons convicted or cautioned for indictable offences is that some offences were reclassified as summary offences under the Criminal Justice Act, 1988 (from 12 October 1988). These were: taking a motor vehicle without authority (TWOC)[3] (17 000 convicted in 1991), common assault (500), criminal damage over £400 and below £2000,[4] and driving while disqualified. These offences, and especially the first, particularly affected the numbers of those aged 14–16 (3400) and 17–20 (9000). (See HOSB 18/92)

The reasons for some of the other changes in the statistics are less evident. A drop in the number of offenders for shoplifting (*CS*, Table 5.13) from 147 000 in 1985 to 93 000 in 1989 has been ascribed (by Farrington 1992 for example) partly to the policy of the police in diverting young people from the criminal justice system. (However, the figure rose again to 116 000 in 1991.)

---

[3] This largely accounts for the change from 1985 to 1991. (From April 1992 an offence called aggravated taking of a motor vehicle without authority has been defined, and is triable-either-way.)

[4] From October 1992 criminal damage below £5000 became summary under CJA, 1991. See p. 19 above.

Those offenders guilty of individual summary offences are discussed in less detail than indictable offences in *Criminal Statistics*, but examination of the court proceedings tables reveals several interesting matters. In 1991, 324 000 males and 130 000 females were convicted of non-motoring summary offences (corresponding figures in 1981 were 365 000 and 65 000). The offences are mainly gender-related, the main offences by males being under the Public Order Act, 1986 (29 000), TWOC (17 000), drunkenness (27 000), criminal damage (26 000), motor vehicle licence offences (95 000) and TV licence evasion (49 000). For females the most common offence was overwhelmingly TV licence evasion (87 000), then motor vehicle licence offences (12 000) and soliciting (10 000). Many of the summary offences depend on pro-active policing by the police or other law-enforcement agencies (such as the Post Office). These may also caution offenders, but they would not come to the notice of the police on this account.

The numbers published of those convicted of summary offences (including some summary motoring offences) are almost certainly under-estimates, since if there were a conviction for an indictable offence at the same time as a summary offence it would not be included in the tables. Besides this, the Home Office believes that the returns made by the police for some summary offences, and in particular motoring offences, are not always accurate. Separate Statistical Bulletins give details of offenders dealt with for drunkenness (e.g. HOSB 20/93), and summary motoring offences (e.g. HOSB 34/93). There are also supplementary tables giving details of how offences related to motoring are dealt with. In 1991, 635 000 males and 64 000 females were convicted of summary motoring offences, but *changes* in the numbers prosecuted are difficult to interpret because there are increasing numbers of these offences which are being dealt with by other means. The Statistical Bulletin gives the number of offences dealt with in different ways – fixed penalties, written warnings, and Vehicle Damage Rectification Scheme notices, but not the numbers of offenders.

'Standard list offences' form another classification group of offences (see p. 6). The Home Office's Offenders' Index contains information of all convictions for these offences since 1963, merged to form criminal histories, and is a valuable resource for research purposes. It is based on tables giving results of court proceedings provided by the police and the courts. Cohort studies of samples of offenders born in 1953, 1958, 1963, 1968, and 1973 have been carried out (see HOSB 32/89 and Tarling 1993). The 1953 sample, for example, estimated that 36 per cent of males have had at least one conviction for a standard list offence by the age of 35, and one in 14 at least one conviction for a violent offence. Nine per cent of females had at least one conviction by the age of 35. Standard list offences are often referred to as 'serious', but this is not the case. All offences of criminal damage are included and some of these may be quite minor offences. On the other hand some serious offences such as drunken driving are excluded.

SENTENCES

There have been fairly consistent patterns in the changes in sentencing for indictable offences since 1981, the main features being an increase in the proportions receiving a discharge (which are almost entirely conditional discharges) from 12 per cent to 19 per cent and a decrease in the proportions fined, from 45 per cent to 35 per cent. Community service orders (CSO) have become more available, and increased from 5 per cent to 9 per cent. The overall proportions receiving immediate custody have stayed at about the same – 15 per cent.

However, these overall percentages mask differences between males and females, differences between age groups, and differences in the sentences given for different offences. A higher proportion of males receive a sentence of immediate custody, and there are other differences: proportionately more males receive a fine or CSO, and fewer receive a discharge or probation order. (See Chapter 9 for a discussion of gender differences.) If the proportions of those sentenced who are male change over the years, this could in itself affect the overall sentencing pattern.

There has been legislation affecting the disposal available for some age groups and not others, and also legislation affecting the classification of offences which may affect the sex and age groups differently.

An examination of sentencing patterns can be carried out from the published tables, but this is not, of course, the same as examining the sentencing process. This must involve looking at the characteristics of the offence (apart from its Home Office classification), the offender, and possibly previous convictions and aggravating and mitigating circumstances, as well as the court of sentence. These can only be studied in detail in a small number of courts because of the time and expense involved (see Farrington and Morris 1983; Hood 1992).

Besides differences between males and females, there are differences in the sentencing patterns of different age groups; those aged 21 and over tend to receive more severe sentences (probably on account of having more previous convictions). The proportion of male offenders in this age group has increased from 52 per cent in 1981 to 65 per cent in 1991, this being mainly due to increases in the age range 21 to 29. On the other hand, although the percentage of all females who are aged 21 and over has increased from 63 per cent to 70 per cent, the proportion in the age range 21 to 29 has decreased (see Table 3.1). These variations in the percentages in the different sex and age groups could bring about changes in the overall distribution of sentences, even if the sentencing pattern within each sex and age group remained the same.

Looking at offence groups, for all offenders (1991 figures) robbery had the highest percentage receiving immediate custody (69 per cent), then sex offences (39 per cent), burglary (28 per cent), violence (16 per cent) drug offences (19 per cent), fraud and forgery (13 per cent), with slightly fewer in other groups. These figures could be regarded as giving a rough ordering of the seriousness of the offences in the different offence groups, but clearly some offences within each group are less serious than others. Differences or changes in the patterns of offences will affect the sentencing patterns. Bearing these complexities in mind, only the factors affecting males aged 17–20 will be examined here in detail, over the period 1981 to 1991. Prior to 1981 there were many changes, in particular due to the Courts Act, 1970 and the Criminal Law Act, 1977, which make interpretation of changes in the sentencing patterns before 1981 extremely difficult (see Walker 1981).

Table 3.3 The distribution of sentences of males aged 17–20, 1981 and 1991, indictable offences

	1981		1991	
	000s	%	000s	%
Discharge	8	7	14	17
Probation	10	9	11	14
Fine	54	48	29	35
CSO	12	11	12	14
AC	1	1	2	3
Suspended sentence	5	4	-	-
Immediate custody	22	19	12	15
Other	1	1	2	2
All	114	100	82	100
Cautioned	3		28	
No/100 000 population	7 049		7 676	

Source: *Criminal Statistics 1991*, Table 7.11.

There were several changes in the sentences of males aged 17–20 from 1981 to 1991, and they appear to have got less severe. There has been an increase in the proportions discharged, from 7 per cent to 17 per cent, and a decrease in the proportion receiving immediate custody, from 19 per cent to 15 per cent. These could be due to (1) legislation, (2) change in offence pattern, (3) change in the percentage sentenced in the Crown Court, (4) other factors which affect sentencing, such as a reduction in the numbers of charges, numbers of previous convictions etc.

1. The main changes affecting this age group were the introduction in 1988 of young offender institutions (replacing Borstals, which were abolished in 1983, detention centres and youth custody). It is not clear whether this would affect the proportion given immediate custody.

   A second change, is the reclassification (in 1988) of certain triable-either-way offences as summary offences; these included TWOC, assault on a constable, and driving while disqualified, which are excluded from the table in the 1981 figures. Since these are, on average, *less* serious offence, removal from the group of indictable offences might be expected to reduce the *numbers* given a discharge, thereby increasing the *percentages* of more severe disposal such as immediate custody, rather than the other way round. It has been shown (HOSB 18/92) that there was a reduction in the overall number of custodial sentences. Unfortunately there is no information on whether there was a change in the acquittal rate.

2. The offence patterns may have changed. The decrease in the percentage receiving immediate custody might come about if the percentage sentenced for robbery, sex offences, and burglary decreased. However, the percentages were virtually the

same in the two years (totalling 34 per cent). The biggest change was that 7 per cent in 1991 and only 4 per cent 1981 were convicted of drug offences, which has a high custodial sentencing rate. This would have had the effect of increasing the custody rate slightly.

3. The percentages committed for trial increased from 20 per cent in 1981 to 21.5 per cent in 1991. This increase might have brought about a higher custody rate, rather than reducing it, as a custodial sentence is more likely in the Crown Court.

    All these factors, might have brought about an *increase* in custodial sentencing, but in fact there was a decrease, which points towards a real change in sentencing for males aged 17–20.

4. Another point worth comment is that the average sentence length appears to have increased since 1981. For all males (the only figures available) the average was 10.3 months in 1981 and 14.7 in 1991. This does not necessarily mean the sentences have been getting more severe. It could be that the less serious offenders have been diverted to CSOs, for example, which would mean that only the more serious were receiving immediate custody. Information on the offences themselves, previous convictions, etc., is not available.

TIME INTERVALS AND WAITING TIMES

The Home Office collects data from the magistrates' courts regarding the time intervals between different events as cases proceed from offence to final disposal (which may mean date of committal) in the magistrates' courts. This is obtained from a sample of one week in each of February, June and October each year for indictable offences and just one week in June for summary motoring and other summary offences. The results are published in Statistical Bulletins, (for example, 22/93 for proceedings in February 1992 and 8/93 for indictable proceedings in October 1992). The latter bulletin includes information on remands, type of proceedings (including plea) and offence, for police force areas and other local areas. A summary is given in *CS*, Table 6.3.

For indictable offences the average number of days from offence to charge or summons is 43 days (1992 figures), from charge or summons to first listing (usually the date of first appearance) 22 days and from first listing to completion 64 days, totalling 129 days from offence to completion in the magistrates' courts. Whereas the first two periods have not increased since 1987 (the first date given) the time *during* court proceedings has increased by nearly two weeks. This is mainly due to the proportion completed at first hearing having decreased from 26 per cent to 20 per cent. Information on whether this was due to an increase in not-guilty pleas would be useful here.

It would clearly be advantageous to the defendant if the police could reduce the time (six weeks) between offence and charge or summons, and this would probably reduce the number of offences committed on bail, a current source of concern. Another three weeks before first court appearance, and an average of nine weeks before completion can surely hardly be justified in terms of the paperwork needed to ensure a just disposal. The Crown Court figures refer, more realistically, to *waiting times* rather than simply *time intervals*. These are published in *Judicial Statistics* and measured in weeks rather than days. The average time between date of committal for trial and start of hearing was 12.6 weeks a quarter being over 16 weeks (in 1991). Cases with not-guilty pleas took 8 weeks longer (averaging 17 weeks) than those with guilty pleas (11 weeks). This means offences to be tried in the Crown Court take about five months before a hearing even commences (that is, 65 days, or 9 weeks from offence to first appearance in magistrates' courts, plus 12.6 weeks to commencement of trial).

APPEALS

Persons convicted of an offence in the magistrates' courts may appeal to the Crown Court against conviction, conviction and sentence, or sentence only. Similarly, those tried or sentenced in the Crown Court may appeal to the Court of Appeal (Criminal Division).

Statistics giving the appeal against decisions by the magistrates are published in Home Office Statistical Bulletins. *Judicial Statistics* (published by the Lord Chancellor's Department) also gives numbers of cases dealt with by the Crown Court on appeal. The HOSB (13/93) points out that the figures in the two sets of tables are not strictly comparable owing to different methods of classification. There is quite a big discrepancy. *Judicial Statistics 1991*, (p. 64) quotes just over 18 000 disposals in the Crown Court in 1991, and the HOSB (Table 5) just under 15 000. The higher figures appear to be partly due to cases of people appealing against both conviction and sentence being counted twice. However, most of the difference is due to appeals against refusals to grant various licences. They are counted in *Judicial Statistics* but not in HOSB.

Appeals to Crown Court against magistrates' decisions

Of those convicted in the magistrates' courts 0.6 per cent or 8500 appealed against conviction and 0.7 per cent appealed against sentence in 1991. Of the former the conviction was quashed in 38 per cent of the cases, compared with 27 per cent in 1981.

Of those sentenced in the magistrates' courts, 3700 appealed against conviction and sentence, and 6300 against sentence only. Fifty-four per cent of the former and 48 per cent of the latter, were 'successful' in having the sentence varied, a slight increase over 1981 figures.

The HOSB (13/93) gives considerable detail about appeals and the result in relation to the initial and final sentence imposed; about a fifth were against unsuspended imprisonment (41 per cent having the sentence retained but reduced in length; 1 per cent had it increased). Fifty-eight per cent were appeals against a fine (57 per cent having it reduced, 1 per cent increased).

Appeals to the Court of Appeal (Criminal Division)

There are two stages in appealing to the Court of Appeal against conviction or sentence by the Crown Court. The applicant has to show that there are reasonable grounds on which to base the appeal, and leave to appeal has first to be obtained. In 1991 there were initially 6300 applications of which 500 (8 per cent) were abandoned and 3500 (55 per cent) were refused, and the latter percentage was virtually the same for the three types of appeal: conviction only, sentence only, or both (HOSB 13/93). *Judicial Statistics* reports just under 9000 cases to be dealt with by the Court of Appeal. The reason for the discrepancy is not clear.

Tables in the HOSB give the number of initial applicants, by offence group, type of sentence, and type of appeal, and also the numbers of appeals heard, for three groupings, and the outcome of the appeals. Where the sentence was changed, details are given. Tables which give the 'success rate' of the appellants are based on the original number of applicants and are therefore considerably smaller than if they were based on the number of appeals heard. Of appeals against conviction heard, 32 per cent had the conviction quashed on all counts; of those heard appealing against sentence only 69 per cent had the sentence varied; of those appealing against both, 61 per cent had either a conviction quashed or a sentence varied. These are in contrast to the rates given based on all applications to appeal, which were 13 per cent and 26 per cent (for the last two groups).

The HOSB gives the numbers of applicants to appeal against conviction for 1981 onwards as fluctuating around 1500 and the percentage with conviction quashed as varying about 10 per cent. The numbers of applicants appealing against conviction and sentence, or sentence only, varied around 6000. About 7 per cent of defendants sentenced in the Crown Court applied, with a peak in 1986 (this would mainly refer to cases sentenced in 1985). Only 16 per cent were 'successful' in that year compared with 20 per cent in 1981 and 26 per cent in 1991.

DISCUSSION

In examining the tables of court proceedings it is important to realize that these refer to the endpoint of a series of decisions made in the relevant court in the relevant year. There is a wealth of material now published in Home Office Statistical Bulletins, not all of which could be referred to here (see p. 88 for a list of the most relevant). Yet they are still certain things one cannot find out. For example, the number initially proceeded against for a particular offence is not available but only the offence for which they are finally acquitted or convicted. There is no linkage between the cases committed for trial for an offence and the outcome in the Crown Court, since the tables relate to those cases completed in a given year and, owing to inevitable delays, many will be tried in the year following that of committal. Besides this, pleas are not recorded, so acquittal rates based on plea cannot be calculated in either court.

The data on offenders which can be obtained from *Criminal Statistics* is limited to sex and age group (or sometimes actual age) of those cautioned and proceeded against in each year. It would be of considerable interest in examining trends in offending if the numbers who were first offenders in each year were recorded, and it has to be remembered that some offenders appear several times in each year. Only longitudinal studies can examine the criminal careers of offenders, but these are mainly only available for convictions (see Tarling 1993). Offenders who are cautioned by the police are less easy to study and offenders *not* dealt with by the police could only be examined by self-report surveys which present methodological and ethical problems.

The information on court proceedings, and the offenders dealt with there, give a snapshot of the operation of one part of the criminal justice system. No set of tables can give an indication of the processes involved, which are a complex interaction of a series of decisions by the defendant, and those involved in the adminstration of justice. The very large amount of data now available certainly constitute a useful starting point for examining these processes. Once again it is important to realize that there is considerable variation, probably at every stage, between different areas of the country and different courts.

Acknowledgement

I wish to thank Patrick Collier and his colleagues at the Home Office Research and Statistics Department for their comments on a draft of this chapter.

REFERENCES

Barclay, G. (1993). *Digest 2: Information on the Criminal Justice System in England and Wales*. Home Office Research and Statistics Department, London.

Bottomley, A. K. and Pease, K. (1986). *Crime and Punishment: Interpreting the Data*. Open University Press, Milton Keynes.

Crown Prosecution Service (1991–1992). *Annual Report*. London.

Farrington, D. P. (1992). Trends in English juvenile delinquency. *International Journal of Comparative and Applied Criminal Justice* **16**, 151–163.

Farrington, D. P. and Morris, A. M. (1983). Sex, sentencing and reconviction. *British Journal of Criminology* **23**, 229–298.

Fowles, A. J. (1993). Crown Prosecution Service: issues of implementation. Paper presented to British Criminology Conference, Cardiff.

Hedderman, C. and Moxon, D. (1992). *Magistrates' Court or Crown Court? Mode of Trial Decisions and Sentencing*. Home Office Research Study 125. HMSO, London.

Hood, R. (1992). *Race and Sentencing*. Clarendon Press, Oxford.

Lord Chancellor's Department (annual). *Judicial Statistics*. HMSO, London.

Phillpotts, G. J. O. and Lancucki, L. B. (1979). *Previous Convictions, Sentence and Reconviction*. Home Office Research Study 53. HMSO, London.

Riley, D. and Vennard, J. (1988). *Triable-either-way Cases: Crown Court or Magistrates' Court?* Home Office Research Study 98, HMSO, London.

Tarling, R. (1993). *Analysing Offending: Data, Models and Interpretation*. HMSO, London.

Walker, M. A. (1981). *Crime: Reviews of United Kingdom Statistical Sources* Vol. XV. Pergamon, Oxford.

4 The police

KEITH BOTTOMLEY AND CLIVE COLEMAN

SOURCES OF STATISTICS ON POLICING

The primary source of statistical data on police work is the annual publication, *Criminal Statistics England and Wales*, with its four additional volumes of Supplementary Tables. Reference has already been made (Chapter 3) to the comprehensive data on police cautioning provided in *Criminal Statistics*. In addition, data is provided on how persons proceeded against at magistrates' courts have been dealt with by the police, prior to first court appearance, including the numbers summonsed, arrested, and bailed by the police, and those arrested and held in custody (p. 27), although some official doubts have been expressed about the quality and accuracy of some of these data on remands on bail and in custody.

Comprehensive information on arrests, by police force areas, is unavailable on a national basis. However, on 15 March 1993, the *Independent* published a 'league table' of arrests, based on published and unpublished Home Office and police force totals. It showed changes in total arrests and recorded crime in 1990 and 1991, as well as the relative positions of the police forces in England and Wales, according to the average number of arrests per officer in 1991. Nottinghamshire came out top of the league, with a figure of 20 arrests per officer, and the Metropolitan Police District bottom with 5.5.

Publication of that table illustrates some of the problems involved in constructing and using such league tables. It is important to note what exactly is being counted. In this instance the figures covered all arrests, as the Home Office refused to supply figures for notifiable crime arrests only. The figures therefore include minor and traffic offences, which normally comprise a sizeable proportion of the total and are notoriously subject to variations in local policy and police discretion. It would be comparatively easy for a force to increase the number of such arrests, which would be a tempting strategy if the figures were being used as a performance indicator. Arrests may differ greatly in terms of their 'quality' in another way – the adequacy of the grounds upon which they are made, which may in turn affect the outcome. Thus, the use of all arrests, undifferentiated in terms of such aspects, may not only be inadequate as a measure of performance but may in itself encourage arrests of doubtful value.

Apart from *Criminal Statistics*, the other regularly published source of national data on aspects of police work is the Home Office Statistical Bulletins, to which detailed reference will be made below in our discussion of statistics relating to the operation of certain powers under the Police and Criminal Evidence Act (PACE). Other relevant Statistical Bulletins cover motoring offences, liquor licensing, the operation of the Prevention of Terrorism legislation, police complaints and discipline, breath test statistics, offences of drunkenness, firearm certificates, betting licensing statistics, and drug seizures.

An interesting but much more variable and less accessible source of information is the annual reports published by the chief constables of each of the 43 police forces in England and Wales. A survey of these reports for 1992 showed that, although some reports incorporate statistics in the main text, the vast majority present statistical tables in separate appendices, typically about 20 pages long, but ranging from 4 to 40 pages. One force published its statistical tables in a separately bound volume.

The scope and format of the statistical data vary greatly, so that it is impossible to make systematic comparisons between forces. All include the required data on certain sections of PACE, and data on recorded crime and persons proceeded against. Additionally, the majority provide statistical information on road traffic accidents, drinking and driving, fixed penalties, establishment staff, recruitment, promotion and commendations, staff training, complaints and discipline, as well as miscellaneous matters such as drug arrests/seizures, firearms licences, burglar alarms, etc. Interesting, but less frequently mentioned, items include public order activities, assaults on officers, forensic and scenes-of-crime work, sudden deaths, number of tape recorded interviews and requests for transcripts (one force), racial incidents (three forces), lay visits (one force), underwater searches, stray dogs and dogs worrying livestock (!), victim support scheme referrals (one force), and child abuse cases (one force). So, at a local level, rich data are sometimes available on the kaleidoscopic range of police duties, but for the purposes of obtaining national or comparative data, the annual reports are an inadequate basis.

Finally, reference must be made to the British Crime Surveys (BCS), of which four have been carried out between 1982 and 1992, providing data on crime victimization and reported crime in 1981, 1983, 1987, and 1991. The BCS data provide unique information not only on the reporting and recording of crime, but also on public fears of crime and attitudes to the police.

It is not possible, in a single short chapter, to provide more than a selective review of statistics relating to police work. In terms of the police role in the initial discovery and recording of crimes, it has already been seen (Chapter 2) that the validity of using the statistic of 'notifiable offences recorded by the police' as an accurate measurement of crime in a particular area, or at a particular time, depends primarily upon the degree to which members of the public take the initial step of reporting the incident or the offender to the police, and whether there is any consistency in the way these initial decisions are taken. Since the publication, in 1983, of the findings of the first British Crime Survey, it has been possible to estimate reasonably accurately the proportion of crimes committed against individuals or households that have been reported to the police, and to discover some of the main reasons underlying the reporting and the non-reporting of crimes.

What is less frequently recognized is that before a reported incident finally appears in the *Criminal Statistics* tables of 'notifiable offences recorded by the police', it is subject to a further filtering process by the police. As a consequence, the recorded crime rate is a complex product of the initial decisions of citizens to *report* crimes and the subsequent investigation and discretionary decisions of police officers as to whether to *record* them as 'notifiable offences'. Two points about the context within which recording takes place should be noted. The first is that most of the incidents that eventually find their way into the statistics of notifiable offences first come to the attention of the police through the activity of members of the public rather than through the activity or observation of the police themselves. Studies in Britain have suggested that between 77 and 96 per cent of offences recorded are initially drawn to police attention by members of the public in various guises (Bottomley and Pease 1986, p. 34). In our own study, for example, the police were directly or indirectly responsible for the discovery of only 14 per cent of incidents which were finally recorded as crimes; 57 per cent were due to personal victims, 23 per cent were reported by representatives of victimized organizations, and 3 per cent by witnesses. The pattern varied according to the type of offence so that, for example, as many as 41 per cent of offences of fraud and forgery were discovered by the police, most often 'indirectly' in the process of investigation or questioning as a result of another, often similar, offence (Bottomley and Coleman 1981, pp. 43–8).

What this means is that although the police play the key role in the recording of crime, this is done within a context in which members of the public and various other organizations or their representatives play a very significant role in bringing information to the attention of the police in the first place. We must therefore take into account the role of such agents as victims, witnesses, store detectives, caretakers, security staff, managers of public and private enterprises, and others in the production of crime statistics. It is these who most frequently take the initial steps (or just as significantly do not) in the process that may lead to a reported crime. This, however, is not to deny the role of police discretion in responding to members of the public and the information they provide. Also, the point is not necessarily true of all offences. Police initiative is likely to be far more pronounced in many non-notifiable offences, particularly those without a clear victim who has an interest in bringing the incident to the attention of the police (e.g. some offences relating to drugs, prostitution, drunkenness, and public order). Here the police are likely to have a more autonomous role in the identification of offences and offenders.

The second point concerns procedures involved in the recording of notifiable offences. In general a document called a crime report is usually started for incidents in which a notifiable offence appears to have taken place, and these become the basis for statistical returns to the Home Office. Upon further investigation, it is possible that new information comes to light or circumstances change in such a way that the police feel able to write off an offence as a 'no-crime'. In the past some interest was aroused by the reasons which led to the use of the procedure and by the fact that different forces had rather different rates of no-crime as a proportion of total recorded crime. One reason for the latter was that forces had different procedures upon receiving crime complaints; the more forces conducted preliminary investigations before starting the crime report, the lower their rates of no-crime tended to be. A number of studies on this area have been helpful in shedding light on police procedure and discretion in recording and writing off incidents (for a summary see Bottomley and Pease 1986, pp. 36–9).

In this chapter we shall begin by looking at the nature and effects of the decisions taken by police officers to record as crimes the incidents that come to their notice, and then examine the significance of the 'clear-up' rates. Finally we shall look at the statistics monitoring certain of the powers under the PACE Act, 1984.

POLICE RECORDING OF REPORTED CRIMES

The British Crime Survey, carried out in 1982, provided the first official recognition of the important gap in our knowledge of the exact nature, extent, and impact of that stage in the production of official crime rates between the reporting and the recording of crime. Not only were BCS respondents asked to indicate the extent of the criminal victimization they had experienced in the previous calendar year, but they were also asked whether they had reported the incident(s) to the police. In this way, not only could estimates be made of the dark figure of unreported crime but also of the 'grey figure' of the number of incidents allegedly reported to the police but apparently not recorded by them. The authors of the first BCS warned that their estimates of the extent of the unrecorded crimes should be treated with particular caution, as the sources of error were more numerous than usual, including:

sampling error in estimating the incidence of offences; sampling error in estimating the proportion of these reported to the police ... non-sampling errors in both estimates (where, for example, respondents might have said that the police were told of an incident when in fact they were not and vice versa) and, finally, errors in the adjustments made to the *Criminal Statistics* figures.

Hough and Mayhew 1983, p. 12

There is also the usual problem of non-response, although this was fairly low at 23 per cent. Hough and Mayhew (1983, p. 12) estimated that 'the police recorded as separate notifiable offences about two-thirds of incidents which involved property loss or damage, and rather less than half of those involving violence'. There are several possible reasons for the shortfall in figures of recorded offences, apart from technical sampling and non-sampling errors. The police may not always regard as crimes those sorts of incident which the BCS classify as such: on further investigation the complainant may turn out to have been mistaken in his or her belief that a crime had been committed (e.g. missing property may turn up) or, for other reasons, may decide to withdraw the complaint; the police may suspect that the complainant was making a malicious report or be partly to blame; or the 'crime' may turn out to have been committed by children under the age of criminal responsibility (see Sparks *et al.* 1977; McCabe and Sutcliffe 1978; Bottomley and Coleman 1981). As previously indicated, if a crime report had already been made out, the incident may have been 'no-crimed'. Some incidents reported to the police may have been recorded by them as notifiable offences, but in different crime categories from those used in comparisons with *Criminal Statistics*.

In the subsequent reports of the British Crime Surveys, carried out in 1984, 1988, and 1992, more precise estimates were given of the proportion of offences reported to the police that were actually recorded by them. In the 1984 survey, for example, these ranged from just 25 per cent of offences of theft from the person/robbery, and 37 per

cent of vandalism, to around 70 per cent of offences of theft from motor vehicles, burglary in a dwelling, and bicycle theft (Hough and Mayhew 1985, Appendix A, Table
A). On the other hand, the number of thefts of vehicles and thefts in a dwelling
recorded in *Criminal Statistics* tend to be *greater* than the BCS estimates of those
reported; in the case of car theft, this is probably due to the various types of error
already mentioned, and the negligible exercise of police discretion to 'no-crime' such
cases. In relation to the much larger discrepancy in thefts in a dwelling, it has been
suggested that this is due to differences in classification, whereby the police might
often ultimately classify as 'thefts in a dwelling' incidents which BCS respondents
initially reported as burglaries.

Similar variations are shown in the 1992 survey, ranging from 27 per cent of thefts
from the person and 34 per cent of attempted motor vehicle thefts to 74 per cent of
burglaries with loss and 94 per cent of thefts of motor vehicles. Overall only 60 per
cent of the type of offences covered by the BCS and reported to the police are subsequently recorded by them. Interpreting these findings, the authors of the 1992 BCS
report suggested that:

One likely reason for the shortfall is that the police do not always accept victims' accounts of
incidents; they may think that a report is mistaken or disingenuous, or may feel that there is
simply insufficient evidence to say that a crime has been committed.

Mayhew *et al.,* 1993, p. 16

Furthermore, 'some incidents may have been regarded as too trivial to warrant formal
police action, particularly if complainants indicated they wanted the matter dropped or
were unlikely to give evidence, or if the incident had already been satisfactorily
resolved' (Mayhew *et al.,* 1993, p. 16).

The figures for levels of police recording of reported crimes 1981–1991, based upon
British Crime Survey estimates, are set out in Table 4.1. Over the last ten years, police
recording of acquisitive crimes reported to them has decreased, whereas it has
increased significantly for vandalism and offences of violence.

In the light of this evidence, greater thought needs to be given and further research
conducted into this area of police decision-making and record-keeping, in order to
make sense of changing trends in recorded offences, which, in some cases, may be as
much influenced by police *recording* practices as by public *reporting* attitudes and
behaviour. It is hardly adequate simply to say that 'reported offences which fall by the
wayside in the police recording process may not be especially serious' (Mayhew *et al.*
1989, p. 12). There are undoubtedly many serious offences of violence against the
person and sexual offences (especially those committed within the family) that fail to
appear as 'notifiable offences recorded by the police', which should give real cause for
concern and extra caution in the interpretation of recorded crime statistics.

INTERPRETING THE CLEAR-UP RATE

The so-called 'clear-up' rate of notifiable offences recorded by the police is probably
one of the most used and abused statistics of all those relating to crime and the criminal

Table 4.1 Levels of police recording, 1981, 1983, 1987, and 1991: BCS estimates

	Proportion of reported incidents recorded by the police			
	1981 %	1983 %	1987 %	1991 %
Comparable with recorded offences				
Acquisitive crime	78	69	66	62
Vandalism	33	37	44	56
Violence	37	36	46	51
All comparable	62	58	60	60
Burglary	71	70	65	63
Attempts and no loss	41	39	37	41
With loss	87	87	84	74
All vehicle thefts	91	75	71	65
Theft from motor vehicles	88	64	68	61
Theft of motor vehicles	106	104	90	94
Attempted motor vehicle thefts	51	53	45	34
Bicycle thefts	91	73	55	58
Theft from the person	26	21	36	27
Vandalism	33	37	44	56
Wounding	41	37	48	53
Robbery	24	36	38	48

Notes:
1. Acquisitive crime includes burglary, thefts of and from vehicles (including attempts), bicycle thefts, theft from the person. Vandalism is to household property and vehicles. Violence includes wounding and robbery.
2. The estimates of recording levels are calculated by expressing adjusted recorded offence figures as a proportion of the estimated number of BCS offences reported to the police.
3. Estimates are only calculable on the sub-set of offences comparable with those recorded by the police; this table therefore excludes common assault, other household theft and other personal theft.
Source: The 1992 British Crime Survey, Table A2.6 (Mayhew *et al.* 1993).

justice process. On the face of it, some readers may wonder what all the fuss is about. The clear-up rate is the proportion of offences recorded by the police which are 'cleared up' (or 'detected') each year. Even at this simple level, the statistics for the last 20–30 years may give rise to some initial concern: thus, whereas in 1962 the proportion of indictable offences recorded by the police that were officially cleared up was 44 per cent, by 1992 the same clear-up rate had plummeted to a record low of 26 per cent. As always, of course, statistics are far more complicated than they might appear at first sight. Very rarely does any statistic have an 'objective' meaning or simple interpretation, but rather the interpretation and meaning – or, more correctly, the many different meanings – of statistics can only properly be begun to be understood in the context of the *purposes for which they are being used.*

For example, if the decline in the police clear-up of notifiable offences since the early 1960s were to be used to make a claim about decreasing police efficiency, then it would at least be necessary to convert the clear-up rates into the *number* of reported offences cleared up and then to relate the annual number of cleared-up offences to statistics of the number of police officers – either in total, or distinguishing between uniform and CID officers. McClintock and Avison (1968, p. 119) carried out a simple but salutary exercise of this kind, in their study of changes in the clear-up rate between 1955 and 1965, when it dropped from 49 to 39 per cent in the short space of ten years. They were able to show that, far from decreasing, the number of crimes cleared up or detected *per police officer* actually *increased*, from 3.3 to 5.3 per officer. Similarly, whereas a 50 per cent clear-up rate in 1938 represented just 141 854 offences, and in 1962 the 44 per cent clear-up rate represented 393 646 offences, the record low clear-up rate of 26 per cent in 1992 represented as many as 1 390 864 offences! Furthermore, when related to the total number of police officers, this represents a five-fold increase in the number of crimes cleared up per officer, from 2.2 in 1938 to 10.9 per officer in 1992.

Apart from very simple adjustments of this sort that are necessary for any meaningful interpretation of trends in the clear-up rate, two other features of this particular statistic must be understood and taken into account in order to make proper comparisons between different police forces. These are (1) the definition and constituent elements of the clear-up rate, and (2) variations between types of offence.

Definition of offences cleared up

The operational definition of what offences the police are permitted or required to count as cleared up is set down in official Home Office requirements, which are subject to periodic revision (see Walker 1992, p. 294; *CS 1991*, p. 190). The main circumstances in which an offence may properly be deemed to have been cleared up include: if a person has been charged, summonsed or cautioned for the offence; if the offence is admitted and has been or could be taken into consideration by the court; if there is sufficient evidence to charge a person but the case is not proceeded with, for a variety of reasons, including the serious illness or death of the offender, complainant, or essential witness before proceedings could be initiated or completed; the offender is under the age of criminal responsibility, or is already serving a long custodial sentence for another offence (and it is decided that no useful purpose would be served by proceeding with the charge); or because the victim is unable or refuses to give evidence.

Although this multi-faceted composition of the clear-up rate has been acknowledged by the Home Office and the police, and well documented by researchers in this country for more than a quarter of a century (e.g. McClintock and Avison 1968; Lambert 1970; Bottomley and Coleman 1981; Burrows and Tarling 1982; Bottomley and Pease 1986), national data giving a breakdown of the methods of clearing up crime have only become available in *Criminal Statistics England and Wales* for the years since 1985 (*CS 1987* paras 2.33–34). Table 4.2 shows the latest breakdown of the clear-up rate according to method.

Table 4.2. Notifiable offences[a] cleared up by the police by method of clear up

England and Wales							Numbers of percentages
Year	Method of clear-up						Total
	Charge/ summons	Caution	Taken into consideration	No further action		All methods	recorded offences
				Interview convicted prisoner	Other		
Numbers of offences (000s)[b]							
1985	607	152	232	159	62	1 212	3 426
1986	592	118	182	175	89	1 157	3 660
1987	629	140	192	190	78	1 229	3 716
1988	637	136	212	188	76	1 249	3 550
1989	657	132	168	199	90	1 247	3 706
1990	687	151	209	221	111	1 379	4 364
1991	691	167	262	246	114	1 479	5 075
Cleared up as percentage of recorded[b]							
1985	18	4	7	4	2	35	
1986	16	3	5	5	2	32	
1987	17	4	5	5	2	33	
1988	18	4	6	5	2	35	
1989	18	4	5	5	2	34	
1990	16	3	5	5	3	32	
1991	14	3	5	5	2	29	

[a] Excluding offences of 'other criminal damage' of value £20 or under.
[b] Estimated from returns from 40 police forces for 1988, 38 for 1987, 35 for 1986, and 26 for 1985.
Source: Criminal Statistics England and Wales 1991, Table 2.12.

As long ago as 1968, McClintock and Avison pointed out that crimes could be recorded as known and cleared up without any *direct* police 'detection' work, citing, in particular, the way in which offenders may be persuaded to have other offences taken into consideration (TIC) by the court. They suggested that a distinction should be drawn between those cleared by *direct* and those cleared by *indirect* methods of detection, particularly if such statistics were to be used as measures of the comparative effectiveness of different police forces (McClintock and Avison 1968, pp. 113–15). The terminology that has now been widely adopted distinguishes between primary and secondary clear-ups, with the former category comprising offences cleared up by charge, summons, or caution, and the latter category covering all other methods.

As can be seen from Table 4.2, between 1985 and 1991 the decline in the overall clear-up rate mainly reflected a drop in the percentage of recorded offences cleared up by charge or summons. There was a decrease in the proportion taken into consideration between 1985 and 1986 – probably mainly attributable to the introduction of the provisions of PACE regulating the conduct and recording of interviews with suspects in police custody – but for the next five years there was no significant reduction in secondary clear-ups. For the first time, the Home Office Statistical Bulletin 9/93 *(Notifiable Offences England and Wales 1992)* presented data on methods of clear-up, using the categories 'primary' and 'secondary': 16 per cent of notifiable offences were cleared up in 1992 by primary means (compared to 21 per cent primary clear-ups in 1987), representing 61 per cent of all clear-ups in that year; the number of primary clear-ups in 1992 fell by only 2 per cent, compared to 1991, whereas the number of secondary clear-ups fell by 13 per cent, which was the first drop of any significance since 1986. It was claimed that 'this reflects a concentration of resources by certain forces on clearing up crime by primary means, rather than following up offenders already convicted' (HOSB 9/93, p. 11). This in turn, it could be suggested, was probably not unconnected with media publicity in the previous year surrounding revelations of the police practice of 'prison write-offs' (i.e. admissions of offences by persons serving prison sentences). Not only was it confirmed that overall clear-up rates vary widely among police forces (see below, for further discussion), but the distribution of clear-ups according to method also varies widely among forces:

(f) The proportion cleared up by primary means [in 1992] ranges from under 50 per cent in three forces (Cleveland, Greater Manchester and Merseyside) to at least 80 per cent in four forces (Cheshire, City of London, Suffolk and Gwent).

(g) 12 per cent of notifiable offences in England and Wales were cleared up by charge or summons, the largest proportion of all the methods. However, in four forces at least 20 per cent were cleared up in this way, headed by Gwent on 32 per cent. Against this, five forces – Avon and Somerset, Cleveland, Devon and Cornwall, the Metropolitan Police District and Thames Valley – cleared up only 9 per cent by this method...

(i) Of the secondary methods, interviews of convicted prisoners accounted for the most clear-ups nationally, with 4 per cent of notifiable offences being detected by this method. However, there was much variation among forces, largely as a result of differing policies towards the employment of this method. Ten forces cleared up 1 per cent or less of notifiable offences using this method, whereas three forces – Merseyside, Greater Manchester, and South Wales – cleared up at least 10 per cent.

HOSB 9/93, p. 11

Once again, therefore, as already seen in relation to the recording of reported crime, variable police policies and practices can and manifestly do have a considerable influence upon some of the important statistics deriving from and frequently taken as a measure of the efficiency of their work in the discovery, investigation, and clearing up of notifiable offences.

Variations by type of offence: offence mix and clear-up rates

A second important feature of clear-up rates that must be recognized before any sensible attempt can be made to draw comparisons between forces is the way that clear-up rates vary according to the type of offence. In particular, the majority of crimes of violence (with the exception of robbery) or crimes of a sexual nature, have clear-up rates that are more than double those of most offences against property. Thus, in each year, 1981–1991, over 70 per cent of sexual offences and offences of violence against the person were cleared up (including well over 90 per cent of homicides and attempted murders) compared with between 23–30 per cent of burglary offences and 28–38 per cent of offences of theft and stolen goods *CS 1991* p. 39, Table 2.8). The main reason for this large gap in the clear-up rates between offences against the person and property offences is simply that in the majority of cases of offences against the person the offender is known to the victim and can be immediately identified or, at the least, described to the police, whereas, in property offences very rarely is there any contact between offender and victim to enable any identification, with the result that the police are faced with very different detection tasks.

A further point to be noted is that there are some categories of offence which are almost automatically 'cleared up' by virtue of having become known to the police. They range from certain sexual offences, such as indecency between males, unlawful sexual intercourse with under-age girls, and incest, to property offences such as handling stolen goods and theft by employee, as well as various forms of fraud. Most of these offences cannot be recorded as such by the police until or unless a suspect is also known, which automatically renders it cleared up.

Another interesting example is the very common offence of shoplifting (or 'theft from shops'), in which the clear-up rate appears artificially high (for property offences) – 80 per cent in 1992 – simply because most shops and department stores only report offences to the police for which a suspect has been apprehended. The message that has to be repeated is that no statistic has to be taken at face value, before careful consideration has been given to the processes, decisions, and circumstances that give rise to the final 'product'.

Comparisons between police forces

The cumulative effect of factors of the sort that have been outlined in this section is to render comparisons between the clear-up rates of different police forces very problematic indeed. Tables in the annual *Criminal Statistics England and Wales* give the clear-up rate by police force area, and show that over the last ten years these have varied from 50 per cent or more in the Welsh forces of Dyfed–Powys and Gwent, to less than 20 per cent in the London Metropolitan Police District (*CS 1991*, p. 42, Table 2.11). Within the main offence groups, there are similar wide variations, from less than 50 per cent to 100 per cent of violent crime, from 10 to 40 per cent of burglaries, and from 40 to 90 per cent of fraud and forgery (*CS 1991* p. 31, Table 2.9). Generally, but not always, the metropolitan forces have lower clear-up rates than the non-metropolitan. In a year when the national clear-up rate was only 26 per cent, forces varied between 53 per cent (Dyfed–Powys) and 16–17 per cent (Metropolitan Police District, Avon and Somerset, and Northumbria). Nine forces cleared up 35 per cent or more of all recorded offences, whereas six forces cleared up 20 per cent or less. The rank order for the distribution between primary and secondary clear-up methods did not correspond precisely to the overall ranking, so that three of the overall top ranking forces (Merseyside, Lancashire, and Greater Manchester – all in the urban north-west of

England) had lower primary clear-up rates than many forces ranked lower than them overall. On the other hand, the percentage of crimes cleared up by prison write-offs in Merseyside and Greater Manchester was between three and four times greater than the national average, and more than twice as high as most of the other forces ranked alongside them for the overall clear-up rate.

Such evidence strengthens the argument for concentrating exclusively on primary clear-ups, if this statistic is to be used to measure police effectiveness in the detection of crime. In their study, McClintock and Avison advocated the calculation, for comparative purposes, of an 'estimated relative detection rate' for each force, based only on crimes cleared by direct (or 'primary') methods. Although the formula they suggested for this calculation was rather 'a curious mixture of people and offences' (Walker 1992, p. 296), their aims were entirely laudable, and were reaffirmed more than 20 years later by the Audit Commission, which suggested that 'if one measure alone is to be used, primary clear-ups per officer is better than the overall clear-up rate' (Audit Commission, 1990, quoted by Walker 1992). The other main message to emerge from research studies is that any comparisons between police forces – even those based solely on primary clear-ups – should take into account the 'offence mix' of recorded crimes in each force, in view of the differential distribution of offences with above average clear-up rates, such as violence, sexual offences, fraud, shoplifting, and handling stolen goods (see McClintock and Avison 1968; Burrows and Tarling 1982; Bottomley and Pease 1986). The authors of a detailed Home Office study concluded:

'Crime mix' was always the most highly related variable [for explaining differences in force clear-up rates] regardless of which other variables accompanied it. This factor, then, appeared to be the most important determinant of the clear-up rate.

Burrows and Tarling 1982, p. 10

Inevitably, in today's political and professional climate, the temptation to use the clear-up rate, or some modification of it, as a measure of police efficiency and effectiveness is almost impossible to resist. However, as the Audit Commission stated:

The simple measure of the clear-up rate of recorded crime is of limited use. Yet it is the subject of media attention and within police forces it is often used as a key indicator of CID performance, even though senior police officers are well aware of its limitations as a measure of police effectiveness.

Audit Commission,1990, p. 9

It further recognized that 'the statistics can be manipulated to produce merely cosmetic improvement' (p. 17) and that no single measure of performance is adequate.

In its report, the Audit Commission presented a diagnostic crime clearance model, which confirmed the inherent complexity of the task of monitoring crime clearance effectiveness and highlighted the major differences between forces' methods of clearing up crimes, especially in the proportions of primary and secondary clear-ups (Audit Commission 1990, pp. 17–20). It is admitted, however, that a model of this kind raises more questions than it answers. For example, Monica Walker has pointed out that no account is taken or information provided of the outcome of primary clear-ups, which include cases of 'no further action' by the police, and might well encourage them to boost their clear-up rate by charging suspects on rather weak evidence (Walker 1992, pp. 302–3). When, in addition, account is taken of CPS discontinuances (which increased sharply between 1985 and 1992), as well as court acquittals/dismissals, it is difficult not to agree with Walker's conclusion that:

even primary clear-up rates, which the Audit Commission consider to be important statistics, can themselves be 'difficult to interpret', although they may be minimally useful as a measure of police activity rather than efficiency.

Walker 1992, p. 302

Clear-up rates should be viewed as (ac)counts of decisions and activities rather than as evaluative measures of police work. Whilst not wishing to go quite so far as Walker in calling for clear-up rates not to be published in *Criminal Statistics,* we would agree with her that high clear-up rates should never be uncritically accepted as valid performance indicators 'by which to judge the policing service delivered to the public' (Walker 1992, p. 305). The more they are used in this way, the greater the risk that they might divert police officers from more important tasks and appear to reward inefficient and professionally dubious practices.

STATISTICS RELATING TO CERTAIN POLICE POWERS UNDER THE POLICE AND CRIMINAL EVIDENCE ACT (PACE)

A number of new or modified police powers were implemented under PACE on 1 January 1986. For certain of these, the Act requires annual reports made by chief officers to include statistics on their use. These relate to stops and searches, road checks, persons detained for more than 24 hours and released without charge, persons detained under warrant of further detention (beyond 36 hours), and intimate searches. Summaries of these statistics for England and Wales are provided in issues of the Home Office Statistical Bulletin. These constitute a major addition to the statistics available on policing. Each category of these will therefore be discussed briefly in turn.

Stops and searches

Statistics are available for each police force area on the number of stop/searches made according to the reason for the search (for stolen property or drugs, for example) and on the resultant arrests according to the reason for the arrest (using the same categories). Summary statistics for England and Wales since 1986 are shown in Table 4.3. All the categories in the table should be fairly clear except the 'other' category. This includes searches under powers that do not fit into the first five categories. The 'other' category in the arrest data should also include these, but might also include arrests due to the behaviour of the person during the stop and search. A survey of records from one force conducted by the Home Office in 1987 found that only 5 per cent of the category were for this reason, but that about a third of the total should have been placed under one of the specific categories (HOSB 21/93, n. 5).

Table 4.3. Searches of persons or vehicles under Section 1 of the Police and Criminal Evidence Act, 1984, and resultant arrests, by reason for search and reason for arrest

England and Wales   Numbers

Year	Stolen property	Drugs	Firearms	Offensive weapons	Going equipped	Other	Total
			Searches made by reason for search				
1986	48 000	32 500	1 450	6 900	10 700	10 700	109 800
1987	48 800	38 300	1 060	8 500	13 600	8 100	118 300
1988	61 000	50 100	1 200	10 400	17 900	9 100	149 600
1989	77 300	79 100	1 590	12 400	23 800	8 600	202 800
1990	97 100	97 800	1 770	14 900	35 500	10 000	256 900
1991	113 700	109 600	2 480	15 800	50 900	11 300	303 800
1992	127 400	124 400	2 740	18 600	63 900	14 700	351 700
			Arrests made by reason for arrest				
1986	7 400	6 200	147	1 340	1 590	2 230	18 900
1987	7 000	6 500	141	1 940	1 780	2 220	19 600
1988	7 500	9 100	182	2 130	2 000	2 770	23 700
1989	9 800	14 000	245	2 700	2 500	3 500	32 800
1990	12 000	16 000	275	3 060	3 490	4 470	39 200
1991	15 100	17 500	389	3 370	4 890	5 060	46 200
1992	15 800	18 100	340	3 420	5 530	5 540	48 700

Source: Home Office Statistical Bulletin, Issue 21/93, Table A.

These statistics appear to allow the monitoring of the use of these powers. Three examples of the ways in which these might commonly be used illustrate the possibilities and problems here. Firstly it is apparently possible to monitor changes in the use of the powers over time for England and Wales, or for a particular force area, for searches in general or for a particular type of search. Table 4.3 shows a steady and substantial increase in recorded searches between 1986 (109 800) and 1992 (351 700), with the largest proportional increase for 'going equipped', followed by drugs.

When interpreting such trends, it is important to look at what exactly is being recorded. From April 1991, if a person is in a vehicle and both are searched for the same object and with the same grounds, then only one record need be completed (Home Office 1991, s.A 4.6). It has been estimated that this had the effect of reducing the total number recorded by about 2 per cent per annum (HOSB 21/93, n. 3). The bulletin also suggests that '(a)s the police have become more familiar with PACE, the recording of stops and searches is likely to have become more complete' (HOSB 21/93, n. 2).

There is a valid point here but the use of the term 'more complete' implies that there is a clearly defined set of events out there just waiting to be counted. The legislation and the code of practice also regard a stop and search as a relatively distinct event, in which the officer clearly has, at a particular point in time, the required reasonable grounds for suspicion for exercising the legal power provided. As we have argued elsewhere, the reality is rarely so clear cut, and stop and search is more usefully seen as part of a social process of interaction between officers, suspects, and members of the public (it is not always immediately clear to which of the latter two categories any individual may belong). The concept of reasonable grounds for suspicion, on which guidance was provided in the original code of practice, has had its problems (see Dixon *et al.* 1989), some of which led to reformulation of the guidance in the revised edition published in 1991. Within this context, there are other factors over and above the statutory requirements which play a key role in whether an incident gets recorded. These include: if searches are recorded also for operational/intelligence purposes, as may be the case with drugs; if searches are conducted by a probationary constable or in the presence of a supervisory officer; if senior officers have encouraged officers to record such events (they may be employed as a performance indicator, making record-ing much more likely); if an article is found and an arrest made; if there is any poss-ibility of 'comeback' about a case (e.g. if conducted on a police 'challenger'); if the suspect declines to consent (Dixon *et al.* 1990). In practice, officers are likely to oper-ate by 'consent' as far as they are able and to conduct 'voluntary' searches, which are not required to be recorded. These are now clearly not permitted with those who appear unable to give informed consent, such as juveniles and those suffering from mental handicap or disorder, since the revised code (1991). Again, 'consent' is not a feature that is simply present or absent in any encounter, but may be subject to a range of definitions from the very loose to the most stringent, and the product of a process of interaction between two parties of unequal knowledge and power, at least one of which may be convinced of the irrelevance of any legalistic rights within that context. 'Voluntary' searches therefore provide a realm of events which may not be recorded in the statistics, but practice is likely to be variable over time and space. There is little doubt that 'consent' searches provided a major problem for the authorities in trying to achieve clarity and consistency in procedure and recording (see Dixon *et al.* 1990) and it is unlikely that the problems here have been resolved.

We can only allude to some of the complexities here, but we hope that this brief dis-cussion shows how difficult it is to use the statistics as a simple measure of clearly defined events and to monitor changes in practice over time. Without substantial knowledge of variations here, it is difficult to know how much the increase in the fig-ures since 1986 is due to changes in police practice on the street or in their recording practices. In addition the statistics will not include those searches with which many citizens will be most familiar: those of persons entering sports grounds or other premises, with consent or as a condition of entry (Home Office 1991, s.A1Da).

Similar comments could be made about any attempt to compare the statistics for different police forces. The HOSB has published a map showing the number of searches per 100 000 population for each force area (HOSB 21/93, 4). Here the Metropolitan, City, North Wales and Dyfed – Powys forces clearly come out with the most, each having 1001 or over for 1992. While it is difficult to see exactly why there are such divergences between many forces (e.g. the West Midlands comes in the lowest category of 1 to 200), it seems likely that the figures for some of the front runners are boosted by counter-terrorist activity.

Finally, it is tempting to make judgements about the effectiveness of stop and search by calculating resultant arrests as a percentage of the number of searches, thereby arriving at what is often seen as a 'success' rate. This figure for England and Wales for 1992 was nearly 14 per cent. This figure is often used by some commentators to argue that the power is justified, while, at the other extreme, it is used by others to show how many innocent people have been subject to coercive power. Where one is located in the debate depends on the relative weight given to crime control or due process values (Packer 1968). This apparently simple statistic should be qualified in a number of ways. For example, the percentage will be increased if there is a tendency to record more frequently those searches which result in arrest; in addition, commentators sometimes assume that arrest is the only indication of effectiveness (it is possible to argue that searches serve other purposes, such as the avoidance of unnecessary arrests).

Road checks

Figures for England and Wales and for each police force area are published on: the total number of these; the reasons why they were conducted (namely, to ascertain whether a vehicle was carrying a person who had committed, had witnessed, or was intending to commit a serious arrestable offence, or was unlawfully at large); the number of vehicles stopped; the number of roads obstructed; and the number of arrests resulting, divided into those connected and those not connected with the reason for the check. The total figure since 1986 ranges from 222 (1991) to 445 (1992). This sudden jump was mainly due to the increase in counter-terrorist activity in the City of London (where 202 were conducted 'to ascertain whether a vehicle was carrying a person who was intending to commit a serious arrestable offence' – normally the smallest category in the national picture – the other categories all declined in this year) and the Metropolitan Police District. The total number of vehicles stopped, on the other hand, was slightly fewer in 1992 than in 1991. From all this activity in 1992, 29 were arrested for reasons connected with the check and 83 for reasons not connected.

Persons detained for more than 24 hours without charge

Figures are published on the number of those detained for more than 24 hours under Part IV of PACE, and subsequently released without charge. These totals are then broken down into numbers of those released within 36 hours and those detained under a warrant of further detention. It is noticeable how the total figure declined steadily from 1986 (1187) to 366 in 1991, and then increased by 10 per cent in 1992 to 402. One interpretation of the overall decline is that police forces have been successful in reducing the use of 'unnecessary' detention, as PACE was intended to do. No doubt the actual picture is more complex than that. In each year since 1986, between 84 and 90 per cent of these persons were released within 36 hours, while for the remainder a warrant of further detention was granted. The figures for individual police forces show marked variations in the total number of such detentions; for example, in 1992 some had no cases at all while South Wales had the most (38). Without more information, it is difficult to comment on these variations.

Persons detained under warrant of further detention

The number of applications for warrants of further detention beyond 36 hours also decreased steadily between 1986 (696) and 1992 (235) apart from a jump against the trend to 405 in 1990. In each year very few of these were refused (5 in 1992). Again there are differences in the number of applications for individual forces, for which the explanations are not obvious. Figures given on the numbers charged and not charged indicate that between 74 and 86 per cent of the total were charged in each year since 1986. Figures are also given for the period of time for the warrants, including any extensions, and the time in custody for persons detained under warrant. Here a foot-note indicates that these statistics 'are known to suffer from ambiguity in the record-ing of the data by police forces for 1986 and 1987'. However in 1992, for example, 59 per cent of warrants granted involved periods up to 36 hours and 33 per cent were extended to provide a total period of warrant of over 48 hours. The totals here need to be set against predictions in the mid-1980s that detentions for four days would be routine under PACE.

Intimate searches

The total number of these (which involve the searching of body orifices) made under section 55 of PACE has varied between 104 (1986) and 50 (1989). Information is given on whether searches were conducted by suitably qualified persons, in the pres-ence of such, or by a police officer (the latter is extremely rare). These totals are then broken down to show the reason for the search (drugs or articles which could be used to inflict bodily harm) and whether such articles were found. In 1992, 49 searches were for Class A drugs under the Misuse of Drugs Act, 1971, in 10 of which such items were found; in those for harmful articles (22), one search resulted in an article being found. The figures for individual forces again show variations, with, for exam-ple, 22 forces recording none in 1992 and only three recording ten or over. The latter are force areas where one might expect drug couriers to be active, but again, as with many statistics in this section, explanations are, at best, speculative.

CONCLUSIONS

We hope that this chapter demonstrates the wide range of statistics available on aspects of policing, even if some of these are patchy in coverage. There are three gen-eral points that we should like to reiterate: first, that an understanding of such statistics must take into account the purposes for which they are being used both inside and out-side police organizations; second, that wherever possible attention should be given to the various rules, processes, decisions, and circumstances that lie behind the final product; and third, that there is often a need for research studies and further informa-tion in order to appreciate the reasons for variations and trends in these statistics. In this respect, we know far more about crime and clear-up rates than we do about the statistics relating to PACE. It should be clear that the use of statistics for evaluative purposes is a difficult enough enterprise, but can be positively hazardous where used without due care and knowledge of the context in which they are produced.

REFERENCES

Audit Commission (1990). *Effective Policing: Performance Review in Police Forces.* HMSO, London.

Bottomley, A. K. and Coleman, C. A. (1981). *Understanding Crime Rates: Police and Public Roles in the Production of Official Statistics.* Gower, Farnborough.

Bottomley, A. K. and Pease, K. (1986). *Crime and Punishment: Interpreting the Data.* Open University Press, Milton Keynes.

Burrows, J. and Tarling, R. (1982). *Clearing Up Crime.* Home Office Research Study No. 73. HMSO, London.

Dixon, D., Bottomley, A. K., Coleman, C. A., Gill, M., and Wall, D. (1989). Reality and rules in the construction and regulation of police suspicion. *International Journal of the Sociology of Law* 17, 185–206.

Dixon, D., Coleman, C., and Bottomley, K. (1990). Consent and the legal regulation of policing. *Journal of Law and Society* 17, 345–62.

Home Office (1991). *Police and Criminal Evidence Act, 1984 (s. 66) Codes of Practice,* revised edition. HMSO, London.

Hough, M. and Mayhew, P. (1983). *The British Crime Survey.* Home Office Research Study No. 76. HMSO, London.

Hough, M. and Mayhew, P. (1985). *Taking Account of Crime: Key Findings from the Second British Crime Survey.* Home Office Research Study No. 85. HMSO, London.

Lambert, J. R. (1970). *Crime, Police and Race Relations.* Oxford University Press, London.

Mayhew, P., Elliott, D., and Dowds, L. (1989). *The 1988 British Crime Survey.* Home Office Research Study No. 111, HMSO, London.

Mayhew, P., Aye Maung, N., and Mirrlees-Black, C. (1993). *The 1992 British Crime Survey.* Home Office Research Study No. 132. HMSO, London.

McCabe, S. and Sutcliffe, F. (1978). *Defining Crime: A Study of Police Decisions.* Blackwell, Oxford.

McClintock, F. H. and Avison, N. H. (1968). *Crime in England and Wales.* Heinemann, London.

Packer H. (1968). *The Limits of the Criminal Sanction.* Stanford University Press, Stanford, Ca.

Royal Commission on Criminal Justice (1993). *Report.* Cm 2263. HMSO, London.

Sparks, R. F., Genn, H. G., and Dodd, D. J. (1977). *Surveying Victims: a Study of the Measurement of Criminal Victimization.* Wiley, Chichester.

Walker, M. A. (1992). Do we need a clear-up rate? *Policing and Society* 2, 293–306.

5 Community sentences and the work of the Probation Service

JEAN HINE

On 1 January 1991, there were 138 721 offenders currently under the supervision of the Probation Service. During 1991, 129 463 offenders commenced a period of community supervision or post-custodial licence with the service. These figures from *Probation Statistics England and Wales 1991* show that well over a quarter of a million offenders were subject to supervision by the Probation Service at some time during that year, a volume often not appreciated by people outside the service.

Similarly, the range of work of the Probation Service is broader than many people realize. Table 5.1 shows the range and volume of the types of case supervised by the service between 1981 and 1991. The work of the service covers the following:

(1) supervising and administering probation orders, combination orders, and suspended sentence supervision orders to which offenders are sentenced by the courts;

(2) organizing the work for and administering community service orders and combination orders to which offenders are sentenced by the courts;

(3) supervising and administering young offender supervision orders, parole, discretionary and automatic conditional release licences for offenders released from prison or young offender institutions;

(4) supervising offenders released from prison on life licence or on conditional discharge requirement from psychiatric hospital;

(5) providing assistance and support to prisoners released from custody who are not subject to licence;

(6) supervising and administering money payment supervision orders made by courts to support offenders who need assistance to pay their fines;

(7) preparing pre-sentence reports for magistrates and judges to assist with the sentencing of offenders;

(8) preparing a range of reports about serving prisoners to inform sentence planning, home leave arrangements, and decisions about release on parole licence;

(9) preparing information for the Crown Prosecution Service about offenders' circumstances to inform decisions about custodial remands;

(10)   preparing reports for Family Courts and County Courts to assist their decisions about the custody, access, (now residence and contact) and welfare of children in divorce and adoption proceedings;

(11)   supervising and administering a range of welfare orders made by Family Courts relating to the support of children following divorce proceedings.

The service also supervises young (juvenile) offenders sentenced under the terms of the Children and Young Persons Acts, but over the last ten years this area of work has reduced considerably, partly because there has been a decrease in the numbers of such orders made by the courts, and partly because work with juveniles has more and more moved to Social Services departments as the Probation Service has concentrated on working with adult offenders (i.e. those aged 17 or more).

This chapter will focus on the work which the Probation Service undertakes in supervising adult offenders sentenced to supervision in the community by criminal courts. It will not cover work with prisoners during sentence or on licence, reports for criminal courts or institutions, or work for family courts (civil work).

SOURCES OF STATISTICS

Probation Statistics England and Wales

Published reports about the work of the Probation Service began with the *Report on the Probation and After-care Statistics 1975* and *1976*. Prior to that, summary information was made available to chief probation officers and government departments only. Since that first report the production of an annual publication about the work of the Probation Service has been established, and *Probation Statistics, England and Wales* is now a regular, substantial, and detailed document.

The development of this publication has been made possible by a change in the way in which statistical information has been collected from the Probation Service, the milestone being the establishment of the National Probation Index in 1978–9. Under the previous system, returns were made to the Home Office in the form of monthly summaries from each Probation Service, briefly outlining the numbers of terminations and current cases of different types, with very little detail other than age group and gender. Information about the number of commencements was obtained by the Home Office from figures about proceedings in criminal courts, obtained from returns made by the police and courts.

The current system of collecting information has been in operation since 1978 when the computerized National Probation Index was established. The 55 Probation Services in the country submit information about each individual case which is supervised by a probation officer, at three points during its life:

(1)   the offender's name, date of birth, and gender, the type of case, most serious type of offence for which the order or custodial sentence was given, date of sentence, length, additional requirements and court making the order are submitted when the case commences, along with a simple summary of the offender's previous sentences;

Table 5.1. Numbers of persons commencing supervision by the Probation Service by type of supervision, 1981–91

Type of supervision	1981	1982	1985	1986	1987	1988	1989	1990	1991
Court orders									
Probation	35 850	36 810	41 750	39 690	41 540	42 440	43 280	46 282	44 067
C&YP supervision	11 840	10 950	7 860	5 970	5 020	4 060	3 330	2 971	2 307
SSSO	1 930	1 810	2 000	2 080	2 340	2 540	2 390	2 371	2 272
MPSO	5 950	5 860	5 240	4 840	5 250	5 900	6 460	6 364	5 674
Community service	28 040	30 880	37 560	34 730	35 670	35 010	34 040	38 173	41 190
Total Court orders	79 140	81 950	89 460	82 770	84 910	84 730	83 780	89 405	88 707
After-care									
YOI	23 640	23 720	25 750	22 360	2 220	20 350	16 440	13 991	13 561
Parole	4 680	4 510	12 120	12 840	12 700	12 140	12 180	12 373	10 552
Other licence	410	400	430	460	470	460	420	379	365
Voluntary after-care	22 320	23 410	29 590	28 420	30 400	30 310	27 880	24 945	25 296
Total after-care	49 800	50 780	61 390	57 710	59 780	57 690	52 030	46 914	45 805
Total Criminal supervision	**123 560**	**127 240**	**143 920**	**134 890**	**138 850**	**136 580**	**130 420**	**131 157**	**128 976**
Domestic supervision	4 120	3 920	2 420	1 920	1 540	1 060	930	706	488
Total number of persons commencing supervision	**127 660**	**131 160**	**146 330**	**136 810**	**140 380**	**137 640**	**131 350**	**131 863**	**129 463**

Data for 1983 and 1984 are not available because of industrial action by some members of the National Association of Probation Officers.
C&YP = Children and Young Persons Act
SSSO = suspended sentence supervision order
MPSO = money payments supervision order (sometimes called a fines supervision order)
YOI = young offender institution
Source: *Probation Statistics 1991* Table 1.1, p. 5.

(2) details of the date of termination, reason for termination, and whether breach proceedings have been taken are submitted at the end of the work;

(3) details of release from custody, where appropriate, are submitted at release.

It is a 'transaction'-based system which is very complex to administer, requiring a considerable number of validation checks within the system. Errors which are found have to be returned to areas for investigation and rectification. Thus, although designed to enable the Home Office to be able to 'snapshot' the current caseload position at any time, it is, in fact, always several months out of date, and this has affected the publication date of the annual statistics in the past.

A greater and more complicated impact of the National Probation Index has been that information about commencements of cases has been available from this source, direct from probation officers. However, in order to maintain continuity with previous publications, figures continued to be included in *Probation Statistics* about 'commencements' calculated from courts proceedings data. This leads to considerable problems in interpreting some of the data, and these are discussed in more detail on pp. 73–74.

Criminal Statistics England and Wales

The data published in *Criminal Statistics* are based on the work of the police and the courts, and provide much information about recorded crime and how offenders are dealt with by the courts. They provide two sorts of data about community supervision orders which are not available from *Probation Statistics*: sentencing rates and information about breach proceedings in probation and community service orders.

Sentencing rates

The sections about sentencing are important when looking at the work of the Probation Service, as they enable the calculation of rates of sentence as opposed to raw numbers of orders. *Criminal Statistics* provides a range of tables which give information about sentencing rates, which leads to the need to decide which one gives the most appropriate information for the task.

Table 5.2 shows the number and percentage of offenders sentenced to probation orders and community service orders by all courts for all types of offence between 1987 and 1991. They show little variation over time, with probation orders being constant at 3.2 per cent of all offenders sentenced for both 1990 and 1991, and community service orders showing a slight increase from 2.5 per cent to 2.8 per cent. These figures give the impression that both disposals are used very rarely, but this is misleading. Table 5.3 illustrates that probation and community service orders constitute a much higher proportion of indictable offences than summary offences. It is therefore better to use *rates* of sentencing from indictable offences only, to compare trends. These figures should not, however, be used when the actual number of orders made is of interest because, as we can see, several hundred orders are made for summary offences – 13 300 probation orders in 1991, which was just over a quarter of all the offenders sentenced to probation in that year.

The rates of sentencing to probation and community service for indictable offences have shown little variation during the years 1981–91. Table 7.2 in *Criminal Statistics 1991* shows that the rate for probation orders has gradually increased from 7 per cent of all sentences for indictable offences in 1981 to 10 per cent in 1989, a figure which remained constant to 1991. Community service sentencing has also gradually

Table 5.2. Number and percentage of offenders sentenced for all offences to probation and community service orders 1987–91

	1987	1988	1989	1990	1991
Total number of offenders sentenced	1 544 800	1 555 400	1 534 100	1 513 900	1 503 900
Total number sentenced to probation orders	42 200	43 600	44 200	47 700	47 500
Total number sentenced to community service orders	35 900	35 300	33 900	38 600	42 500
Probation orders as a percentage of all sentences	2.7%	2.8%	2.9%	3.2%	3.2%
Community service orders as a percentage of all sentences	2.3%	2.3%	2.2%	2.5%	2.8%

Source: *Criminal Statistics England and Wales 1991* Table 7A, p. 127.

Table 5.3. Number and percentage of all offenders sentenced who were sentenced to probation and community service orders in all courts in 1991, by type of offence

Gender	Type of offence	Probation orders		Community service orders	
		Number	%	Number	%
Males	Indictable	27 100	9.2	27 600	9.4
	Summary (excluding motoring)	5 800	1.8	5 200	1.6
	Summary motoring	6 400	1.0	7 500	1.2
	All males sentenced	**39 300**	**3.1**	**40 300**	**3.2**
Females	Indictable	7 100	16.9	1 900	4.5
	Summary (excluding motoring)	700	0.5	200	0.2
	Summary motoring	400	0.6	100	0.2
	All females sentenced	**8 200**	**3.5**	**2 200**	**0.9**
All Offenders	Indictable	34 200	10.2	29 500	8.8
	Summary (excluding motoring)	**6 500**	**1.4**	**5 400**	**1.2**
	Summary motoring	6 800	1.0	7 600	1.1
	All offenders sentenced	**47 500**	**3.2**	**42 500**	**2.8**

Source: *Criminal Statistics England and Wales 1991* Table 7.4. p. 145–6.

increased over the years, from 5 per cent in 1981 to 9 per cent in 1991, this figure being 1 per cent more than the 1990 rate of 8 per cent.

Table 5.3 illustrates that the overall rates of sentencing mask marked variations between males and females, and, as we shall see, different age groups also have different sentencing patterns. The overall figures are skewed by males aged 21 and over who accounted for 61 per cent of all adults sentenced for indictable offences in 1991. Table 5.4 shows the sentencing rates for probation and community service orders for the years 1981 to 1991 for males and for females in the 17–20 and 21 and over age groups. The most striking feature of this table is not the trends in sentencing over time, but rather the different rates of sentencing between the four groups. Males have a lower rate of probation orders than do females, and older offenders of both genders have a lower rate than the 17–20 year olds. Probation orders were given to 21 per cent of 17–20 year old female offenders in 1991, making them much more likely to be sentenced to a probation order than any other group. Second most likely to receive an order were female offenders aged 21 and over, at 17 per cent. These were followed by 17–20 year old male offenders at 14 per cent, and lastly male offenders aged 21 and over, at 8 per cent. Community service orders, on the other hand, were most likely to be given to male offenders aged 17–20, 14 per cent of whom were sentenced to community service in 1991. Second most likely were males aged 21 and over, at 8 per cent, followed by 17–20 year old female offenders at 6 per cent and female offenders aged 21 and over, at 4 per cent. These figures show that probation is more likely to be given to women than to men, whilst community service is more likely to be given to men than to women. We will return to this topic later.

The picture about which group is most likely to receive a particular order is very different if viewed from the perspective of the probation statistics. Commencements of probation orders in 1991 (*Probation Statistics 1991* Table 2.2) show that most orders (49 per cent) were on male offenders aged 21 or over, followed by males aged 17–20 who accounted for 32 per cent of orders, females aged 21 and over with 13 per cent of all probation orders, and finally females aged 17–20 with just 5 per cent of commencements. This is a complete reversal of the ranking obtained from sentencing rates in *Criminal Statistics*. Thus, although female offenders aged 21 and over had a much higher rate of sentencing to probation than the other groups, they actually constituted only a very small proportion of the probation order caseload. This reflects the way in which the underlying structure of the sentenced offender population feeds through into the caseload of the probation service; i.e. because the majority of persons sentenced for indictable offences are males aged 21 and over their numbers will dominate the probation order caseload even though their sentencing rate for probation orders was lower than the other groups. *Probation Statistics* can be used to look at the balance of work within the service and changes within that, but should not be used to draw inferences about sentencing practice – *Criminal Statistics* data about sentencing patterns should be used for that.

Table 5.2 shows that the probation order's 'market share' seems to have remained stable, despite a very slight decrease in the actual number of orders made. The decision about which set of figures to use is very much determined by your purpose. If you

Table 5.4. Percentage of offenders sentenced for indictable offences only who were sentenced to probation and community service orders 1981–91, by gender and age group

Year	Males		Females	
	Aged 17–20 years	Aged 21 and over	Aged 17–20 years	Aged 21 and over
Total number sentenced 1991, all sentences	82 400	190 000	10 300	29 200
Probation orders				
1981	9	6	21	16
1982	9	6	21	16
1983	9	6	21	17
1984	10	7	21	17
1985	11	7	21	18
1986	12	7	22	19
1987	12	8	22	18
1988	12	8	22	18
1989	12	8	22	17
1990	13	8	21	18
1991	14	8	21	17
Community service orders				
1981	11	5	4	2
1982	11	6	4	2
1983	13	7	4	2
1984	13	7	5	3
1985	13	7	5	3
1986	14	7	5	3
1987	13	7	5	3
1988	13	7	6	3
1989	13	6	5	3
1990	13	7	6	4
1991	14	8	6	4

Source: *Criminal Statistics England and Wales 1991* Table 7.10–7.13. p. 151–2.

were looking at the workload of the Probation Service you would take the raw figures and the decline; if you were looking at changes in sentencing you would use the sentencing rate figures and the stability.

Breach proceedings

Some information is collected from Probation Services about breaches during probation and community service orders, but a) it is very limited, and b) what is collected is unreliable. The only data published in *Probation Statistics* is the number and percentage of orders which terminate because of the failure to comply with the order. There are many breaches proved where the order is allowed to continue, especially community service orders. Where a breach is proved and the order revoked this may not always be recorded accurately, especially, as often happens, if the breach is dealt with at the same time as a new offence. In these cases the order is often recorded by probation staff as terminated because of conviction of another offence. *Criminal Statistics* does not indicate how such offenders are dealt with in their figures.

Probation order breaches Table 5.5 shows that both the number and percentage of offenders dealt with by the courts for breaches of probation orders increased gradually between 1981 and 1991. There were 5000 orders breached in 1981, which was estimated at 14 per cent of persons sentenced to probation in that year. In 1991 the corresponding figures were 9600 and 20 per cent of sentences of probation. Thus, although the actual number of breach proceedings almost doubled, the rate increased by less than a half. The increased rate of breaches reflects the changed offender profile of persons being given probation orders, whilst the still relatively low rate of 20 per cent shows how well they have been contained.

The likelihood of an offender being given a custodial sentence from breaching a probation order shows an interesting trend over time. The rate increased from 43 per

Table 5.5. Offenders breaching probation and community service orders 1981–91, number and percentage breached and number and percentage sentenced to immediate custody

	Probation				Community service			
Year	Number of offenders breaching order	Breaches as % of offenders sentenced	Number sentenced to immediate custody	% use of immediate custody	Number of offenders breaching order	Breaches as % of offenders sentenced	Number sentenced to immediate custody	% use of immediate custody
1981	5 000	14	2 100	43	4 500	18	1 700	37
1982	5 600	15	2 500	45	5 300	18	2 000	38
1983	5 700	15	2 700	47	5 600	16	2 100	37
1984	6 200	15	3 300	52	6 400	16	2 500	38
1985	7 100	17	4 000	56	6 500	17	2 600	41
1986	7 200	18	3 700	52	6 200	18	2 300	36
1987	8 000	19	4 300	54	6 600	18	2 300	35
1988	8 300	19	4 300	52	8 200	23	2 600	31
1989	8 200	19	4 000	49	9 600	28	2 500	26
1990	8 900	19	3 800	42	11 000	30	2 300	21
1991	9 600	20	4 300	45	11 900	29	2 400	21

NB: Percentages are based on raw figures and this may not correspond exactly to percentages obtained from the rounded figures in this table.
Source: *Criminal Statistics and Wales 1991* Table 7.28, p. 169.

cent in 1981 to 56 per cent in 1985; it remained at 52 per cent or more until 1988 at which time it began to fall, to 42 per cent in 1990 and 45 per cent in 1991. These figures show that more than half of the breach proceedings resulted in the continuation of the probation order. National Standards for probation orders were introduced in 1992, and it will be interesting to see whether breach proceedings data for probation orders are affected in the same way as those for community service orders have been (see below).

Community service order breaches We see a very different pattern in Table 5.5 for breaches of community service orders. Whilst the number of breaches increased between 1981 and 1984 and remained fairly stable until 1988, the rate of breaches showed little variation during that period. 1988 however saw a substantial increase in both the number and the rate of breaches. The reason for this was the introduction of National Standards for community service orders by the Home Office. They were not officially operative until 1989, but draft standards were issued for consultation early in 1988 and began to be implemented in practice during that year. One of the key elements of National Standards concerned the rules about when an offender should be returned to court for breach of an order. Prior to that time, community service schemes had discretion to initiate breach proceedings as it was felt appropriate, and there was variation in policy and practice around the country. The new standards required that breach should be initiated for all offenders who failed to attend for community service without acceptable reason on three occasions within a six-month period. This led to a big increase in breach proceedings in some parts of the country and is reflected in these figures. Since 1989 the rate of breaches has stabilized although the actual numbers have continued to increase, reflecting the increased numbers of community service orders made by the courts.

The rate of sentencing to custody for breach also shows a significant shift in 1988. Between 1981 and 1987 the rate fluctuated between 41 per cent and 35 per cent. In 1988 it began a substantial decline to 21 per cent in 1990 and 1991. It reflects how the nature of breach proceedings has changed: prior to National Standards, breach proceedings were often a 'last resort' and so a high proportion could be expected to go into custody. National Standards required that breach proceedings be taken earlier and used as a warning to offenders, with the expectation that most would be required to continue their order. This is reflected in our figures, and interestingly the actual number of people given a custodial sentence for breach of a community service order has been remarkably stable over time.

PROBLEMS OF UNDERSTANDING

Both *Probation Statistics* and *Criminal Statistics* include an appendix about factors which affect the statistics within the volumes and thus the reader's understanding of those statistics. The factors are of three broad kinds: changes in legislation; counting procedures; and accuracy of recording.

Changes in legislation

Changes in legislation which have affected criminal supervision orders in the last ten years are as follows.

1. *The Criminal Justice Act, 1982* introduced a range of new additional requirements which could be included in probation orders, particularly specified activity and day centre requirements (often referred to as Schedule 4A and 4B). They were implemented from 31 January 1983, but not all probation services were in a position to make the provision available at that time. Part of the reason for the increase in such requirements since then has been the gradual development of these facilities by all the probation services in the country. New additional requirements were also made available for inclusion in supervision orders on juveniles made under the Children and Young Persons Act, 1969.

2. *The Criminal Justice Act, 1982* also made provision for community service orders to be given to 16 year olds, with a sentence length of between 40 and 120 hours. This facility was made available on an individual Probation Service basis between 1 June 1983 and 1 August 1985.

3. *The Criminal Justice Act, 1988* reclassified some groups of triable-either-way offences as summary. Those involved were common assault, taking a motor vehicle without consent, driving whilst disqualified, and criminal damage of less than £2000. This has compounded the difficulties of trying to make sense of any changes in patterns of offences for those subject to particular types of disposal. More detail about the changes can be found in Chapter 3 and Home Office Statistical Bulletin HOSB18/92.

Counting procedures

Probation Statistics

'Persons commencing an order during a year' refers to the number of people who have commenced one *or more* orders of a particular type during the year. If one individual has received two community service orders in the same year s/he will be counted as one community service order. If that individual also commenced one probation order during the same year, that too would be recorded in the figures about probation orders. However, where there are sub-totals within tables of commencements which relate to the number of persons commencing court orders during the year (as in Table 5.1) our person will be counted once only, despite commencing three orders. Not only does this mean that the figures on commencements will be an under-recording of the actual number of orders made by the courts (which in turn helps to explain why figures from the two sources vary), but the figures given in the sub-totals will be less than the figure obtained by adding together each of the elements of work within it.

When the recording of community service orders was first introduced each individual order made at a court appearance was recorded. In practice, courts would frequently mix a number of concurrent and consecutive orders at one court appearance, with the result that recording practice became very confused. In 1986 the practice was changed so that one order was recorded per court appearance, and this would record the total number of effective hours to be worked by the offender. The system of counting one order only per year for each offender meant that data about commencements would not be affected by this confusion, but data about terminations would be. It is thus especially difficult to re-+concile commencements and terminations for community service, and inferences drawn about changes in terminations before and after 1986 should be treated with caution.

'Persons supervised/current at the year end' are dealt with in exactly the same way as commencements, which again leads to some under-recording of work. This is a different basis of counting from that used in *Criminal Statistics*.

'Terminations', however, record each individual order which is terminated in the year, even if the same person has finished two orders of the same kind. This means that it is not easy to reconcile figures about commencements and terminations.

'Court proceedings' information relates to data collected on an 'all persons basis', which means that each disposal is recorded irrespective of whether or not it is the principal one.

Criminal Statistics

'Persons sentenced' refers to the number of sentencing events in court. An offender is recorded only once for each continuous set of court proceedings about a particular offence or offences.The offender is recorded against the principal offence, which in turn is determined by the heaviest sentence imposed at the court appearance, should there be more than one sentence passed.

Accuracy of recording

Data checking

Criminal Statistics acknowledges some under-recording in the figures, especially for summary offences. The recording of information about summary offences is said to have deteriorated in recent years, a problem exacerbated by not having inputting checks on data accuracy. Changes in numbers proceeded against for summary offences may also be affected by changed recording practices of the Metropolitan Police Department. Data about indictable and triable-either-way offences are not affected by inaccuracy to the same extent, and thus are safe to use for our purposes.

Probation Statistics, as already mentioned, is produced from a system which contains a comprehensive range of data validation checks, and cases which fail them are rejected until the data is corrected. This considerably reduces the amount of inaccuracy in the system, but of course it cannot detect data which is valid but wrong – for instance an offender being recorded as male instead of female.

Late returns

Probation Statistics figures for the year of publication are liable to be revised in the next year's publication, taking account of late returns from Probation Services. Whilst the scale of such change is unlikely to be great, it is unwise to use the precise numbers from the current year's figures, especially where they are low.

Large-scale recording

There is an overall disclaimer in both publications that the figures are subject to the inaccuracies inherent in any large-scale recording system, and that the precise figures may not be accurate. It is likely, however, that the general patterns and trends will be accurate, and that the percentage figures will be safe.

Offence type

Probation Statistics contains a problem with the data it presents about offence types. Court proceedings data provides a different picture from that obtained form Probation Service data, and 'Because of their greater involvement in the classification of offences, it is thought that the police are likely to be more accurate in this respect' (*Probation Statistics 1991* p. 119). Thus tables which give an analysis of offence types use an offence breakdown based on returns of court proceedings as well as a breakdown based on the returns made by the Probation Service.

This is a problem which relates back to the change in the system of recording. *Probation and After-care Statistics, England and Wales 1979*, the first publication which contained information derived from the National Probation Index, contains tables which give details of commencements of orders by type of offence. The tables included two columns of data for that year: the first came from court proceedings data and was included to aid comparability with previous years, and the second came from the National Probation Index. Table 6, for example, gives 'Persons placed on probation by type of offence'. The first important difference is in total numbers, with probation service returns showing 27 006 orders and courts proceedings returns showing 27 812 orders. The former figure would indicate an 0.9 per cent increase in cases whilst the latter indicates a 3.9 per cent increase! The reason for this difference is the different counting base used by the two sources as described above.

There is even more variation when looking at the number of orders for individual offences, where the numbers are *very* different. For instance, the number of probation orders made for offences of burglary in 1979 was 4194 according to court proceedings data but 3024 according to Probation Service data; orders for summary offences numbered 3634 according to court proceedings data, but 1238 according to Probation Service data. The reason for this is twofold. Firstly, where there is only one offence, or where the most serious offence is very clear, there may be different interpretations of the category of offence. A frequent misunderstanding, which was compounded by the change of categories for some offences in the Criminal Justice Act, 1988, is whether an offence is indictable or summary. For instance, common assault is now a summary offence but is frequently recorded as an indictable violence offence. It is in these cases where court proceedings data is likely to be more reliable than Probation Index data.

Secondly, a large number of orders are made at a court appearance where the offender is convicted of more than one type of offence; for instance burglary and theft often appear together. In these circumstance each of the two sources of information have to decide the 'principal offence', but the way in which they do it is different. Court proceedings data take the heaviest sentence imposed and code the particular offence which is related to that sentence. The Probation Service has available details of all the offences dealt with at the court appearance at which the probation order was given, and subjectively decides which is the most serious. On most occasions the category chosen from the different perspectives will be the same, but sometimes it will not and this will create the problems highlighted in Table 6 in *Probation and After-Care Statistics 1979*.

The reasons for the differences were not explained in any detail in the 1979 publication. In the following year, 1980, the tables referring to the type of offence contained an additional footnote to the figures for 1979 and 1980. It said that the total figure for the overall number of orders came from the Probation Service returns, but that this had been apportioned between different types of offence according to the proportions obtained from court proceedings data. The column containing the actual Probation Service figures was again included, once more showing significant differences with court proceedings data between the offence groups, even though the difference in overall numbers of orders had been removed. This convention has been retained in current publications, with most figures being based on court proceedings data, but a final column in the tables giving the current year's figures from Probation Service data – and still the differences continue without explanation other than the unreliability of Probation Service data.

Despite reservations about the quality of the Probation Service data relating to offences, *Probation Statistics* since 1980 have made additional use of it. 1980 saw the first inclusion of Table 8 which related the current type of offence to the most serious previous sentence served by the offender.

The figures are interesting, showing, for example, that offenders commencing probation for an offence of burglary was the offence group least likely to be first offenders. We know from the previous table in that volume that burglary was recorded 25 per cent less by Probation Service data than court proceedings data would suggest was correct. It is possible that those who were differently recorded in an offence type other than burglary contain a substantial number of first offenders, completely negating the impression gained from the table. It is thus very important to treat these tables containing information about offence type with considerable caution.

Reconciling data from *Probation Statistics* and *Criminal Statistics*

Reconciling data about the same subject which has been compiled from two different sources is always difficult, and the same is true of *Probation Statistics* and *Criminal Statistics*. As already mentioned, the establishment of the National Probation Index in 1979 and the availability of the information from it about numbers of new cases in a year created the difficulty of reconciling data from Probation Services with that from court proceedings. Figures about the actual number of orders given in a year vary between the *Probation Statistics* and the *Criminal Statistics* for any given year. This is well illustrated by comparing the figures in Table 5.1 and 5.3: Table 5.1 (based on Probation Service returns) indicates that 44 067 persons commenced probation orders during 1991, which was a fall of 5 per cent from the previous year's figure of 46 282. Table 5.3 (based on court proceedings data) gives a total figure of 47 500 offenders sentenced to probation orders during the year, a fall of less than 0.5 per cent on the previous year's figure of 47 700. Not only do court proceedings data show a different trend, but they indicate that 3433 more probation orders were made by the courts than were commenced by the Probation Service.

The reason for the difference is the basis used for the figures in the two sets of data. Both sets of statistics are concerned to reduce the possibility of double counting of offenders. As described above, *Criminal Statistics* counts each offender once only for each occasion on which s/he is sentenced by the court, and records the most severe penalty which was given on that occasion. Thus if an offender appears in court and is convicted of three offences for which sentences of a probation order and two fines are given, that is recorded as one offender sentenced to probation in the statistics. If that same offender appears in court later in the year for one offence for which a sentence of another probation order is given, that too is recorded in *Criminal Statistics* as one offender sentenced to probation. This one offender will therefore appear in *Criminal Statistics* as two offenders sentenced to a probation order in Table 5.3.

Probation Statistics on the other hand records the number of persons commencing *one or more* probation orders during the year. Thus, in this publication, our offender in the example above will appear as one commencement of probation during the year. It is by no means unusual for an offender to be given more than one probation order during a year, and this would account for the difference between 44 067 persons in *Probation Statistics 1991* and 47 500 offenders in *Criminal Statistics 1991* – around 3400 persons who apparently were given more than one probation order during 1991, almost 8 per cent of the Probation Service commencements in the year.

A further complication has been added to the problem of reconciling data from two sources by the recent inclusion in *Probation Statistics* of new tables which show the number of persons sentenced by age group, giving the total sentenced for indictable and summary offences, the percentage of those offenders who were given probation orders or community service orders, and the total number of persons commencing probation or community service for all offences. The figures come from court proceedings data and are produced on an 'all persons basis' which means that all disposals are included. The numbers given in many instances are different to those found in *Criminal Statistics*, and there is no directly comparable data in *Criminal Statistics* for the sentencing rates for probation and community service. Despite this, the inclusion of the tables in *Probation Statistics* is very helpful, as they bring together the required sentencing information in an easily digestible form, and eliminate the need to search and rework *Criminal Statistics* for indictable and summary offences.

A GUIDED TOUR OF *PROBATION STATISTICS ENGLAND AND WALES 1991*

Overview of contents

Probation Statistics is broken down into twelve chapters:

(1)   Summary

(2)   Probation

(3)   Community service orders

(4)   After-care

(5)   Children and Young Persons Act, 1969

(6)   Suspended sentence supervision orders

(7)   Money payment supervision orders

(8)   Domestic supervision

(9)   Reports and conciliation work

(10) Manpower

(11) Average caseloads and numbers of reports completed

(12) Expenditure and costs.

Each chapter begins with a description of its contents or the topic which it covers. It then provides a summary of the main points drawn from the information in the chapter, before providing a series of detailed tables containing information about the topic. Many of the tables and charts contain comparable information for each of the years since 1981, thus showing trends over 11 years. Each table is suitably annotated with relevant information about significant factors which affect the data it contains, and there is an appendix giving details of definitions, data sources, counting procedures, and changes in legislation which will affect interpretation of the data within the tables. Important aspects of this chapter are outlined on pp. 69–73. Some of the chapters contain information about the work of individual Probation Services, allowing comparison for the current year. This information has been included since 1981.

Trends in criminal supervision orders 1981–91

Table 5.1 shows that the total numbers of criminal court orders commenced[1] have increased from 79 140 in 1981 to 88 707 in 1991, a 12 per cent increase. At the same time the number of persons currently under supervision at the end of 1991 was 89 318, 3 per cent less than the figure of 92 330 under supervision at the end of 1981. These figures reflect an increase in turnover of work, such that more people are in contact with the service, but generally for shorter periods of time. This is reflected in a detailed look at the orders commenced where we see that the shorter timescale cases, i.e. community service orders which are generally completed within a year and probation orders of one year or less, have increased, whilst longer timescale work, e.g. three-year probation orders and supervision orders on juveniles, have decreased.

The age and gender distribution of persons subject to criminal supervision at 31 December has changed over time. The number of females has fallen from 24 060 in 1981 to 15 944 in 1991, whilst the number of males has increased from 121 310 to

---

[1] Unless otherwise specified, figures in this section relate to returns made by the Probation Service, not to court proceedings data.

123 513. Thus males have become even more of a majority of the current caseload of the service, increasing from 83 per cent in 1981 to 89 per cent in 1991. There has also been a general increase in the ages of the people receiving criminal supervision, with the under 21s falling from 64 880 in 1981 to 36 958 in 1991. In 1981 this age group made up 44 per cent of the criminal supervision work of the service, but this had fallen to 26 per cent in 1991. This in part reflects changes in cautioning and sentencing practices, but also reflects the demographic changes which have occurred in the age structure of the general population over this time which have filtered through into the criminal justice system.

Probation orders

Table 5.1 shows that the overall number of probation orders commenced during a year has risen from 35 850 in 1981 to 44 067 in 1991, a 23 per cent increase. The increase has not been evenly spread over time, with a big increases in 1990, and decreases in 1986 and 1991.

Gender Proportionately and numerically, fewer probation orders commenced on female offenders, from 33 per cent of all orders being on women in 1981 to 18 per cent in 1991. Whilst the general developments outlined above apply, this change also reflects the service's increasing commitment to deliver equitable services to men and women. In the early 1980s, probation orders for women had been recommended and supported on welfare grounds where the seriousness of the offence may not have justified such an intervention. In 1981, 11 680 probation orders commenced on women; 36 per cent of the women were first offenders, with only 9 per cent having previously committed an offence which warranted a custodial sentence. By 1991 the position had changed such that just 8074 orders were commenced on women; 21 per cent of them were first offenders and 16 per cent of them had served a previous custodial sentence. Whilst this picture is still different from that of men who commenced probation orders (9 per cent first offenders and 43 per cent previous custody in 1991) it is moving in the right direction with more careful targeting of probation orders for both women and men.

Age The proportion of new probation orders made on offenders aged 30 or over has decreased; this group accounted for 31 per cent of new probation orders in 1981 but just 24 per cent of new orders in 1991. There was a corresponding increase in the 21–29 age group, with the proportion of new orders on those aged 17–20 remaining much the same, at 38 per cent. Women who commenced probation were generally older than the men, men being much more likely to be aged 17–20. Whilst the shift in older age groups occurred for both men and women, women have continued to be generally older than men, having proportionately more in both of the 21–29 and 30+ age groups.

Demographic changes in the age structure of the general population are well documented and can be seen reflected in criminal justice statistics. The table on pages 16/17 of Chapter 2 of *Probation Statistics 1991* shows that the numbers of 17–20 year old offenders sentenced for both indictable and for summary offences has fallen significantly since 1986. Interestingly, the proportionate use of probation orders for these offenders has actually increased over that time, reflecting the significant initiatives taken over the years in how best to deal with young adult offenders. The trend is the same for over 21 year olds, but the scale is nowhere near the same magnitude.

Offence type This item of data is subject to the difficulties outlined on pp. 72–3, but interestingly the reclassification of offences by the Criminal Justice Act, 1988 is clearly illustrated. Between 1981 and 1987 there was very little change in the distribution of offences types; 1988 and 1989 saw a gradual shift to much higher proportions of summary offences, as would have been expected. The detail of these changes is described on p. 70 and in Chapter 3.

Previous criminal record This item is more accurately described as most serious previous sentence, as that is what is recorded. The most serious offenders are those who have served one or more previous custodial sentences, with the least serious being those who have no previous convictions at all, i.e. the order or licence which is recorded arose from their first conviction. The proportion of probation orders commenced on people with previous custodial experience increased from 24 per cent in 1981 to 38 per cent in 1991. The proportion of first offenders has fallen gradually from 23 per cent in 1981 to 11 per cent in 1991. The reliability of the data recorded over this time has improved, with the proportion of cases where the previous sentences are not known falling from 10 per cent in 1981 to 5 per cent in 1991. The change in previous criminal record patterns dramatically reflects the changing focus of probation orders during the 1980s.

There were four strands of development during the 1980s which led to this change. Firstly, the 'just deserts' model of criminal justice gained acceptance, and the view that offenders should not be given probation orders on purely welfare grounds generally accepted. This meant that alternative sources of help were found for offenders whose current and previous offending was not serious enough to warrant the significant infringement of liberty effected by a probation order. This approach to sentencing was embodied in the Criminal Justice Act, 1991. Secondly, the Probation Service has significantly developed its work with offenders, focusing its work on offending behaviour and the factors in a offender's life which are linked to their offending. This work is most effective with offenders who have a history of offending. A third feature was the development of the probation order as an 'alternative to custody' a label which was used as part of a strategy to target probation orders at offenders who were likely to be given a short custodial sentence. Fourthly, and finally, the financial climate within the Probation Service changed, culminating in the introduction of cash limits in 1991. This required the service to use its more limited resources to greatest effect. All of these developments meant that the Probation Service became much more proficient at targeting probation orders at more serious offenders – both those with a current very serious offence and those with a serious criminal history.

Additional requirements Almost a quarter (24 per cent) of the new probation orders in 1991 had an additional requirement, compared with 12 per cent of new orders in 1981. The big increases began in 1983 when the new schedule 4A (specified activities) and 4B (day centre) options made available by the Criminal Justice Act, 1982 became operative. The immediate impact cannot be seen because figures for 1983 and 1984 are not available due to industrial action by some members of the National Association of Probation Officers during those years. Figure 2.4 in *Probation Statistics 1991* graphically displays the changes between 1985 and 1991: the pie charts show that residential requirements have gone down from 7 per cent of orders to 5 per cent, whilst specified activity and day centre (4A and 4B) requirements have increased from 6 per cent to 19 per cent of all probation orders commenced. (NB, there is a problem of interpretation with these charts because an order can have more than one additional requirement attached. Each individual requirement is included in the pie, but as a percentage of the total of orders. The total of percentages is 104 per cent, implying that 4 per cent of orders have more than one requirement.)

Lengths of orders Probation orders are getting shorter: 54 per cent of all new orders in 1991 were for 12 months or less, compared with 33 per cent in 1981. This reflects the Probation Service's emphasis on more focused short-term work with offenders. The change is shown graphically: the most dramatic changes are the increase in one-year orders and the decrease in two-year orders.

Terminations Information about the terminations of probation orders is very limited, with just two tables being provided in *Probation Statistics 1991*. The first shows the reasons for termination for the orders which terminated in each of the years 1981 to 1991: 79 per cent of probation orders terminated successfully in 1991, i.e. they expired at the end of the time ordered by the court, or the probation officer successfully applied to the court for early discharge of the order for good progress. This was 1 per cent higher than in 1990, but 1 per cent less than in 1981. There has been little change in the pattern of terminations over time despite the significant changes in the previous criminal histories of the offenders being given probation orders. This highlights the Probation Service's success in containing serious offenders who have a high risk of failing their order. The second table contains information for 1991 only and relates the reason for termination to the length of the order and the age of the offender at the start of the order. Orders of less than one year were most likely to terminate successfully for all age groups, but the 17–20 year old offenders were the most likely to have their order revoked because of conviction of another offence during that time. The most striking feature of this table is the relationship between age and length of order with the likelihood of the order being terminated because of conviction for another offence. As would be expected, the longer the order the greater the likelihood of the order terminatiing because of further conviction, because the time at risk increases. However, the likelihood of this happening is much greater for young offenders whatever the length. Figure 5.1 illustrates this picture. The 17–20 year olds were also more likely to have their order revoked for failure to comply with the conditions for all lengths of order, but here the differences are not so marked, nor is there the correlation with the length of the order.

Breaches of probation orders were discussed on p. 68.

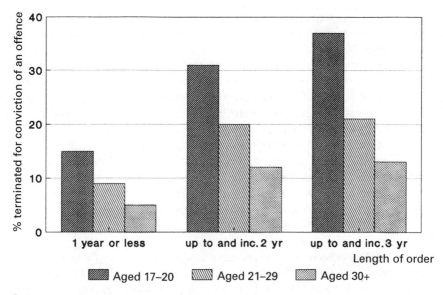

Source: *Probation Statistics England and Wales 1991* Table 2.14, p. 36.

Fig. 5.1. Percentage of all probation orders terminated in 1991 which were terminated for conviction of offence, by length of order and age of offender.

Community service orders

The history of community service has been beset with debates about the place of the order in the sentencing 'tariff'. When first proposed in 1970 in the Wootton Report it was suggested that community service orders should be reserved for offenders where the sentencer was seriously considering an immediate custodial sentence, i.e. it should be used as an alternative to custody. When the Criminal Justice Act, 1972 introduced the sentence, the wording required that community service orders be used for offences which *could* be dealt with by a custodial sentence. In practice, many offenders sentenced for imprisonable offences are given a sentence other than custody. This meant that the place of community service became unclear, with some sentencers using the original strict interpretation and others seeing the disposal as a sentence in its own right for all imprisonable offences. Many Probation Services had an internal policy of proposing community service to the courts only where the probation officer felt there was a significant chance of a custodial sentence. They also entered into considerable discussion with local sentencers about their use of the order. However, in practice, individual sentencers made the decisions about how community service was used. Variation in sentencing practice is well known (see, for example, Hine 1990), and the continuing debate during the 1980s significantly influences interpretation of figures about community service, particularly those relating to previous criminal record.

The Criminal Justice Act, 1991 ended the debate and the confusion, saying that a community service order could be imposed for any offence the sentencer felt was 'serious enough' to warrant a community sentence. This has led to a substantial increase in the number of community service orders made, and it will be interesting to see the effect in *Probation Statistics 1993*.

Community service orders have been an outstanding success for the Probation Service, with the number of orders being made increasing gradually since they were introduced in 1975. Table 5.1 shows that 1991 commencements were the highest ever at 41 190. This was 8 per cent more than the previous year, and a 47 per cent increase overall since 1981, despite fallbacks in 1986, 1988 and 1989. Table 5.4 shows that the proportion of offenders of all groups sentenced for indictable offences who received community service orders has increased consistently since 1981, this trend being most marked for male offenders. One possible contributing factor to this may have been increased unemployment rates during the 1980s. Unemployed offenders cannot afford to pay fines but they do have time available to perform community service and thus the 'fine on time' often seemed appropriate.

Gender Numbers of community service orders have increased for both males and females between 1981 and 1991, with a 47 per cent increases for males and a 43 per cent increase for females. The vast majority of community service orders are still made on male offenders: 94 per cent of all orders in both 1981 and 1991. This is in marked contrast to the picture for men and women and probation orders. The reasons why there is this difference are complex. However, community service has developed an image of being a physical work disposal, more suitable for men than for women, and there has been a common misunderstanding that offenders with dependants (particularly women with young children) could not be accommodated within community service. This will have contributed to the position that sentencers are more likely to see probation as a first course of action for women and community service as a first course of action for men. Most probation areas have undertaken a range of initiatives to show that women are often suitable for community service and that they can and do successfully complete their orders.

Age The age of offenders given community service has gradually increased, with the proportion of 17–20 year olds being 50 per cent in 1981 and 39 per cent in 1991. This change in age distribution applies to both men and women, but women subject to community service orders still have greater proportions in the older age groups than do men; 31 per cent of females in 1991 were in the 17–20 age group compared with 39 per cent of males commencing community service. Community service was made available to 16 year olds in 1983, but was not available throughout the country until 1985. Numbers began high with 2000 offenders aged 16 being given an order in 1985, but since then have gradually fallen, to just 1181 in 1991.

Type of offence The differences between Probation Service sources and court proceedings sources are as great for community service order commencements as for probation order commencements. Again, the most significant change over time occurred with the reclassification of offences by the Criminal Justice Act, 1988. There are some differences between the pattern of offences for community service orders and probation orders, the differences being similar whichever set of figures is used. The most common type of offence for both orders was theft and handling stolen goods, but this category accounted for 32 per cent of community service orders (Probation Service figures) and 37 per cent of probation order commencements. Offences against the person (including robbery and sexual offences) had much the same proportion for both orders, as did fraud, criminal damage, and summary offences. The only other difference was for 'other indictable offences' with community service having 18 per cent compared with 13 per cent for probation. Many of the offences in this group are public order offences such as affray, for which reparation to the community by means of a community service order may seem particularly appropriate to sentencers.

Type of court This information is provided for community service orders, but not probation, the figures being compiled from returns of court proceedings and adjusted to the totals obtained from the Probation Service. The vast majority of community service orders were made by magistrates' courts in 1991 – 73 per cent. The nature of the offences from Crown Court and from magistrates' courts varies considerably, as might be expected. There were very few orders made for summary offences in Crown Court, and a much higher proportion of orders made for offences of violence and burglary.

Previous criminal record The previous sentencing history of offenders commencing community service orders has become less serious over time, with the proportion of first offenders increasing from 10 per cent in 1981 to 14 per cent in 1991, and the number with a previous custodial sentence decreasing from 40 per cent to 34 per cent. This trend is very different from that which we saw for probation orders, where criminal histories were becoming more serious. Targeting of community service orders and probation orders was an important issue for the Probation Service during the 1980s. The rise in the number of orders has been more dramatic for community service than for probation. Probation orders are unlikely to be given by the court without being proposed by a probation officer in a social inquiry (now pre-sentence) report. The same does not apply in relation to community service orders where substantial numbers have been made on offenders who either did not have a report prepared by a probation officer or whose report proposed something else. It has therefore been less easy for the Probation Service to influence sentences of community service directly. The apparent downward trend in seriousness shows that the Probation Service has been less successful in targeting community service than probation orders. The Criminal Justice Act, 1991 requires that a pre-sentence report be prepared before passing any community sentence, including community service orders, which in theory could give more scope for succesful targeting.

This reduction in the seriousness of the criminal record is particularly marked for the under 21s, but difficult to interpret as policy initiatives within the criminal justice system during the 1980s have been geared towards increasing the use of community sentences and decreasing the use of custodial sentences, particularly for young adult offenders. The reduction in the proportion of offenders with a previous custodial sentence is greater than the increase in the proportion of first offenders. This may be an indicator of the success of this policy, with community service orders being more likely to be imposed *before* a custodial sentence. There has also been an interesting increase in the proportion of offenders whose most serious previous sentence was a community service order, perhaps indicating a greater propensity to use community service orders as a repeat option.

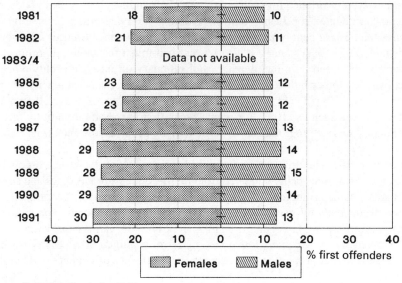

Source: *Probation Statistics 1991*
Table 3.5, pp. 45–46

Fig. 5.2. Proportion of males and females who commenced community service orders who were first offenders, 1981–91.

The difference between men and women in relation to most serious previous sentence cannot go unremarked. Females of all ages who receive a community service order are much more likely to be first offenders than are men, and this tendency has increased much more for women than it has for men. Figure 5.2 highlights this. We can see that overall the increase in first offenders amongst males commencing community service was relatively small: from 10 per cent to 13 per cent. The same figures for females commencing community service are from 18 per cent to 30 per cent. These figures show that not only was the gap between men and women wide, but it has been getting wider over time.

Interpretation of these figures is not easy. At face value it looks as though women who are given community service are being dealt with more harshly than men, but the information about whether women are sentenced more or less seriously than men is ambiguous (see for example Mair and Brockington, 1988; Hine, 1993; and Chapter 9). As discussed on p. 66, the structure of the population of offenders being sentenced is crucially important to any debate about sentencing practice. Published sentencing figures do not give information about previous offending, but we do know that fewer women commit crimes than men, and a higher proportion of women are likely to be first offenders than are men. This will naturally feed through into the cases of the Probation Service.

Lengths of orders Orders have generally been getting shorter over the period 1981 to 1991, with both the actual numbers and the proportions of orders in the longest category (200–240 hours) reducing: the proportion fell from 22 per cent in 1981 to 12 per cent in 1991. There has also been a decrease in the proportion of orders which are between 100 and 200 hours, but to a lesser extent. The proportion of orders in the shortest category (40–100 hours) has significantly increased to compensate, from 16 per cent in 1981 to 31 per cent in 1991. The trend has been much the same amongst the orders on both males and females, but the base from which females started was very different. Orders on females have always had a much higher proportion in the shortest category, and this has increased from 28 per cent to 45 per cent compared with an increase from 15 per cent to 31 per cent for males.

Terminations Again, the information in *Probation Statistics* about terminations of community service orders is much sketchier than that for commencements. However the tables show that 70 per cent of community service orders terminated in 1991 successfully completed the hours ordered. This was 1 per cent more than in 1990, but 4 per cent less than in 1981. There has been an increase in the proportion of orders which terminated on revocation for failure to comply with the requirements of the order, from 13 per cent in 1981 to 17 per cent in 1991. The change really occurred between 1987 and 1989 (from 12 per cent to 17 per cent) and coincides with the introduction of National Standards for community service orders in April 1988 (a discussion of breaches of community service and the introduction of National Standards can be found on p. 69). Interestingly, this is also the point at which there is a reduction in the proportion of orders which terminate on revocation for conviction of another offence, but it is not so substantial (from 10 per cent to 8 per cent). This could reflect different recording practices following the standards, or it could indicate that the National Standards have picked up offenders who might otherwise have gone on to be convicted of another offence. The national study of community service orders (Thomas *et al.* 1990) showed that many offenders on community service orders are charged with further offences during the processing of breach proceedings for failure to comply with their order. Very often the breach proceedings would be dropped and the information about failure to comply with the order would be fed into the court at the time the further offence was dealt with, which would mean that, strictly speaking, the order was revoked for reconviction and not for failure to comply, even though the failure to comply was likely to have been an important factor in the decision about whether to allow the order to continue or not. The introduction of National Standards made Probation Services more aware of the need to ensure that breach proceedings were seen to be processed to the end, and this change may have fed through into the statistics.

Greater detail is provided about the community service orders terminated in 1991 than about probation orders. As would be expected, shorter orders were more likely to have their hours completed successfully (78 per cent of 40–100-hour orders to 60 per cent of 200–240-hour orders), whereas the proportion of orders terminating because of failure to comply increased with the length of the order (from 13 per cent of 40–100-hour orders to 23 per cent of 200–240-hour orders). The proportion of orders revoked for conviction of a further offence also increased with length, from 4 per cent to 9 per cent. As the likelihood of successful completion decreased with the length of the order, so it increased with the age of the offender. Unfortunately no tables are provided about the relationship between age and length of order so we cannot say whether the two features are independent. Figure 5.3 illustrates how older offenders on community service were more likely to complete their orders successfully.

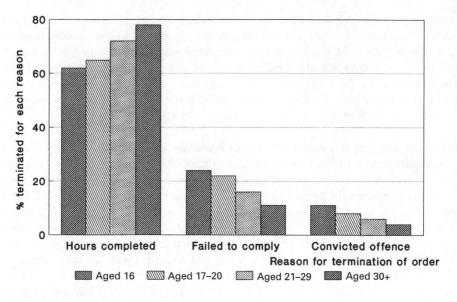

Source: *Probation Statistics England and Wales 1991* Table 3.14, p. 57.

Fig. 5.3. Percentage of all community service orders terminated in 1991 for each age group by reason for termination of order.

The final table provided by *Probation Statistics 1991* about community service orders gives an indication of the amount of time between commencement and termination of orders and relates this to length of order and reason for termination. There are no surprises here – longer length orders take more time to termination, whatever the reason, and orders which are revoked for failure to comply or for conviction of a further offence take longer than those which complete their hours. The time difference here is much greater for the shorter orders, giving an indication of the time involved in processing breach and reconviction proceedings through court. For example, orders of 40–100 hours where the hours were completed took an average of 4.4 months, whereas the same length order which was revoked for failure to comply with requirements took an average time of 8.3 months. Long orders (200–240 hours) where the hours were completed lasted an average of 10.4 months, whereas the same length order lasted 11.3 months if it was revoked for failure to comply.

Supervision orders under the Children and Young Persons Act, 1969

The total number of C&YP supervision orders made by courts fell considerably during the 1980s in line with juvenile justice policy. Figures from courts proceedings show that there were 18 690 orders made following criminal proceedings in 1981 and this figure had fallen to 6525 orders made in 1991. Table 5.1 shows a corresponding decrease in the number of these orders supervised by the Probation Service, from 11 830 in 1981 to 2307 in 1991. These figures also represent a significant reduction in the proportion of orders which are supervised by the Probation Service, from 63 per cent in 1991 to 35 per cent in 1991. Policy decisions have been made in most Probation Services, following negotiations with Social Services departments, and have resulted in agreements for local authority Social Service departments to supervise more juveniles, with some Probation Services supervising offenders aged under 17 only in exceptional circumstances. These services have been focusing their work on adult offenders.

Length As with probation orders, there has been a shift towards the making of shorter orders for more focused work, with the proportion of one-year orders increasing from 29 per cent in 1981 to 66 per cent in 1991.

Additional requirements Among the orders which have been supervised by the Probation Service the proportion with additional requirements has decreased, from 23 per cent in 1981 to 18 per cent in 1991. Types of additional requirement have also changed, with intermediate treatment falling from 20 per cent to 10 per cent and supervised activity requirements gradually increasing from their introduction in 1985 to 8 per cent in 1991.

Terminations Overall, the proportion of orders terminating satisfactorily has remained fairly stable – 85 per cent in 1981 and 86 per cent in 1991 – but within that there has been a shift toward more orders running their full term and fewer being terminated early for good progress. This would link in with the change in lengths of order made, as short orders are less likely to be terminated early.

Suspended sentence supervision orders

Suspended sentence supervision orders (SSSOs) have had their ups and downs, but as Table 5.1 shows, the overall trend has been slightly upwards, from 1930 orders in 1981 to 2272 orders in 1991. The implementation of the Criminal Justice Act, 1991 has caused a very significant reduction in the number of suspended sentences both with and without supervision orders, and thus will have abruptly ended this upward trend.

This type of case accounts for a relatively small proportion of the Probation Service's overall caseload, being just under 3 per cent of all the criminal supervision orders commenced in 1991.The orders can only be made in the Crown Court and tend to be used for more serious offenders: in 1991 50 per cent of the orders commenced had an offence of burglary or violence against the person and 50 per cent had previously served a custodial sentence. (These are separate items of information and there will be some overlap.)

Terminations in 1991 show the continuation of a trend of increasingly successful terminations, with 71 per cent running their full course or being terminated early for good progress in 1981, compared with 79 per cent for the same reasons in 1991. The proportion of orders which had their suspended sentence activated fell from 23 per cent in 1981 to 10 per cent in 1991. The final table in this chapter in *Probation Statistics* indicates that, in 1991, offenders aged less than 30 at the commencement of their order were less likely to complete their order satisfactorily than those aged 30 or more (76 per cent compared with 83 per cent) and were more likely to have their suspended sentence activated (12 per cent compared with 7 per cent). This fits in to the general trend identified with other types of orders that younger offenders are less likely to successfully complete their orders.

Money payment supervision orders

Magistrates' courts may enforce monetary penalties by placing the offender under the supervision of the Probation Service. Numbers of money payment supervision orders (MPSOs) have been remarkably consistent over time (see Table 5.1). Although there have been ups and downs in the interim (a high of 6460 and a low of 4840), the 1991 figure of 5674 commencements is not very different from the 1981 figure of 5950.The general age distribution of persons commencing MPSOs has shifted upwards (49 per cent aged 17–20 in 1981 compared with 42 per cent in 1991). The tables provided do not indicate whether the distribution of males and females has changed over time, but it is clear that in 1991 women accounted for 29 per cent of the orders. As with other orders, the age distribution for the women subject to MPSOs in 1991 was generally older than that of men, with just 23 per cent of women in the 17–20 age group compared with 50 per cent of men.

The proportion of orders terminated on completion of payment has fallen (from 54 per cent in 1985 to 36 per cent 1991), whilst the proportion of terminations for 'other' reasons has increased from 16 per cent in 1986 to 31 per cent in 1991. It is difficult to find a reason for this, but the most likely is increasing applications to court to terminate orders which no longer require the involvement of the Probation Service, either because the payment of the fine is progressing well and the offender no longer needs support, or because payment has broken down and no useful purpose is served by the continuation of the order.

EFFECTS OF THE CRIMINAL JUSTICE ACT, 1991

The most significant piece of legislation in recent years has been the Criminal Justice Act, 1991. The Act was passed in the last year to which the figures covered in this chapter relate, but many of the changes which it contained, particularly those which affected the Probation Service and the administration of community sentences, did not come into effect until 1 October 1992. The effects of this Act on sentencing and the work of the Probation Service have been dramatic. *Probation Statistics 1992* contains some information, but this is inevitably limited because the terms of the Act were only operative for a quarter of the year. *Probation Statistics 1993*, when it is published, will tell us much about the effect of the Criminal Justice Act and we await it with interest. Unfortunately, however, at the time of writing some aspects of the Act have already been repealed by the CJA, 1993 and a new criminal justice bill is weaving its way through the parliamentary process. This presents a real challenge to the Home Office Statistics Department to make data available in a way which will help us to interpret the effects of the legislation.

To help readers of *Probation Statistics 1992* or *1993*, the following are the elements of the Act which have affected criminal supervision orders:

1. Combination orders, a new criminal supervision order (now called community disposals or sentences) was introduced. It combines a 1–3 year probation order

with 40–100 hours of community service. It was made available for any court to pass for any offence which the sentencer felt was 'serious enough' to warrant a community disposal.

2. Community service orders: the maximum length order for 16 year olds was raised to 240 hours, in line with persons over 16 years.

3. Probation orders could be made on 16 year olds at the discretion of the courts, the decision being guided by the court's view of the 'maturity' of the offender.

4. Provision was made for new additional requirements in probation orders for drug and alcohol treatment. As with other new additional requirements, not all Probation Services have been in a position to make them available straightaway, and thus their introduction and use will vary around the country.

5. Supervision orders made under the Children and Young Persons Act, 1969 could be made on 17 year olds at the discretion of the courts, again the decision being guided by the court's view of the 'maturity' of the offender.

A word about *Probation Statistics 1992*

To help with assessing the impact of the Criminal Justice Act, 1991, Chapter 1 of *Probation Statistics* separates information for the last quarter of 1992 (the point at which the Act was implemented) from that of the previous three months. This allows comment on the impact of the Act.

This section should be treated with some caution as the points identified do relate to just three months of a year, and there is some indication that they have already changed again. However the important effects are as follows:

(1) a decline in the number of probation orders overall;

(2) an increase in the number of probation orders with additional requirements;

(3) a big increase in the number of community service orders;

(4) a high number of combination orders.

Probation Statistics 1992 also includes a new chapter giving information about reconvictions for people given probation and community service orders. This follows from Home Office Statistical Bulletin HOSB18/93, and may become a regular feature.

OTHER HOME OFFICE PUBLICATIONS CONTAINING INFORMATION ABOUT COMMUNITY SENTENCES

Home Office Statistical Bulletins

The Home Office has been producing Statistical Bulletins (HOSB) for many years, about all aspects of work covered by that department, not just criminal justice. In recent years the quality of presentation of these bulletins has improved substantially, and charges for them have been dropped. They can be obtained free from the Research and Statistics Department at the Home Office, Croydon. Many bulletins contain information relevant to an examination of criminal supervision orders, often in a detail not found in the larger, general annual publications. The following are some examples of recent relevant bulletins.

1. *HOSB 24/93: Cautions, Court Proceedings and Sentencing England and Wales, 1992* Published annually, this bulletin gives some summary information about persons cautioned by the police or dealt with by the courts during the previous year. It is a way of making basic data about court proceedings easily available before the publication of *Criminal Statistics England and Wales.*

2. *HOSB 18/93: Reconvictions of those given Probation and Community Service Orders in 1987* This bulletin reported an analysis of the criminal records of a sample of offenders given probation and community service orders during 1987, the samples being drawn from the National Probation Index. The bulletin presents some very interesting data relating the reconviction rates to type of order, age at sentence, gender, and criminal history prior to the sampled sentence. This data was updated for 1988 and included in *Probation Statistics England and Wales 1992* and looks as if it may well become a regular feature.

3. *HOSB 17/93: Summary Probation Statistics England and Wales 1992.* A bulletin is usually issued around the middle of the year giving summary probation statistics for the previous year. This document provides some basic information about the work of the service prior to the official publication of *Probation Statistics,* which is not usually published until towards the end of the year.

4. *HOSB 30/93: Statistics of Drug Seizures and Offenders Dealt with, United Kingdom 1992; HOSB 20/93: Offences of Drunkenness, England and Wales, 1991; HOSB 1/93: Motoring Offences, England and Wales, 1991.* Each of these bulletins focuses upon one particular type of offence and how it is dealt with. This will give an indication of the use of criminal supervision orders for those particular offences. These bulletins are now issued regularly. Supplementary tables give details of all disposals for motoring offences.

5. *HOSB 35/92: Main Sources of Statistical Data on the Criminal Justice System collected by Central Government.* This is a very useful document which does precisely as the title suggests. It does not provide any data but outlines in some detail exactly what information is collected, and provides references for published data and contact points for data which is unpublished.

6. *HOSB 18/92: Effect of Reclassification of Offences in the 1988 Criminal Justice Act.* Contains a detailed explanation of what was reclassified and how the change affected criminal court statistics between 1988 and 1989. The bulletin looked in detail at the offences which had been reclassified, including their outcome.

7. *HOSB 13/92: Statistics on Community Service Orders.* Contains a detailed analysis of persons sentenced to community service orders in 1990, much of which is

in more detail than provided in *Probation Statistics*. It also provides information about breaches of community service orders, again data not present in *Probation Statistics*. This bulletin was not repeated in 1993.

Digest of Information on the Criminal Justice System in England and Wales

This digest is one of several initiatives designed to 'improve understanding of the criminal justice system'. It aims to 'present a comprehensive picture of crime and justice in England and Wales without becoming too technical or lengthy', and in doing so uses a lot of graphics and colour. The chapter on sentencing contains some simple and graphic information about community-based disposals, including an interesting chart on breaches of orders.

CJA, 1991, Section 95: Race and the Criminal Justice System, 1992; CJA, 1991, Section 95: Gender and the Criminal Justice System 1992

Both of these publications were produced at the end of 1992 as 'Home Office publication under section 95 of the Criminal Justice Act 1991', with the expectation that they would become annual publications. They again bring together information from a wide range of sources, including research, about all aspects of the criminal justice system, but focusing on the specific aspect of race or gender. The booklet about race contains very little about the work of the Probation Service, but this will be included in future publications following the introduction of race and ethnic monitoring during 1992. The booklet about gender includes quite a lot of information about sentencing and the Probation Service, together with useful discussions of why there are significant differences between the statistics for women and men.

THE FUTURE OF *PROBATION STATISTICS*

There are some current developments which will significantly affect *Probation Statistics* in the next few years, improving the reliability of the data as well as extending the range of information available.

Race and ethnic monitoring

At the end of 1992 race and ethnic monitoring of all offenders who come into contact with the service was introduced. This data is translated into the race categories used in the OPCS census and transmitted to the Home Office in summary form in relation to commencements and termination of a range of orders, and about proposals and sentences in pre-sentence reports. This data should be included in *Probation Statistics 1993*, as well as in the next issue of *CJA Section 95: Race and the Criminal Justice System*.

Offence classification

A new offence classification system has just been introduced to record the type of offence for which an order is given. The system will be implemented throughout the country by 31 March 1995. The new classification is much more detailed than the current broad category system, having just over 80 codes. Detailed guidance is being produced about how the new classification should be used, together with considerable documentation to enable the person recording the offence to identify the correct code. This new system should be much more reliable than the existing system, and hopefully will remove some of the current anomalies.

National case recording system (CRAMS)

A considerable amount of effort has been expended in the last two years by the Home Office and by Probation Service organizations in specifying requirements for a national computerized case record monitoring system. The specification is now complete, programming has begun and the first services to use the system will have it installed by early 1995. All probation areas will transfer from their current systems to the national system by 1999. This new system will improve consistency of recording between probation areas, and improve the transfer of information to the Home Office who will no longer maintain the National Probation Index in its current form. This new national system will also assist the transfer of data between different agencies of the criminal justice system which are also currently developing national computerized systems.

REFERENCES

Hine, J. (1991). 'Standards and sentencing: a magical mystery tour'. Paper presented to conference entitled 'Community Service Orders: the Impact of National Standards', Trent Polytechnic, September 1991.
Hine, J. (1993). 'Access for women: flexible and friendly? In *Paying Back: Twenty Years of Community Service*, (ed. D. Whitfield and D. Scott). Waterside Press, Winchester.
Home Office (1989). *National Standards for Community Service Orders*. Circular 18/89.
Home Office (1992). *National Standards for the Supervision of Offenders in the Community*. HMSO, London.
Mair, G. and Brockington, N. (1988). 'Female offenders and the Probation Service'. *Howard Journal,* **27**, pp. 117–26.
Thomas, N., Hine, J., and Nugent, M. (1990). '*Study of Community Service Orders: Summary Report*'. University of Birmingham.
Wootton, B. (1970). *Non-custodial and Semi-custodial Penalties*. Report of the Advisory Council on the Penal System, HMSO, London.

6 Prison

ROD MORGAN

INTRODUCTION

This chapter has three purposes: first, to provide the reader with a guide to the sources of statistical data on prisons and prisoners; second, to provide a brief resumé of the principal findings which can be derived from those data; and, third, to explore some of the pitfalls involved in comparing prisons data internationally.

DEFINITIONS AND SOURCES

What counts as the prison population? The answer is not quite as straightforward as it might appear and, since comparisons are increasingly made between the size and character of prison populations internationally (see Council of Europe 1992), commentators need to be aware of the precise basis on which calculations are made in each jurisdiction: they are not everywhere the same.

Until recently the prison population in England and Wales (Scotland and Northern Ireland are separate jurisdictions with their own prison systems and statistics) simply comprised those persons committed to prison by the courts and held in establishments run by the Prison Service.[1] Two recent developments have compromised that simple formula.

Since 1980, when industrial action by members of the Prison Officers' Association led to a refusal to admit additional prisoners to prisons deemed overcrowded, there has been a statutory provision (the Imprisonment Temporary Provisions Act, 1980) enabling prisoners – colloquially known as 'Home Office prisoners' – to be held in police stations. Between 1980 and summer 1992 this temporary provision was almost permanently used either to cope with the consequences of industrial action, or the unexpected loss of prison accommodation (as, for example, following the riots at Strangeways Prison, Manchester and elsewhere in April 1990), or to avoid excessive overcrowding in particular establishments. At the time of writing (autumn 1993) police stations are being used for prisoners once again.

The second development is the decision to contract out to commercial companies the management of prisons. In April 1992 and May 1993 two new purpose-built estab-

---

[1] The arrangements for administering prisons have undergone various changes in recent years. Until 1962, when the Prison Department, a department within the Home Office, was formed, prisons were the responsibility of the Prison Commission outwith the Home Office. In 1985 the Prison Department was re-titled the Prison Service and on 1 April 1993 the Prison Service became a 'Next Steps' agency outwith the Home Office.

lishments–the Wolds and Blakenhurst – opened under the management of Group 4 Security and UK Detention Services respectively. Furthermore, there is provision in the enabling legislation, the Criminal Justice Act, 1991 section 84, for the contracting out of existing state-run establishments. Though the first competitively-tendered contract for a state-run establishment has been given to the Prison Service – that for Strangeways Prison, Manchester in July 1993 – it seems probable that further contracts will be won by commercial companies. However, the Prison Service remains ultimately responsible for prisoners held in commercially run establishments and self-evidently these prisoners are part of the prison population. It follows that the prison population must now be defined as: those persons committed by the courts to prison and for whom the Prison Service exercises direct or indirect responsibility.

Most prisoners – currently over 95 per cent – are the direct responsibility of the Prison Service, a Crown agency accountable, financially and administratively, for approximately 130 prisons and young offender institutions (for prisoners aged under 21). We know what the prison population is from the accounts given by the Prison Service. The service is obliged by the Prison Act, 1952 to report annually to parliament. This it does currently in the form of three publications. The first (see Home Office 1992a) comprises a largely prose account of the work of the service during the previous year. It includes, *inter alia*, a list of establishments, their functions, the type and amount of accommodation provided, and average and greatest occupancy levels. It also includes staffing and financial data, miscellaneous information on aspects of prison management ranging from the number of escapes from and deaths in custody, to prisoner employment and hours spent in educational classes. It also provides a list of recent in-house or contracted research publications on prison-related matters. The second text is the so-called statistical report on prisons *Prison Statistics 1991* provided by the Home Office Research and Statistics Department. This volume is exclusively concerned with the number and characteristics of all prisoners irrespective of where they are held, the data being presented in tabular form accompanied by brief prose accounts. Many tables usefully present data series for ten years, thereby obviating the need for investigators tiresomely to have to consult many annual reports. The third text, also from the Home Office Research and Statistics Department, presents statistics, by institution, on offences against prison discipline and the punishments imposed (see Home Office 1992b).

The quantity and quality of statistical data produced by the service has generally increased over the years and, until the formation of the Prison Department in 1962, the annual account, statistical and prose, was contained in a single volume. To the extent that the number of statistical data collected and published has grown, and recording conventions have changed, it is not always possible to make precise comparisons between years, though the basic data relating to prisoners have not changed greatly since the early 1960s.

Though the annual reports from the Prison Service and the Home Office on prisons are without doubt the most important data sources, they have shortcomings and need supplementing. First, by definition, they appear only once a year and, in the case of the statistical reports, much later than the periods reported on. This makes the monthly population returns produced by the Research and Statistics Department (available from S2 Division), the parliamentary statements which the Home Secretary makes from time to time in response to oral or written questions, and the interim Home Office Statistical Bulletins on the prison population (see, for example HOSB 7/93 on 1992), valuable advance notices of short-term population movements. Second, the annual reports are almost entirely historical. For this reason a good deal of attention is focused on the occasional Home Office Statistical Bulletins projecting the prison population for the decade ahead (for the most recent, see HOSB 10/92, 6/93). Third, the annual Prison Service reports have hitherto provided little information of assistance to analysts interested in assessing the quality of life provided for prisoners (and, by implication, staff) in either particular prisons or generally. For example, though the annual reports provide global figures about the overall number of prisoners sharing cells, or the proportion of prisoners employed and the manner of their employment, no information is provided about the number of hours spent in cells, the *de facto* generosity of visiting arrangements, and so on. The absence of such data arguably reflects the priorities of the system.

This failure to provide much quality-of-life data may change.The new Prison Service agency has published corporate and business plans (Prison Service 1993*a*; 1993*b*) setting out organizational goals and specifying key performance indicators. This makes it likely that more sophisticated measures of service delivery will be developed and reported in future annual reports. For example, though the Prison Service has for several years been collecting 'regime monitoring data (RMD) which are becoming more inclusive of prisoner activities (see Home Office 1992*a*, paras 59–62), few have so far been published. RMD – comprising aggregate figures purporting to show the number of hours spent in organized activities by prisoners in different types of establishment – were first officially used in the White Paper setting out the government's response to the Woolf Report on the prison disturbances at Strangeways Prison, Manchester and elsewhere in April 1990 (Home Office 1991, Table 1). The data may not be accurate and are certainly narrowly focused (see Morgan 1992). Until now, therefore, a good deal of reliance has had to be placed by commentators on the various reports published by the Prisons Inspectorate.

The Prisons Inspectorate, which is independent of the Prison Service though part of the Home Office, is charged with reporting to the minister 'on the treatment of prisoners and conditions in prison' (Prison Act Section 5a(3)) and does so by: conducting inspections of individual establishments (40 prisons were inspected during 1991/2, 20 fully and 20 briefly); undertaking occasional thematic reviews of aspects of policy (topics so far covered have included sanitation, the complaints system, security classification, and suicide and self-harm); investigating major incidents such as the spate of prison disturbances in 1986; and reporting annually on his work to parliament (most recently in HMCIP 1993). All the Chief Inspector's reports are published.

The problem with inspectorate reports is that they have tended to be rather long on subjective description and rather short on objective measurement (see Morgan 1985). This has made it difficult to gauge why and to what degree a particular establishment has been judged deficient, or to make precise comparisons between institutions or successive reports on particular institutions. This defect is gradually being addressed. Inspectorate reports now include a reasonable array of hard data about facilities, programmes, and regimes, though coverage remains uneven so that it is still difficult to make comparisons between institutions or gauge changes in the delivery of services within institutions over time.

The lacunae in the official data on delivery of services within the prison system have meant that there is a good deal of uncertainty, and thus controversy, as to whether the significant increases in real expenditure on prisons of recent years (Home Office 1986, Table 1; 1992*a*, Table A), and the greatly improved staff prisoner ratios achieved (Morgan 1983; *Prison Statistics 1991* p. 39), have been matched by any, let alone commensurate, improvements in outputs. Some light can be shed on these issues by turning to the findings of independent researchers. For example, the limited comparisons of regime data collected during the course of successive projects by King and his associates suggests that the delivery of measured services to prisoners during the period 1970–87, had either not improved or had deteriorated (King and McDermott 1989; 1991; 1992). King's work is rare, however. Though aspects of life in prisons, including sensitive aspects, have been studied by several groups of independent researchers – race relations (Genders and Player 1989), suicide (Leibling 1992) and the operation of special security or control units (Walmesley 1989; Bottomley and Hay 1991) – their data have not been longitudinal or of a nature enabling us to map how prison conditions have changed. The key performance indicators now being developed by the Prison Service – an overcrowding index, 'the number of prisoners with 24-hour access to sanitation', 'the number of hours a week which, on average, prisoners spend in purposeful activity', the proportion of prisoners held in establishments where prisoners have the opportunity to exceed the minimum visiting entitlement', and so on (Prison Service 1993*b*) – should make analysis of service delivery easier, but the evidence suggests that more work needs to be done on the sophistication and accuracy of the performance indicators.

The official statistics tell us much more about prisoners than the conditions in which they live, though what they tell us is almost entirely to do with prisoners' legal characteristics. Prisoners are defined principally in terms of their legal status – unconvicted, convicted but unsentenced, sentenced (including fine defaulters), and civil prisoners (including persons held under the Immigration Act) – their sex, age, and ethnicity and, if sentenced, their length of sentence and offence. Further, a good deal can be calculated from prison reception and release dates. The latter are vital, for there is an important distinction between portrayals of the prison population derived from receptions data and average daily population (ADP) data. A simple illustration will suffice to make the point. Figures 6.1 and 6.2 show that whereas the overwhelming majority of offenders sentenced to imprisonment are serving relatively short sentences – 70 per cent are serving eighteen months or less – long-term prisoners dominate life in prison; 42 per cent of the sentenced population at any one time is serving four years or more. Most prisoners are relatively transient, but a minority stay a long time and, as Figures 6.1 and 6.2 indicate very clearly, that minority is growing.

Relatively little is discernible from *Prison Statistics* about the social character of the prison population, thus the importance of the recent one-in-ten survey of the prison population conducted by the Office of Population Censuses and Surveys (OPCS) on behalf of the Home Office (Walmesley, Howard and White 1992). When combined

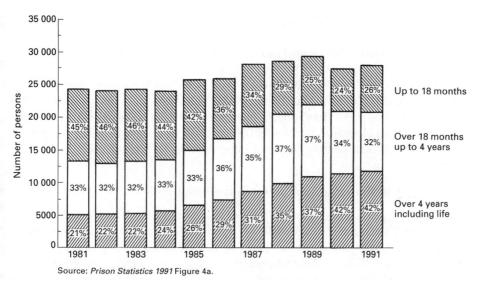

Source: *Prison Statistics 1991* Figure 4a.

Fig. 6.1. Population of adult males under sentence on 30 June: by length of sentence, 1981–91.

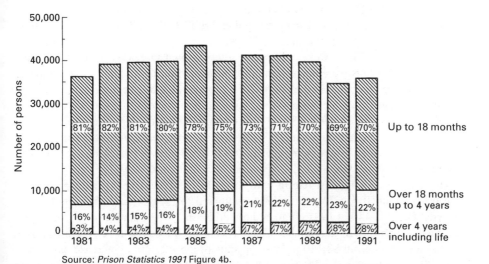

Source: *Prison Statistics 1991* Figure 4b.

Fig. 6.2. Receptions of adult males under sentence of immediate imprisonment: by length of sentence, 1981–91.

with other studies the OPCS data provide a sound base with which future surveys will be able to make comparisons.

There is as yet no comparable array of information about prison staff, though the OPCS undertook a survey of staff attitudes in 1981 (Marsh *et al.* 1985).

TRENDS AND FINDINGS

The prison population has approximately tripled in size since 1945 with all the consequences that one might expect for the number of institutions and staff and the size of
the prisons budget. In 1946 there were approximately 15 000 prisoners, about 40 prisons and around 2000 staff (Home Office 1947). Today there are approximately 46 500
prisoners, between 130 and 140 prisons (new prisons are still being opened and unecon-
omic institutions closed) and nearly 36 000 staff, the latter statistic being particularly
revealing. In 1946 the prison officer to prisoner ratio was 1: 7.1, today it is 1: 1.3.

The growth of the sentenced prison population

It is a commonplace among penal policy analysts that the incarceration rate for a country – generally calculated as the ADP per 100 000 population – is to only a limited
degree influenced by the crime rate (see discussion below). Penal policy in England
and Wales since 1945 has been characterized by some countervailing trends which
illustrate the complex determinants of incarceration rates. In 1945 the incarceration
rate was 37.6 per 100 000: today it is 90.0 per 100 000.

The first point to note is that the increase in the ADP is substantially smaller than
the increase in recorded crime (see Chapter 2). In the period 1945–55 the number of
offences recorded by the police fluctuated around the half million level: in 1992 5.0
million offences were recorded by the police (HOSB 9/93). This represents a more
than ten-fold increase in the number of recorded offences per head of population
(Barclay 1993, p. 7). However, the remorseless annual increases in recorded crime
since the early 1950s were accompanied by a proportionate decline in the number of
offenders being convicted in the courts – the product of a decreasing clear-up rate and
the greater use of police cautions – and also proportionately less use of custody for
convicted offenders. In 1950 63 per cent of convicted offenders over the age of 17
sentenced in the higher courts and 18 per cent of those dealt with in the magistrates
courts received a custodial sentence. In 1960 the figures were 54 and 13 per cent
respectively and by 1990 43 and 4.5 per cent (*CS 1950; 1961; 1991*).

This explains the modest rise in both the number of sentenced prisoners received
into prison annually[2] – 72 313 in 1991 compared to 34 119 in 1945 – and the sentenced ADP – 35 440 in 1991 compared to 13 275 in 1945 – relative to the increase in
recorded crime. Indeed the number of sentenced receptions has fallen significantly in
the last ten years, from 88 110 in 1981, in spite of the substantial increase in recorded
crime. It is noteworthy that the rise in the ADP between 1945 and 1991 – 167 per cent
– is substantially larger than the rise in the number of receptions – 112 per cent. The
reason is the changed distribution of sentence lengths.

---

[2] It is not sensible to aggregate and compare all prison receptions because the same person may be
received into prison several times during a particular court sequence, first as an unconvicted remand, second
as a convicted but unsentenced prisoner, and third as a sentenced prisoner (see *Prison Statistics 1991*, p. 4).
It follows also that it has never been possible to say from the published statistics exactly how many different
persons are imprisoned annually. Quite apart from the above complication, the same person may be imprisoned more than once in a year for different offences.

There has been a substantial increase in the length of some sentences handed down by the courts, a proportionate decline in the imposition of very short sentences and, in spite of the introduction of discretionary executive release (see Chapter 7), a consequential rise in the average period of custody served. In 1945 approximately 80 per cent of custodial sentences were for six months or less, life sentences were rare and prisoners serving determinate sentences of over ten years almost unknown. The picture today is very different. Fewer than 40 per cent of sentences are now for six months or less and the number of offenders sentenced to life or determinate sentences of more than ten years is such that at any one time there are more than 4000 of them in prison. We have already seen from Figs 6.1 and 6.2 how this trend has widened the gap between the character of prisoners received and the sentenced ADP during the last decade. The parole system has complicated the picture further.

When parole was introduced in 1967 (see Chapter 7) it was superimposed on an existing system, which had been in operation since 1940, of one-third remission for good conduct on all determinate sentences. After a cautious beginning, when parole was seen very much as a privilege, successive initiatives meant that an increasing proportion of short- and medium-term sentenced prisoners received parole almost routinely. Indeed, after 1987, all prisoners serving sentences of 12 months or less were automatically released without assessment at the half-way point in their sentences. Yet long-term prisoners continued to be subject to tightly controlled discretion which, following Leon Brittan's highly controversial measures in 1983, have became tougher.

This combination of changes in sentencing *and* executive release policy has led to what Bottoms, in a prescient 1983 article, called bifurcation: the attempt to distinguish 'ordinary' or 'non-threatening' from 'exceptional' or 'dangerous' prisoners (Bottoms, 1983). The consequence of the policy as implemented has been the differentially widening gap between the length of sentences passed and sentences served and the increasing importance of the distinction between receptions and ADP data.

Consider the pattern during the last decade. In 1981, 54 prisoners were received with determinate sentences of more than ten years. In 1991, in line with the steadily upward trend, the number was 230. Life sentence prisoners also have become more numerous. In 1965, when the death penalty was abolished, 76 life sentence prisoners were received. By 1981 the figure was 171 and by 1991 223 (*Prison Statistics 1991*)[3]. By contrast both the number and proportion of prisoners received with sentences of less than twelve months had markedly declined. The increased proportion of prisoners received with long-term sentences, and the increased length of their sentences (a long-term sentence is technically one of four years or more (Criminal Justice Act, 1991, section 33) has been matched by an increase in the proportion of those long sentences that prisoners have been required to serve in prison. In 1981, for example, the average time served by life sentence prisoners released on licence was 10.2 years. By 1991, in line with the steadily upward trend, the figure was 12.1 years (*ibid*. Table 8.5). Both murderers, for whom the life sentence is mandatory, and discretionary life sentence prisoners, are generally required to remain longer in custody now before being conditionally released.

---

[3] The number of offences currently recorded as homicide in 1981 was 499: in 1991 it was 675 (*CS 1991* Table 4.2). But see Chapter 9.

The general tendency towards bifurcation in executive release policy is well illustrated by Table 6.1. It is apparent that the dividing line is around the four years mark. Prisoners serving sentences of three years or less have gradually been required to serve proportionately less of their sentences in prison – around 60 per cent in 1981 declining to 41–43 per cent in 1991 – while prisoners serving four years or more continue to be required to serve approximately half their longer sentences.

To sum up, bifurcation has impacted the prison system at three levels: an increase in the proportion of receptions with long-term sentences; an increase in the length of those long-term sentences; and an increase in the proportion of those longer long-term sentences being served. The consequence is that long-term prisoners have come to dominate the culture and policies of the prison system.

The growth of the remand population

The proportion of the ADP made up of remand prisoners, that is, suspects awaiting court appearance or trial and offenders awaiting sentence, has greatly increased in recent years. In 1945 remand prisoners comprised only 7.5 per cent of the ADP, a proportion that was much the same in 1960. By 1970, however, the figure was 11.9 per cent, by 1981, 16.2 per cent and by 1991, 22.1 per cent. Such is the burden on the prison system now represented by remand prisoners that they have become a major focus of policies designed to reduce their number (see Morgan 1989; Morgan and Jones 1992). In order to evaluate these reductivist initiatives – the provision of bail information schemes, increased bail hostel places, the phasing in of custody time limits under provisions introduced by the Prosecution of Offences Act, 1985, and so on – it is important to understand precisely why the remand population has increased.

First, it is the unconvicted whose numbers have grown, not the convicted but unsentenced: in 1991 unconvicted prisoners comprised 81 per cent of all remand prisoners (*Prison Statistics 1991* Table 1.1). Second, though the number of unconvicted receptions has increased, the principal explanation for the increased population is the increased duration of their custody. Figure 6.3 tells the story eloquently. Whereas male unconvicted remands spent an average 15–20 days in custody in the 1960s, in 1991 the figure was 51 days. Female remands were typically in custody for a shorter period – on average 40 days – but this represented no less of an increase on the 1960s.

This increased duration of custody is not primarily the consequence of court delays, though that has been a problem which is rightly being addressed (see Lord Chancellor's Department 1990*a*). There are currently three times as many untried prisoners at any one time who have been in custody for six months or more than ten years ago (*Prison Statistics 1991* Table 2.3). It is rather the result of increased committal and committal-in-custody rates. Whereas the proportion of defendants dealt with summarily whose cases are remanded and refused bail has declined from 16 per cent in 1978[4] to 10 in 1991 (*CS 1991*, Table 8.5) the proportion of either-way offences committed by magistrates for trial in the Crown Court rose steadily in the period 1979–87,

---

[4] 1978 is the appropriate starting point for any analysis of trends in the use of bail because it was in that year that the prevailing statute, the Bail Act, 1976 came into force.

Table 6.1. Average time served in prison under sentence[a] by adult male prisoners discharged[b] from determinate sentences on completion of sentence or on licence: by length of sentence

Adult males

Length of sentence[c]	1981	1982	1983	1984	1985	1986	1987	1988	1989	1990	1991
Average time served under sentence											Months
Up to 3 months	1.2	1.2	1.2	1.2	1.2	1.2	1.1	0.8	0.8	0.8	0.9
Over 3 months up to 6 months	3.2	3.2	3.2	3.2	3.2	3.1	2.7	2.2	2.3	2.2	2.3
Over 6 months up to 12 months	6.0	5.9	5.8	5.6	5.4	5.3	4.8	4.0	4.2	4.1	4.2
Over 12 months up to 18 months	8.6	8.6	8.5	7.6	6.6	6.8	6.8	6.8	6.5	6.8	6.9
Over 18 months up to 3 years	13.3	12.9	12.8	11.3	10.1	11.8	11.8	11.8	12.0	11.7	11.8
Over 3 years up to 4 years	22.1	21.4	20.8	20.2	21.1	21.7	21.7	21.5	22.3	21.5	22.3
Over 4 years up to 5 years	28.7	27.2	27.3	28.0	29.2	29.6	28.7	29.2	29.3	28.9	28.4
Over 5 years up to 10 years	40.5	41.3	40.6	42.5	45.0	45.8	46.7	44.9	45.3	43.9	44.9
Over 10 years less than life	74.7	73.5	70.4	80.4	101.5	86.3	89.3	96.4	87.3	87.8	87.2
Percentage of sentence served in custody under sentenc											Percentage
Up to 3 months	60	60	61	60	60	58	52	41	42	42	42
Over 3 months up to 6 months	59	60	60	60	60	59	51	42	42	43	43
Over 6 months up to 12 months	60	60	58	56	54	53	48	40	41	41	41
Over 12 months up to 18 months	60	59	58	52	45	42	41	41	39	41	42
Over 18 months up to 3 years	53	52	52	46	41	43	43	43	43	42	42
Over 3 years up to 4 years	48	47	46	44	47	48	48	47	49	48	49
Over 4 years up to 5 years	49	47	47	48	50	51	49	50	50	50	49
Over 5 years up to 10 years	49	49	49	53	55	55	55	54	54	53	53
Over 10 years less than life	46	47	44	49	59	56	54	59	53	58	49

[a] Excluding time served in custody on remand awaiting trial or sentence, which counts towards the discharge of sentence.
[b] Excludes discharges following recall after release on licence, non-criminals, and persons committed for non-payment of a fine.
[c] On discharge; the sentence may change after reception if there are further charges or on appeal.
Source: *Prison Statistics 1991* Table 4.16.

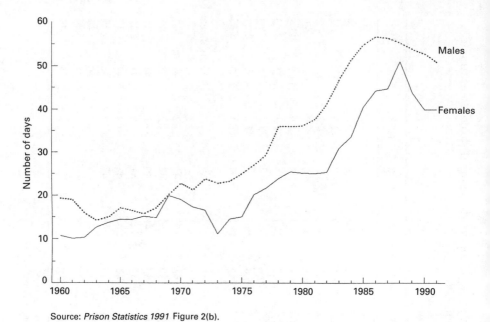

Source: *Prison Statistics 1991* Figure 2(b).

Fig. 6.3. Estimated average time spent in custody by untried remand prisoners before conviction or acquittal, 1960–91.

and the proportion of this rising tide of committals refused bail was as high in 1991 as it was in 1975 prior to the Bail Act 1976 (see Morgan and Jones 1992, pp. 37–8). In fact the 1991 figures were an improvement. Between 1979 and 1987 the number of either-way cases committed increased from 55 000 to 93 500, an increase from 15 to 23 per cent of all defendants proceeded against. Since 1987, as a result of the reclassification of some either-way offences as summary under the Criminal Justice Act, 1988, and the issue of committal guidelines (Lord Chancellor's Department 1990*a* and 1990*b*), both the number and proportion of cases committed has declined somewhat, including the proportion committed in custody. This respite in the late 1980s is evident from Figure 6.3.

The growth and decline of overcrowding

Talk of overcrowding is meaningless without reference to a definition of uncrowded accommodation. Therein lies a problem which goes to the heart of a major controversy regarding prisons policy: the relative absence of minimum standards (see Maguire, Vagg and Morgan 1985, particularly Chapters 5 and 6).

All prison accommodation must be certified as adequate for use (Prison Act, 1952, section 14) and the certificate must state how many prisoners the accommodation is capable of containing (Prison Rule 23(2)). However, though the Prison Service has laid down space standards for new establishments – standards which, controversially, permit the construction of cells designed to be shared – no standards have been promulgated for older prisons. Thus what is termed the 'certified normal accommodation' (CNA) of a prison has historically been something of a moveable feast. Nevertheless, analysts have no alternative but to rely on the CNAs given for each establishment in the annual reports of the Prison Service, the total CNA being the aggregate of single cells, double cells, cubicles, and rooms or dormitories. It is also important to distinguish institutional from system overcrowding. When the total capacity of the system is exceeded by the prisoner population then, unless the excess is housed in police cells or emergency camps, there must by definition be institutional overcrowding. However, even when there is apparently substantial spare capacity within the system, it is likely there will still be institutional overcrowding. The available accommodation may be of the wrong type or in the wrong location and there is said to be need for a 5 per cent margin to cater for refurbishment and decoration, temporary loss of spaces as a result of accidental fire, deliberate damage, and so on. Though there was no system overcrowding in 1945, as there was not again in the summer 1992, there has never been a time since 1945 when there was no overcrowding in some prisons.

In 1945 the ADP was almost exactly matched by the number of prison places. However, the population grew steadily after 1945 and in spite of various initiatives to increase the capacity of the system, overcrowding steadily increased. In the 1950s the population exceeded the number of available places by on average 0.5 per cent. This overload increased to 5.4 per cent in the 1960s, 8.5 per cent in the 1970s and 14–15 per cent in the first half of the 1980s. It was not until 1992 that system overcrowding was eliminated. With approximately 47 500 prisoners occupying a system with some 47 000 places, there is currently almost parity, a situation which, as Fig. 6.4 illustrates, the service forsees continuing until towards the end of the century.

The growth in prison capacity since 1945 has been achieved in roughly three phases. Scarcely any new prisons were built in the last quarter of the nineteenth and the first half of the twentieth century. Thus the establishments that survived the Second World War were nearly all Victorian radial establishments built in the period 1840–80: these were the old county gaols in urban centres and the ex-government convict prisons, several in inaccessible rural locations. Between 1945 and 1955 approximately 10 000 extra places were added by recommissioning disused prisons and converting country houses and ex-service camps: most of the latter became open prisons and remain so today. In the late 1950s new purpose-built prisons began to be completed and these were opened at a rate of about two a year until the late 1970s. Between 1955 and 1980 these new establishments, together with new cell blocks built on or alongside existing sites, produced a further 16 000 places. After the election of the Conservative government in 1979 there began the largest prison building programme since the mid-Victorian period. By 1994, 19 500 places will have been added to the system, 21 new prisons providing 11 300 places and an additional 8200 places constructed on existing sites. It follows that, contrary to the impression created by the continued use of the Victorian landmark prisons, most of the prison estate is purpose-built and relatively modern.

Finally, it should be noted that whatever overcrowding exits within the system, it has never been evenly distributed between the establishments. Overcrowding has always been concentrated in the largely Victorian local prisons and modern remand

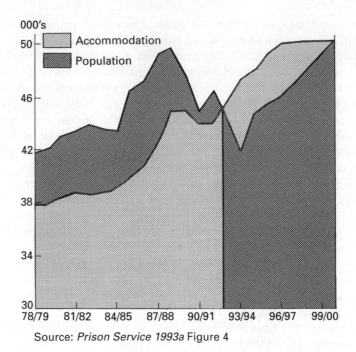

Source: *Prison Service 1993a* Figure 4

Fig. 6.4. Average accommodation and population, 1978/9–1999/2000.

centres. It follows that remand prisoners in particular, and local prison populations generally, have been subject to the most oppressive conditions within the system (King and Morgan 1976; Morgan 1993a).

The social composition of the prisoner population

The prison population in England, as elsewhere, is overwhelmingly male – 97.6 per cent in 1991 – and young. In 1991 34 per cent of untried receptions, 42 per cent of unsentenced receptions, 27 per cent of sentenced receptions and 19 per cent of the ADP were under 21 years of age: the modal age for both male and female sentenced prisoners is 25 or 26. Moreover imprisonment is largely deployed against repetitive property offenders (in 1991 only 21 per cent of all sentenced receptions, young and adult, male and female, were convicted of violent, sexual, or robbery offences and 58 per cent of those adults whose previous offences were recorded on reception had six or more)[5] from socially and economically disadvantaged backgrounds. Prisoners are disproportionately black or from other ethnic minorities originating from outside the British Isles (16 per cent of male and 30 per cent of female prisoners compared with

---

[5] The figure for previous convictions is provided for adults only because, for reasons which are not apparent, equivalent data are not published in *Prison Statistics* for young adult and juvenile receptions. Further, the figure of 58 per cent is derived from *Prison Statistics 1990*, Tables 4.9 and 5.9) because a computer error in February 1991 resulted in the majority of 1991 receptions being recorded as having no previous convictions (Home Office 1993a, Introduction, para. 9).

less than 5 per cent of the general population)[6] and working class (83 per cent of male prisoners are from manual, partly skilled or unskilled groups compared to 55 per cent of the population generally – see Walmesly *et al.* 1992).

There are more telling signs of social disadvantage. According to the recent OPCS survey no fewer than 38 per cent of prisoners under 21, and 26 per cent of all prisoners, report having been in local authority care as children,[7] 13 per cent said they had no permanent residence prior to their incarceration, 43 per cent said they left school before the age of 16 (compared to 11 per cent of the population generally), 43 had no qualifications whatsoever and one-third were unemployed immediately prior to their imprisonment (almost three times as many as one would expect to find in the population generally *(ibid.)*. Perhaps even more serious is the finding from another survey that, of the adult sentenced population of males and females, 2.4 and 1.1 per cent respectively were suffering from pyschoses; 5.8 and 15.4 per cent from neuroses; 8.8 and 16.1 per cent from personality disorders; and almost one quarter of all males and approaching one third of all females were regular substance abusers or were substance dependent (Gunn *et al.* 1991). Surveys of the remand population suggest that their psychiatric problems may be even more acute (Dell *et al.* 1991).

Given these multiple disadvantages it is unsurprising that on release so high a proportion of prisoners are reconvicted: some two – thirds of young offenders, approximately one half of all adult males and between a third and two-fifths of all adult females are reconvicted within two years of discharge *(Prison Statistics 1989* Table 9.1).[8]

As with all general statements about a given population, it is important to recognize that there is significant differentiation between prisoner sub-groups. For example, female prisoners are typically older, serving shorter sentences, less likely to be serious recidivists, more likely to be first offenders, and markedly less likely to have committed violent offences, than male prisoners *(Prison Statistics 1991* Chapters 4 and 5). These differences have led some commentators to conclude that there should be even fewer women in prison (Carlen 1990). However, there is no evidence that women, first offenders or otherwise, are more likely to receive a prison sentence than men.

Finally, the survey data are cross-sectional: until data are available from successive surveys our appreciation of the changing culture of prison life will be limited. The distinction between reception and ADP data is once again striking, however. Violent offenders may be a small minority of those sentenced immediately to prison, but they now constitute 41 per cent of all prisoners at any one time and on 30 June 1991 there were no fewer than 3108 sentenced prisoners convicted of sexual offenders (a high

---

[6] *Prison Statistics* include analyses of the population in Prison Service establishments on 30 June each year. For several years these analyses have included a breakdown of the population by ethnic origin *(Prison Statistics 1991* Tables 1.10 and 1.11). The much higher proportion of female black prisoners is largely explained by the imprisonment of West African nationals for drugs offences (see Green, 1991).

[7] The OPCS does not reveal what proportion of these prisoners had been taken into care as a result of a criminal offence.

[8] The annual *Prison Statistics* normally includes a chapter, hitherto Chapter 9, on prisoners' reconvictions. However, due to severe delays in producing the data on prisoners discharged in 1987, no reconviction data were included in the reports for either 1990 or 1991. The most recent available data, for 1989 on prisoners released up to 1986, have been quoted. The Home Office Research and Statistics Department has promised a statistical bulletin on the missing data as soon as possible (see *Prison Statistics 1991* Introduction, para. 1) but at the time of writing it had not yet appeared.

proportion of whom had to be segregated for their own protection) and 2896 serving
life sentences or detained for an indeterminate time under Section 53 of the Children
and Young Persons Act, 1933. There can be little doubt that the prison population is
now more intractable than in the past, as far as the seriousness of prisoners' offences is
concerned.

Trouble

It is easier to assess the amount of trouble occurring in prisons – prisoners' offences
against the disciplinary code, prisoner group disturbances, staff industrial actions and
absenteeism, the use of segregation, mechanical restraints and punishments against
prisoners, incidents of prisoner self-harm and suicide, and so on – than it is to establish
how much crime and fear of crime there is in society. Because prisoners are under the
control of the state, which owes them a corollary duty of care, a great deal that happens in prison has formally to be recorded and the data published. Nevertheless several prison offences are defined in vague terms (see Prison Reform Trust 1993) and a
wide discretion rests with individual prison officers as to whether to charge prisoners
with offences against the prison disciplinary code. The same discretion attends the use
of other control measures. Moreover, the degree to which prisoners seek protection
through segregation (under Prison Rule 43 or Young Offender Rule 46) in part
depends on the level of safety and orderliness which the physical layout and social
management of the institution affords the mainstream population. By the same token
policy initiatives undoubtedly impact administrative decision-making and recording.
For example, it seems probable that the 70 per cent increase in recorded incidents of
self-harm 'with or without apparent suicidal intent' between 1989/90 and 1991/92
(Home Office 1992a, Appendix 6) owed more to official expressions of concern that
the problem of suicide and self-harm be recognized and prevented (HMCIP 1990;
Prison Service Circular Instruction 20/89) than to an epidemic of prisoner self-
destruction and despair.

Yet, despite these reservations, all the evidence suggests that the prison system *is*
now more troubled than in the recent past. For example, concerted acts of prisoner
protest or indiscipline were rare in the 1940s and staff industrial action unheard of
(Fox 1952, p. 160). Today prison disturbances are relatively commonplace (see Home
Office 1984; Woolf Report 1991, paras 9.7–9.18) and controlling prison staff became
almost as difficult a task for prison managers in the 1970s and 1980s as controlling
prisoners. There have been major inquiries into both problems (May Committee
Report 1979; HMCIP 1987; Woolf Report 1991). Further, to the extent that prisoner
disciplinary proceedings reflect the incidence of prisoner offences (which they may
not), or are an index of a stable order (which they may be), then the number of
offences punished per head of prisoner population has increased in recent years (Home
Office 1992b). The increase has been in every type of establishment except those for
women, where the number has fallen but still remains far higher than that for men
(*ibid*. Table 2). Further, though the use of mechanical restraints has not increased, the
segregation of prisoners in protective rooms on medical grounds, and in special cells
on non-medical grounds, has increased three-fold in ten years (*Prison Statistics 1991*

Table 9.3) and there is now a higher proportion of segregated prisoners on Rule 43 or 46 or held in one of 18 designated Vulnerable Prisoner Units – 3139 prisoners or 6.8 per cent of the ADP in 1991 – than ever before (Home Office 1992a, para. 13 and Appendix 5).

Moreover, in spite of repeated official calls that high security provisions[9] be used more sparingly (Prison Department 1981, Home Office 1984; HMCIP 1984; Hadfield and Lakes 1991, Woolf Report 1991 paras 1. 204–6), the proportion of prisoners subject to high security, and thus the proportion of the prison estate equipped for their high security custody, has until very recently gone on rising inexorably. Until the early 1960s there was no talk of dangerous or high security prisoners and no maximum security accommodation in the system (see King and Morgan 1980, Chapter 3). Moreover, it was originally envisaged that no more than 120 prisoners would be labelled category A (Mountbatten 1966). Today there are more than 3000 places in the six high security and control units (SSUs and SUs, of which there are currently three of each) and approximately 400 category A prisoners (Home Office 1992a, para. 16).

High security eats up the prison budget as much as it cuts into human liberty. In 1991 the net operating cost of keeping a prisoner in a high security dispersal prison (those in which most category A prisoners are held) was £807 per week, almost twice as much as that of holding such prisoners in any other type of adult male establishment (*ibid.*, Appendix 7, Table D). One of the most interesting questions for analysts of Prison Service financial and security data in the years ahead will be to see the degree to which current media attention on, and government embarrassment about, the increased number of prison escapes and absconds in recent years will place even more emphasis on security or, alternatively, will lead to stress being placed on the benefits, financial as well as in terms of human potential, of extending greater trust to prisoners and therefore taking greater security risks.

The future

Predicting the future size and composition of the prison population is an uncertain and, hitherto, has been an unrewarding business. In England the method employed has only to a limited extent been based on planning decisions *designed* to achieve a certain outcome: the estimates produced from time to time by the Home Office Research and Statistics Department are largely projections of existing sentencing policies with allowance made for demographic trend factors. It follows that the more volatile the factors determining the workload and existing responses of the courts, and the further into the future the projections are made, the less reliable a guide to the future the estimates are likely to prove. No better example of these uncertainties is provided than by the two latest Home Office projections of May 1992 (HOSB 10/92) and March 1993 (HOSB 6/93). Whereas the former projected an ADP of 57 500 for

---

[9] All prisoners are security classified A, B, C, or D following the recommendations of the Mountbatten Report 1966. Category A prisoners are those 'whose escape would constitute a danger to the public, the police or the security of the state', category D prisoners are those suitable for open conditions and whose escape would not excite public alarm. Indeed prisoners making unauthorized exits from open prisons are termed absconders not escapees.

the year 2000, the latter projected it to 50 400, a reduction of 12.4 per cent which, as we saw from Figure 6.3, rather neatly dovetails with the prison accommodation which will be available by the end of the century. It follows that if the earlier pessimistic projections are borne out there will, by the year 2000, be a return to system overcrowding on the scale which dogged the Prison Service in the 1970s and early 1980s.

It is not sensible within the limited space of this chapter to detail why the 1992 and 1993 projections were so different (the factors are fully explained in the bulletins) not least because, no sooner were the latest projections published than the Home Secretary announced, in response to extraordinary short-termist media and other pressures, that he proposed making changes to two of the pivots on which the Criminal Justice Act, 1991, an Act only implemented in October 1992, rested. Suffice it to say that most commentators predict that the precipitate abandonment (in the Criminal Justice Act, 1993) of unit fines and section 29 (regarding the weight which sentencers may give to previous convictions when estimating the seriousness of current offences) is likely adversely to affect the future size of the prison population. If that prediction proves justified then it seems probable that the next population projection bulletin will revise the figures for the beginning of the 21st century upwards as dramatically as the last bulletin revised them downwards. There could be no better illustration of the relative absence of penal policy planning.

COMPARING PRISON STATISTICS INTERNATIONALLY

There has long been theoretical interest in the profound differences in punishment levels, particularly resort to imprisonment, over time and between countries (for reviews of that literature, see Young 1993; Zimring and Hawkins 1991). Further, statistical comparisons between countries are increasingly employed by penal pressure groups campaigning for change. For example, English groups have consistently lambasted the government during the last decade for the fact that England allegedly has one of the highest incarceration rates within the Council of Europe (see Cavadino and Dignan 1992, pp. 12–13), the implication being that the English are peculiarly punitive. Such comparisons have spawned comparative interest in how other European jurisdictions have such low rates (see Downes 1988 on the Netherlands) or how reductivist initiatives are being pursued elsewhere (Rutherford 1986, Chapter 6; Graham 1988; Feest 1988). In concluding this chapter, therefore, it is important that we consider briefly how valid and sensible the comparison of incarceration rates is.

First, it is not surprising that the statistic most commonly employed to make use-of-prison comparisons comprises a ratio with the ADP as numerator and the country's population (generally in units of 100 000) as denominator. It is a simple measure: it tells us the 'stock' in prison which, because of double-counting and other uncertainties discussed above, is almost certainly a more reliable measure than reception and discharge data measuring 'flow'. We should note, however, that even as a measure of 'stock' an ADP may be deficient. It tells us nothing about the 'depth' or 'weight' of custody being employed (in some jurisdictions such as Texas in the USA most prisoners are subject to high security whereas elsewhere allocation to open prisons is the norm) and questions need to be asked about how prisoners on home leave (which in some countries is generously granted) or transferred to hospital are accounted: in some countries or states these absentees are included in the ADP, in others they are not. In Queensland, Australia, for example, offenders serving prison sentences intermittently at weekends are included in the ADP.

Second, similar ADP/general population ratios may be the product of very different sentencing policies and vice versa. A high ratio could be the outcome of extensive use of short sentences, or proportionately low resort to custody but the imposition of a few very long sentences – what Young (1993) has termed the 'breadth' or 'intensity' of prison use. Without 'flow' data it is not possible to explain why ADP/general population ratios are high or low and thus how change can best be achieved. Moreover one needs to know a good deal about local counting conventions before drawing conclusions from the make-up of ADPs. In several of the continental European jurisdictions, for example, sentenced prisoners within the time limits available for appeal against conviction or sentence continue to be accounted remand prisoners, thereby greatly inflating the proportion of the ADP apparently comprising pre-trial prisoners. And in Germany sentenced prisoners are counted according to the duration of their current sentence even when they have been sentenced to consecutive terms, thus misleadingly inflating the proportion of the ADP apparently serving short sentences (Feest 1992).

Third, and most importantly, even if ADP/population ratios were comparable measures of stock, are they good indicators of punitiveness? Pease describes them as worthless on the grounds that they tell us nothing about the condition to which imprisonment is a response, namely crime. He quotes Lynch's findings (Lynch 1987) that if the use of imprisonment for selected crimes is related to arrests data for the same crimes, then the United States, which is generally regarded as a punitive state because of its extraordinary high incarceration to population ratio, is little different in its use of imprisonment from England or Germany. Pease argues that if we really wanted to compare punitiveness then we should undertake controlled studies of the response of sentencers in different jurisdictions to similar crimes (arguably only the first step because of the operation of executive release policies and the wide disjunction in many countries between sentences passed and sentences served). Or we should employ a ratio in which a crime-related statistic rather than the general population served is the denominator. Pease favours convictions for the denominator (Pease 1992).

Though most analysts have concluded that there is a weak relationship between crime levels and resort to imprisonment (Zimring and Hawkins 1991), such a ratio would certainly tell us something about the connection between the amount of offending behaviour being handled by the courts and the ADP. But it would still be an imperfect indicator of punitiveness. There are significant differences between countries in the use made of cautions or other diversionary devices, quite apart from the degree to which public attitudes impact police records of crime and their effectiveness in clearing it up. There are also differences between countries in the degree to which young or mentally disordered offenders are drawn into the criminal justice system and, to the extent that they are, whether, if convicted and detained, they are held in prisons or establishments administered by other agencies. Which brings us back to counting conventions. The truth is that all international comparison of prison data is fraught with difficulty. Single indices should always be treated with extreme caution. The more one can approach penal practices from several statistical angles the better.

Acknowledgement

I am grateful to Ken Pease for his advice regarding the international comparison of prison population data.

REFERENCES

Barclay, G. (1993). *Digest 2: Information on the Criminal Justice System in England and Wales*. Home Office; London.

Bottomley, K. and Hay, W. (1991). *Special Units for Difficult Prisoners*. Centre for Criminology, University of Hull.

Bottoms, A. E. (1983). Reflections on the renaissance of dangerousness. *Howard Journal* **16**, 70–96.

Carlen, P. (1990). *Alternatives to Women's Imprisonment*. Open University Press, Milton Keynes.

Cavadino, M. and Dignan, J. (1992). *The Penal System: an Introduction*. Sage, London.

Council of Europe (1992). *Penological Information Bulletin*. Council of Europe, Strasbourg.

Dell, S., Grounds, A., James, K. and Robertson, G. (1991). *Mentally Disordered Remand Prisoners: Report to the Home Office*. Cambridge Institute of Criminology, Cambridge.

Downes, D. (1988). *Contrasts in Tolerance: Post-War Penal Policy in the Netherlands and in England and Wales*. Oxford University Press.

Feest, J. (1988). *Reducing the Prison Population: Lessons from the West German Experience*, NACRO, London.

Feest, J. (1994). Germany prior to reunification. In *Prevention and Punishment: Dangerousness, Long-term Prisoners and life Imprisonment, an International Perspective*. (ed. J. Vagg) (forthcoming).

Fox, S. L. (1952). *The English Prison and Borstal System*. Routledge, London.

Genders, E. and Player, E. (1989). *Race Relations in Prison*. Clarendon, Oxford.

Graham, J. (1988). *The Declining Prison Population of the Federal Republic of Germany*. Home Office and Planning Unit Research Bulletin 24. Home Office, London.

Green, P. (1991). *Drug Couriers*. Howard League for Penal Reform, London.

Gunn, J., Maden, A. and Swinton, M. (1991). *Mentally Disordered Prisoners*. Home Office Research and Planning Unit, London.

Hadfield, R. and Lakes, G. (1991). *Summary Report of an Audit of Custody Arrangements for Category A Prisoners*. Prison Service, London.

Her Majesty's Chief Inspector of Prisons (1984). *Prisoner Categorisation Procedures*. Home Office, London.

Her Majesty's Chief Inspector of Prisons (1990). *Suicide and Self Harm in Prison Service Establishments in England and Wales*. Cm 1383. HMSO, London.

Her Majesty's Chief Inspector of Prisons (1993). *Report of Her Majesty's Chief Inspector of Prisons 1992–3*. HMSO, London.

Home Office (1947). *Report of the Commissioners of Prisons and Directors of Convict Prisons for the Year 1946*. Cmd 7271, HMSO, London.

Home Office (1984). *Managing the Long-term Prison System: the Report of the Control Review Committee*. HMSO, London.

Home Office (1986). *Criminal Justice: A Working Paper*. HMSO, London.

Home Office (1991). *Custody, Care and Justice: The Way Ahead for the Prison Service in England and Wales*.Cm 1697, HMSO, London.

Home Office (1992a). *Report on the Work of the Prison Service April 1991-March 1992*. Cm 2087, HMSO, London.

Home Office (1992b). *Statistics of Offences against Prison Discipline and Punishments, England and Wales 1991*. Cm 2066, HMSO, London.

King, R. D. and McDermott, K. (1989). British prisons 1970–1987: The ever-deepening crisis. *British Journal of Criminology*, **29** 107–28.

King, R. D. and McDermott, K. (1991). A fresh start: managing the Prison Service. In *Beyond Law and Order* (ed. R. Reiner and M. Cross). Macmillan, London.

King, R. D. and McDermott, K. (1992). Security, control and humane containment in the Prison Service in England and Wales. In *Unravelling Criminal Justice* (ed. D. Downes). Macmillan, London.

King, R. D. and Morgan, R. (1976). *A Taste of Prison: Custodial Conditions for Trial and Remand Prisoners*. Routledge, London.

Leibling, A. (1992). *Suicides in Prison*. Routledge, London.

Lord Chancellors's Department (1990a). *Report of the Working Group on Pre-Trial Issues*. LCD, London.

Lord Chancellor's Department (1990b). *National Mode of Trial Guidelines*. LCD, London.

Lynch, J. P. (1987). *Imprisonment in Four Countries*. US Bureau of Statistics, Washington DC.

Maguire, M., Vagg, J., and Morgan, R. (eds.) (1985). *Accountability and Prisons: Opening Up a Closed World*. Tavistock, London.

Marsh, A., Dobbs, J., Monk, J., and White, A. (1985). *Staff Attitudes in the Prison Service*. Office of Population Censuses and Surveys, Social Survey Division, HMSO. London.

May Committee Report (1979). *Report of the Committee of Inquiry into the United Kingdom Prison Service*. Cmnd 7673, HMSO, London.

Morgan, R. (1983). How resources are used in the prison system. In *A Prison System for the '80s and Beyond: The Noel Buxton Lectures 1982–3* . NACRO, London.

Morgan, R. (1985). Her Majesty's Inspectorate of Prisons. In *Accountability and Prisons: Opening up a Closed World* (ed. M. Maguire, J. Vagg and R. Morgan). Tavistock, London.

Morgan, R. (1989). Remands in custody: problems and prospects. *Criminal Law Review* **481–92**.

Morgan, R. (1992). Regime monitoring for prisoners. *Prison Report*, **18**, 8–9.

Morgan, R. (1993a). Prisons accountability revisited: *Public Law,* 314–32.

Morgan, R. (1993b). An awkward anomaly: remand prisoners. In *Prisons After Woolf* (ed. M. Jenkins and E. Player). Routledge, London.

Morgan, R. and Jones, S. (1992). Bail or jail. In *Justice Under Stress* (ed. E. Stockdale and S. Casale). Blackstone, London.

Mountbatten Report (1966). *Report of the Inquiry into Prison Escapes and Security*. Cmnd 3175, HMSO, London.

Pease, K. (1992). Punitiveness and prison population: an international comparison. *Justice of the Peace*, 27 June, 405–8.

Prison Department (1981). *Report of a Working Party on Categorisation*. P5 Div., Prison Department, London.

Prison Reform Trust (1993). *Prison Rules: A Working Guide*. Prison Reform Trust, London.

Prison Service (1993a). *Corporate Plan 1993–6*. Prison Service, London.

Prison Service (1993b). *Business Plan 1993–4*. Prison Service, London.

Rutherford, A. (1986). *Prisons and the Process of Justice*. Oxford University Press.

Walmesley, R. (1989). *Special Security Units*. Home Office Research Study No. 109. HMSO, London.

Walmesley, R., Howard, L., and White, S. (1992). *The National Prison Survey: Main findings*. Home Office Research Study No. 128. HMSO, London.

Woolf Report (1991). *Prison Disturbances April 1990: Report of an Inquiry by the Rt Hon. Lord Justice Woolf (parts I and II) and His Honour Judge Stephen Tumin (Part II)*. Cm 1456, HMSO, London.

Young, W. (1986). Influences upon the use of imprisonment: a review of the literature. *Howard Journal* **25** (2) 125–36.

Young, W. (1993). Influences upon the use of imprisonment: trends and cross-national comparisons. In *Crime and Justice: An Annual Review of Research*, Vol. 12 (ed. M. Tonry) University of Chicago Press, Chicago (forthcoming).

Zimring, F. and Hawkins, G. (1991). *The Scale of Imprisonment*. Chicago University Press, Chicago.

7 Parole

JOHN DITCHFIELD

INTRODUCTION

The 1965 White Paper 'The Adult Offender' proposed that prisoners who had shown promise or determination to reform should be able to earn a further period of freedom on parole (i.e. over and above the one-third remission they already earned) of up to one-third of sentence. It argued that:

Prisoners who do not of necessity have to be detained for the protection of the public are in some cases more likely to be made into decent citizens if, before completing the whole of their sentence, they are released under supervision with a liability to recall if they do not behave ... What is proposed is that a prisoner's date of release should be largely dependent upon his response to training and his likely behaviour on release. A considerable number of long-term prisoners reach a recognisable peak in their training at which they may respond to generous treatment, but after which, if kept in prison, they may go downhill.

As such, the new scheme was conceived of in thoroughly rehabilitative terms but, as the Carlisle Report was later to point out, the motivations for its eventual introduction were more mixed than this. In fact, the debate on the Criminal Justice Act, 1967 (which embodied the recommendations of the White Paper) tended to see parole as part of a package of measures to control the prison population (which, between 1964 and 1967, had risen from 29 000 to 35 000), rather than a rehabilitative innovation in its own right. For example, the other main measure included by the Act had been the suspended sentence (which had received much more attention), and when the Bill was debated, it was the scheme's potential for controlling numbers that was emphasized rather than it reformative aspects. The result, as Carlisle noted, was that 'the theoretical basis for the scheme was never very clearly enunciated' (Carlisle 1988).

The scheme itself was introduced on 1 April 1968. Although the White Paper had spoken of the 'long-term prisoner', the scheme applied to all prisoners serving a determinate sentence of more than 18 months.[1] This was because prisoners became eligible for release on parole after serving one-third of their sentence or 12 months, whichever came latest (the 'minimum qualifying period' or 'MQP' as it later became known).

---

[1] Under the 1967 Act, 'custody' included any period of time between conviction and sentence which was spent in custody, but was amended by schedule 5 of the Criminal Justice Act, 1972 to include time spent on remand in custody awaiting trial.

The Secretary of State may, if recommended to do so by the Parole Board, release on licence a person serving a sentence of imprisonment, other than imprisonment for life, after he has served not less than one-third of his sentence or twelve months thereof, whichever expires the later.

Section 60 (1)

In practice, the minimum period of custody which an offender had to serve before he became eligible for parole was 19 1/2 months. This was because of an administrative requirement for parole to make a minimum difference of one month between release on licence and release at the two-thirds point of sentence. The sentence which produced a two-third point of 13 months (i.e. one year – the minimum qualifying period – plus one month) was 19 1/2 months. Release, if granted, was on licence and under the supervision of a probation officer until the prisoner's earliest date of release, i.e. the date on which he would have been released – with remission for good conduct – if he had not been paroled (Nuttall *et al.* 1977).

The position with regard to young offenders was slightly different in that they remained subject to supervision until the end of sentence (i.e. they continued to be supervised during the one-third remission which other prisoners earned). Those sentenced to life imprisonment were also eligible for early release. However, they remained on licence for the rest of their lives and were subject to recall at any time.

The Criminal Justice Act, 1967 set up a three-tier system of selection for parole consisting of Local Review Committees (LRCs) attached to each prison; the Parole Board, a national body; and the Home Office acting on behalf of the Secretary of State (Nuttal *et al.* 1977).

THE PAROLE INDEX

From the outset, there was close cooperation between the administrative division of the Home Office concerned with parole (the Parole Unit) and the Home Office Research Unit. One of the earliest fruits of that cooperation was the Parole Index. This was set up to meet the need which both units had for information about the individuals subject to the scheme which was not already on the Prison Index, in particular information on their criminal records and their social backgrounds. The index has since been used to carry out research, to answer parliamentary questions, and to produce the statistics in each of the Parole Board's annual reports since 1970. All the tables, and virtually all the statistics quoted in this chapter, have originated from the index.

THE EXPANSION OF PAROLE 1968–83

To begin with parole was awarded frugally. During 1968 some 9271 cases were dealt with, excluding those declined the opportunity of a review. Of these, 1157 (12.5 per cent) were recommended for parole.

There was disappointment at the initial cautious approach of the Parole Board. Even so the paroling rate had been rising steeply during 1968 (it reached 23 per cent in December) and continued to rise during 1969 to 27.1 per cent; thereafter it rose more modestly to 28.2 per cent in 1970 and 30.6 per cent in 1971 (Table 7.1).

Thereafter, the scheme enjoyed considerable expansion and development. For example, until 1973 all favourable recommendations by the LRCs had had to go through the additional stage of being considered by the Parole Board. However, the Criminal Justice Act, 1972 extended the powers of the LRCs to let them decide certain categories of cases themselves:

If any case falling within such class of cases as the Secretary of State may determine after consultation with the Parole Board, a Local Review Committee recommends the release on licence of a person to whom subsection (1) of Section 60 of the Criminal Justice Act 1967 applies, the Secretary of State shall not be obliged to refer the case to the Parole Board before releasing him under that subsection and, unless he nevertheless refers it to the Board, may so release him without any recommendation by the Board.

Section 35 (1)

This section of the Act came into force on 1 January 1973. To begin with, the policy was applied fairly cautiously and only to men serving sentences of less than three years for property offences. Any favourable recommendation had to be unanimous. In 1974, the procedure was extended to property offenders serving sentences of three years (Nuttall *et al.* 1977).

Then in July 1975 the Home Secretary, Roy Jenkins, told the NACRO Annual General Meeting, 'I believe there is scope for making parole progressively more acceptable, so that the parole system can make a greater contribution to reducing the prison population' (Cavadino, Hinton, and Mackey undated).

He subsequently announced in the House of Commons (on 4 August 1975) that greater use would be made of his powers under Section 35 of the Criminal Justice Act, 1972 to enable LRCs to deal with a greater number of cases. He said that after consultation with the Parole Board he had agreed that, on the unanimous favourable recommendation of the LRC, prisoners serving sentences of up to and including four years, except where the offence involve sex, violence, drug trafficking, or arson, could be released without reference to the board. Prisoners serving sentences of up to two years for the above excluded offences could also be released solely on the unanimous favourable recommendation of the LRC. All other cases with favourable recommendations from at least one LRC member were to be considered by the Parole Board. He also said that some prisoners were likely to get parole earlier in their sentence.

An important effect of these changes was an increase in paroling rates (i.e. paroles granted as a percentage of cases considered). Before the changes, the board inevitably disagreed with some of the LRCs' positive recommendations. After the changes, a favourable LRC recommendation was sufficient in a large number of cases to secure release without reference to the board.

At the same time, the smaller number of LRC favourable recommendations which the board had to deal with meant that it had the opportunity to review (and in some cases reverse) a larger proportion of the LRCs' unfavourable or negative recommendations.

Table 7.1. Parole reviews and decisions, 1969–1992

England and Wales

Year	Eligible	Opted out	Opt outs as % of eligibles	Local Review Committees			Parole Board				Number of reviews/percentage	
				Considered	Recommended	Recommended as % of considered	Considered	Considered as % of total considered	Recommended	Recommended as % of considered	Paroles granted	Paroles granted as % of cases considered by LRCs
1969	7 264	490	6.7	6 774	2 189	32.3	2 562	37.8	1 835	71.6	1 833	27.1
1970	8 454	641	7.6	7 813	2 570	32.9	3 566	45.6	2 210	62.0	2 201	28.2
1971	10 388	735	7.1	9 653	3 460	35.8	4 584	47.5	2 971	64.8	2 956	30.6
1972	9 644	710	7.4	8 934	3 410	38.2	4 450	49.8	2 926	65.8	2 915	32.6
1973	10 614	768	7.2	9 846	3 932	39.9	4 421	44.9	2 531	57.2	3 328	33.8
1974	10 681	804	7.5	9 877	4 047	41.0	5 145	52.1	2 831	55.0	3 502	35.5
1975	10 154	699	6.9	9 455	3 894	41.2	4 662	49.3	3 106	66.6	4 029	42.6
1976	10 660	583	5.3	10 077	4 865	48.3	4 289	42.6	2 880	67.1	4 991	49.5
1977	10 989	645	5.9	10 344	5 221	50.5	4 796	46.4	3 200	66.7	5 210	50.4
1978	10 829	646	6.0	10 183	5 160	50.7	5 303	52.1	3 193	60.2	4 808	47.2
1979	10 814	658	6.1	10 156	5 128	50.5	4 997	49.2	2 846	57.0	4 758	46.8
1980	10 756	686	6.4	10 070	5 032	50.0	5 006	49.7	3 090	61.7	5 077	50.4
1981	10 243	623	6.1	9 620	5 063	52.6	5 058	52.6	3 363	66.5	5 271	54.8
1982	9 779	586	6.0	9 193	5 028	54.7	4 626	50.3	3 158	68.3	5 180	56.3
1983	10 077	543	5.4	9 534	5 196	54.5	5 218	54.7	3 460	66.3	5 346	56.1
1984	19 592	521	2.7	19 071	12 080	63.3	5 884	30.9	3 463	58.9	11 886	62.3
1985	23 477	565	2.4	22 912	14 886	65.0	6 401	27.9	3 293	51.4	14 406	62.9
1986	25 066	686	2.7	24 380	15 829	64.9	7 655	31.4	3 560	46.5	14 790	60.7
1987	24 432	654	2.7	23 778	15 199	63.9	7 508	31.6	3 524	46.9	13 994	58.9
1988	23 771	635	2.7	23 136	13 914	60.1	7 703	33.3	3 749	48.7	12 760	55.2
1989	24 445	673	2.8	23 772	14 814	62.3	8 423	35.4	4 614	54.8	13 751	57.8
1990	23 937	767	3.2	23 170	13 826	59.7	7 373	31.8	3 224	43.7	12 885	55.6
1991	23 041	741	3.2	22 300	13 178	59.1	8 582	38.5	3 819	44.5	11 899	53.4
1992	25 593	545	2.1	25 048	15 211	60.7	8 201	32.7	3 713	45.3	14 311	57.1

Source: *Report of the Parole Board 1992*

In fact, the overall parole rate increased from 35.5 per cent in 1974, to 42.6 per cent in 1975, 49.5 per cent in 1976, and 50.4 per cent in 1977 (see Table 7.1) (Nuttall *et al.* 1977).[2]

Except for 1978 and 1979, the paroling rate continued to increase and reached 55 per cent in 1981 and 56 per cent in 1982. In fact, except in the first two years of the scheme, the annual number of parole reviews had remained remarkably stable at around 10 000, while the number of prisoners released had risen steadily from around 2000 to over 5000 each year. Carlisle notes that:

To the extent that parole was about getting out of prison those who could safely be released it had clearly proved to be a success. By 1983 there were, at any one time, about 3000 people on parole licence who, but for the scheme, would still have been in prison. Despite the occasional notable example of serious reoffending, the failure rate, measured by the percentage of licences revoked for further offending or other breaches of conditions, remained consistently low at around 10 per cent.

Carlisle 1988, paragraph 25.

RETRENCHMENT 1983–92

1983 was a watershed in the history of the scheme. Two major legislative changes had the (largely unintentional) effect of transforming it from a system concerned, ostensibly at least, with the rehabilitation of the medium- and long-term offender, to one much more focused on the short- and medium-term offender.

The 1983 changes

On 30 November 1983, the Home Secretary, Leon Brittan, stated that while he did not want to significantly affect the parole system, he had to take account of the general public's concern about the increase in violent crime and the growing criticism of the gap between the length of sentence passed and the length of sentence actually served in certain cases:

I have therefore decided to use my discretion to ensure that prisoners serving sentences of over five years for offences of violence or drug trafficking will be granted parole only when release under supervision for a few months before the end of a sentence is likely to reduce the long-term risk to the public, or in circumstances which are genuinely exceptional.

Quoted in the report of the Parole Board, 1986

The offences concerned were those specified in section 32 and schedule 1 of the Criminal Justice Act, 1982. In 1982 about 240 prisoners sentenced for these offences

---

[2] In November 1989, the range of cases whereby parole could be approved on the basis of the LRC recommendation alone (i.e. under section 35 of the Criminal Justice Act, 1972) was increased. With effect from that date the section 35 arrangements were revised to apply to all cases with sentences of two years and under four years regardless of offence. Cases with sentences of under two years were mostly brought into the parole scheme after July 1984 as 'section 33' cases and could also be implemented without further reference to the board.

had been recommended for parole before their final review. The Home Secretary commented that 'in future, there will have to be the most compelling reasons before I would agree to parole being granted in such cases' (report of the Parole Board 1986).

The toughness of the new policy was underlined by the fact that it was made to apply to prisoners who had already been sentenced and not merely to new prisoners.

The most immediate effect of this 'tougher' policy was to reduce the proportion of longer sentence inmates paroled. As Table 7.2 shows, the proportion of eligible offenders serving over five years who were granted parole fell from 33.5 per cent in 1983 to 19.6 per cent in 1984 and it was to remain around this level until 1991.

Moreover, the effect of the new restricted policy was not confined to those in the over-five-year category. It also impacted on offenders sentenced to five years (whose paroling rate fell from 39.1 per cent in 1983 to 33.5 per cent in 1984) and offenders in the two-to-five year category, whose rates fell from 62.2 per cent in 1983 to 60.4 per cent in 1984 and 56.9 per cent in 1985. In fact it is estimated (*Prison Statistics England and Wales 1987,* that the policy added some 2000 to the annual average prison population between 1983 and 1986, of which 500 were among inmates directly subject to the policy.[3]

Other consequences were to increase the number of reviews before release and to reduce average licence lengths in the five-year and over-five-year sentence categories (Table 7.3). The average licence length for those serving over five years fell from 441 days in 1983 to 272 days in 1984 and 198 in 1985. For those serving five years, the corresponding figures were 365, 334, and 279 respectively.

In summary, a much more cautious approach to paroling long-term offenders became evident following the introduction of the restricted policy. Indeed, introducing the report of the Parole Board for 1986, the chairman, Lord Windlesham, was quoted as saying: 'with the mounting concern about the level of criminality, especially when the offender has been before the courts before, a closer degree of scrutiny is expected'. He noted that board members were more critical than in the early 1980s and said, 'I think the water has got colder in the last few years' (*Daily Telegraph*, 2 July 1987).

Short sentence prisoners

The other change in 1983 concerned short sentence prisoners. In many ways, this had an even more dramatic impact on the parole system than the restricted policy.

As noted above, section 60 of the Criminal Justice Act, 1967 had originally stipulated that 12 months should be the minimum period of custody qualifying for parole. But during the passage of the 1982 Criminal Justice Bill, the government accepted an amendment from the Parliamentary All-Party Penal Affairs Group (which became section 33 of the Act) which enabled the Home Secretary to reduce by order the 12-month minimum qualifying period to an 'unspecified period'.

The Home Secretary subsequently exercised his discretion (under the Eligibility for Release on Licence Order, 1983) by reducing the specified period from 12 months to 6 months. This came into operation on 1 July 1984.

---

[3] The restricted policy was lifted on 29 June 1992.

Table 7.2. Prisons granted parole by sentence length, 1982–92

England and Wales

Number of reviews/percentage

Year	Cases considered					Paroles granted					Paroles granted as % of cases considered				
	Under 2 years	2 years and less than 5 years	5 years	Over 5 years	All sentences	Under 2 years	2 years and less than 5 years	5 years	Over 5 years	All sentences	Under 2 years	2 years and less than 5 years	5 years	Over 5 years	All sentences
1982	274	6 730	789	1 400	9 193	201	4 134	335	510	5 180	73.4	61.4	42.5	36.4	56.3
1983	265	6 920	926	1 424	9 535	202	4 305	362	477	5 346	76.2	62.2	39.1	33.5	56.1
1984	7 575	9 123	869	1 504	19 071	5 789	5 511	291	295	11 886	76.4	60.4	33.5	19.6	62.3
1985	10 966	9 181	990	1 775	22 912	8 537	5 223	302	344	14 406	77.8	56.9	30.5	19.4	62.9
1986	10 603	10 620	1 077	2 080	24 380	8 332	5 736	324	398	14 790	78.6	54.0	30.1	19.1	60.7
1987	9 397	11 001	1 144	2 236	23 778	7 259	5 974	334	427	13 994	77.2	54.3	29.2	19.1	58.9
1988	7 585	11 617	1 269	2 665	23 136	5 659	6 322	346	433	12 760	74.6	54.4	27.3	16.2	55.2
1989	6 917	12 324	1 345	3 186	23 772	5 286	7 311	493	661	13 751	76.4	59.3	36.7	20.7	57.8
1990	6 536	11 177	1 469	3 988	23 170	4 995	4 546	500	844	12 885	76.4	58.6	34.0	21.2	55.6
1991	5 926	10 161	1 568	4 645	22 300	4 318	5 889	588	1 104	11 899	72.9	58.0	37.5	23.8	53.4
1992	7 055	11 504	1 460	5 029	25 048	5 230	7 061	535	1 485	14 311	74.1	61.3	36.6	29.5	57.1

Source: *Report of the Parole Board 1992*

Table 7.3. Average lengths of parole licence granted: by sentence length 1982–92

England and Wales   Days

		Sentence length			
Year	Under 2 years	2 years and less than 5 years	5 years	Over 5 years	All sentences
1982	63	235	365	475	261
1983	68	228	365	441	250
1984	93	213	334	272	159
1985	99	223	279	198	150
1986	104	214	249	202	152
1987	115	221	260	216	167
1988	129	215	258	192	177
1989	132	209	232	185	179
1990	131	235	252	195	192
1991	132	228	279	204	192
1992	132	241	294	324	212

Source: *Report of the Parole Board 1992*

Again, taking into account the need for parole to make at least one month's difference to being released on EDR, this change meant that it became possible for those sentenced to as little as 10 1/2 months to be granted parole, whereas previously no sentence of less than about 19 1/2 months could attract parole. Prisoners sentenced to over 12 months but under two years, who were brought into the parole scheme by the change in the MQP, came to be known as 'section 33' cases, after the appropriate section of the 1982 Act.

Carlisle (1988, paragraph 34) commented that 'Unlike the restricted change this change caused hardly a murmur at the time. Indeed it was generally welcomed as the answer to the long-standing grievance that short-term prisoners lost out compared to those who had received more substantial sentences' – which seemed to run counter to elementary considerations of 'justice'. (For example, it could happen that a prisoner sentenced to 18 months could find himself serving much the same period of imprisonment as a prisoner sentenced to three years.) It also, in the short-term, brought much needed relief to an over-stretched prison system.

However, even if little thought had been given to the possible implications of the change, the results were dramatic indeed. Table 7.1 shows that those eligible for parole – and thus the Parole Board caseload – almost doubled from 10 077 in 1983 to 19 592 in 1984 and 23 477 in 1985. Within this overall change, the impact on young offenders was even more striking, the numbers eligible for parole rising from 979 in 1983 to 4571 in 1984 and 5991 in 1985. The numbers released on parole increased from 5346 in 1983 to 11 886 in 1984 and 14 406 in 1985 (report of the Parole Board 1985).

Relatively high proportions of the cases brought into the scheme were granted parole, though the amount of time they could be on licence was inevitably limited. This had the effect of raising the overall average paroling rate from 56.1 per cent in 1983 to 62.3 per cent in 1984 (Table 7.1) and, together with the restricted policy for offenders sentenced to over five years, lowering the average licence length from 250 days in 1983 to 159 days in 1984 (Table 7.3).

Finally, it is estimated that, by 1986, section 33 parole had reduced the annual average prison population by about 3000 (Report of the Parole Board 1992).

Given the huge number of short sentence cases which now had to be considered, a special review procedure was adopted in order to process them – the 'section 33 procedure' as it came to be known. The section 33 review procedure was a much abbreviated form of the 'old' section 60 procedure (which continued to be used for prisoners serving more than two years). Behind the procedure there was also a fundamental difference in philosophy; in section 33 parole there was a presumption in favour of parole, and the reporting and selection procedures were directed towards identifying those inmates who might prove to be poor parole risks. The theory behind this approach was that prisoners who qualified for section 33 review were serving shorter sentences, which indicated that their crimes were not so serious as inmates serving two years and over, with a consequent smaller risk to the public from their release (Pascoe 1985).

Even so, it ran counter to the original notion of parole as being something that helped the longer sentence prisoner back into the community with a period of supervision. Judges in the Crown Court were finding it hard to accept that a majority of offenders sentenced to between ten and 18 months imprisonment were being released after six months irrespective of the differential length in the sentences imposed by the court (Report of the Parole Board 1985), and in the autumn of 1985 the Lord Chief Justice drew to the attention of the Home Secretary the mounting concern among members of the judiciary about the way in which parole was operating for those sentenced to less than two years imprisonment.

A Home Office working group was set up at the end of 1985 to consider the problem and proposed that the presumption in favour of parole, which the Home Office and the Parole Board had asked the LRCs to apply in the under-two-years cases, should be withdrawn and all parole cases, irrespective of sentence length, be considered on the basis of the relative risks and benefits.

Even so it had become apparent that a much wider review of parole was required. The Conservative manifesto for the June 1987 election contained a pledge to review the system and a committee under Lord Carlisle was established the following month.

Increase in remission, 1987

In July 1987, the Home Secretary announced that he was going to amend the appropriate Prison and Youth Custody Centre Rules in order to change the rules governing remission so that existing and future sentences of 12 months or less could attract half remission.

Even more than the extension of parole to section 33 cases, this measure was taken in order to reduce demand for scarce prison places and came into force on 13 August 1987.

Its main effect was to reduce the annual parole caseload for those serving under two years (mostly section 33 cases), which fell from 10 603 in 1986 to 5926 by 1991 (Table 7.2 and report of the Parole Board 1991).

Thus, by the end of the 1983–88 period, the parole system had changed almost beyond recognition. The Carlisle Report summarized these changes along the following lines:

1. The caseload of the LRCs was about two and a half times what it had been previously and that of the board more than one and a half times. Little of this increase had been accounted for by growth in the sentenced population.

2. There had been expansion in the size of the LRCs and the Parole Board to cope with this work, but more and more of their work had become, in effect, non-discretionary.

3. Parole licenses were lasting on average for much shorter periods than they used to. In 1983 the average length of licence had been about eight months; in 1987 it was down to 5 1/2 months. This had reflected both the greatly increased number of short-term prisoners eligible for parole and the restricted policy for serious offenders.

4. Those involved in the system found it increasingly difficult to think of it as one system, tending to distinguish between 'section 33 parole' for those serving less than two years and 'real' parole for those serving two years and over.

THE POST-CARLISLE PERIOD

The Carlisle Committee reported in November 1988 and the government's response to its findings and recommendations were set out in the White Paper of February 1990 'Crime, Justice and Protecting the Public'. These closely followed Carlisle's recommendations and were embodied in the Criminal Justice Act, 1991.

General

Carlisle agreed that parole was unsuitable for short sentence offenders. It was difficult for a discretionary system to reach a meaningful view on an individual prisoner's fitness for parole where it had to deal with large numbers and very short periods of time between the sentencing decision and the parole decision. He therefore recommended that a standard proportion of the sentence should be served before short-term prisoners were released (which should be one-half of sentence), with judgements about fitness of individuals for parole reserved to longer sentence prisoners.

With respect to where the threshold for parole eligibility should be, he said: 'In the nature of things an arguable case can be made for a number of possible thresholds but we have come to the conclusion that the two- or three-year threshold which many have suggested would be too low' (paragraph 260). In particular, the shorter the period between sentence and review the more likely it was the parole decision would be based on no more material than had been available to the sentencing judge.

Carlisle himself recommended that discretionary parole should apply only to those serving more than four years. The government felt however that accepting the Carlisle line would lead to the automatic release after serving half their sentence of many prisoners convicted of violence (including robbery), sexual crime, arson, or drugs offences. (About 75 per cent of prisoners serving sentences of *exactly* four years imprisonment were convicted of such offences in 1988.) The line between automatic and discretionary release was therefore set at exactly four years.

The arrangements or system for releasing short-term prisoners became known as the automatic conditional release (ACR) system, and those for prisoners serving four years and over as the discretionary release (DCR) system.[4]

Automatic release

Under the new Act, remission was abolished but all prisoners, including young offenders, serving sentences of less than four years, were to be released automatically at half-sentence (unless 'additional days' were imposed for disciplinary offences).

Except for adults serving less than 12 months, the Act also provided for compulsory supervision up to the three-quarters point of sentence.

It also introduced the concept of being 'at risk', whereby an offender committing an imprisonable offence between release and the 100 per cent point of their sentence is at risk of being returned to custody. It empowered the court dealing with the new offence to order the offender to be returned to custody to serve all or part of the balance of the original sentence outstanding at the time the fresh offence was committed.

Discretionary release

Prisoners serving sentences of four years or more became eligible for parole after having served one-half of their sentence (subject to any 'additional days' imposed). All such cases were to be considered by the Parole Board. Those who were unsuccessful in obtaining parole were to be automatically released on licence at the two-thirds point of sentence. The effect of this was to reduce the parole 'window' from one-third to one-sixth of sentence.

Unlike the old system, however, both those granted parole and those refused were to be on licence until the three-quarters point of their sentence had been reached. One of the criticisms of the parole system had been that those who were thought to pose the

---

[4] The Carlisle Committee was concerned only with determinate sentence prisoners, but during the passage of the Criminal Justice Bill through parliament a provision was introduced for prisoners serving discretionary life sentences (that is life sentences imposed for sexual or violent offences other than murder, for which there is a mandatory life sentence). The Act provides that, in order to conform with the requirements of the European Convention on Human Rights, the decision on the release of discretionary life prisoners will cease to be a matter for the Home Secretary, acting on the advice of the Parole Board. Instead it will be the board, operating under a new judicial procedure, which will take the decision.

worst risks (and thus were denied parole) were the very ones to emerge from prison after two-thirds of their sentence with no obligation to receive supervision from the Probation Service. Carlisle therefore recommended that, irrespective of whether offenders had been granted parole, they should be supervised by the Probation Service until the three-quarters point of sentence had been reached.

They were also to be subject to the same 'at risk' provisions as those serving shorter sentences, i.e. if they were reconvicted of an imprisonable offence committed during the last quarter of their sentence, they were at risk of having all or part of the unexpired portion of their sentence added on to any new sentence that the court might impose.

Abolition of the LRCs

The implications of these new arrangements are considerable. For example, they mean that there will be a considerable reduction in the number of determinate sentence prisoners eligible for discretionary release: it was forecast that when the new system was fully operational, there would be about 4500 such cases per annum instead of the 23–25 000 during the years 1985–92. The Carlisle Committee foresaw that this would mean that there would no longer be a role for Local Review Committees and indeed the new Act made no provision for the appointment of LRCs. It was proposed that they should be phased out over the two years following implementation of the Act (report of the Parole Board 1992).

The more restricted criteria also mean that parole cannot have the same potential impact on the time served in prison as before. For those serving sentences of between 12 months and four years, possible release at the one-third point has been replaced by automatic release at the half-way point. For the kinds of 'non-high risk' prisoners who would have obtained early parole, the new arrangements probably mean spending slightly longer periods of time in prison. But not all prisoners obtained parole before the half-way point and, from their point of view, the new system must represent an improvement.

For those serving sentences of four years and over then, as noted above, the window for release on licence has been reduced from a potential one-third of sentence to one-sixth of sentence.

In assessing the impact of the new arrangements on longer sentence prisoners, a complicating factor has been the abandonment of the restricted policy for those serving over five years. The restricted policy had been heavily criticized during the hearings of the Carlisle Committee, not just by prisoners but also by many prison and probation staff and members of LRCs.

The change had been made administratively rather than by a change in the law. Thus the Home Secretary had modified the criteria for parole without being able to adjust the actual eligibility rules (which would have required legislation). Thus all prisoners still had to be reviewed as before, i.e. after one-third of sentence and, to preserve the legality of the policy, there had to be the possibility of parole in exceptional circumstances. This was wasteful of everyone's time but, more importantly, it posed serious problems for prisoner/family relationships. Unable to appreciate the intricacies of the policy, partners and family expected the prisoner to agree to be reviewed in the normal way and then were inevitably disappointed by the continuing refusals or 'knock-backs' (Carlisle 1988, paragraphs 170–3).

There had also been a long-standing perception that the restricted policy interfered with the sentencing process because it distinguished between offenders on the basis of their offence rather than the length of their sentence – in effect, it was 're-sentencing' them.

In June 1992, the government decided to abolish the restricted policy without waiting for the new criteria to be implemented. There was concern about the possible disparity in outcome between cases handled before and after abolition of the policy and the effect this might have on some inmates if they believed they were being adversely affected by having their cases considered before 1 October 1992 (the implementation date of the Criminal Justice Act, 1991). The government therefore thought it wiser to introduce this particular change as soon as possible.

As a result, there was a significant increase in the proportion of those serving more than five years being granted parole, as well as an increase in the average length of licence granted for this group from around 200 days to 300 days (Tables 7.2 and 7.3).

The abandonment of the restricted policy means that even when the new release procedures come into operation, this group of offenders will continue to benefit. For example, under the restricted policy, those sentenced to more than five years for an offence involving violence, sex, arson, or drugs had their parole restricted to a few months – in practice a maximum of eight months – except in wholly exceptional circumstances. Thus even if a 'six-year' man received as much as six or seven months parole (which would have been very generous), he would only have been paroled (in effect, have been 'eligible'), after he had served some 40 or 41 months. Under the DCR he would be eligible for parole after serving 36 months.

It is clear that the Criminal Justice Act, 1991 changes will impact on the proportion of sentences being served by prisoners in very complex ways and that their combined effect on the prison population will not be discernible for some time.

PAROLE AND PREDICTION SCORES

Introduction

Selection for parole has always implied selecting the best 'risks' for early release on licence and, right from the start, research played an important part in the parole scheme. There was particularly close cooperation between the administrative division of the Home Office concerned with parole (the Parole Unit) and the Research Unit. One of the latter's first tasks was to provide the Parole Unit with information for generating a score for each prisoner eligible for parole, in order to predict the likelihood of his being reconvicted within two years of his release from prison – a reconviction prediction score (RPS).

The RPS was derived from the analysis of a sample of 2276 male prisoners who were discharged in 1965 (i.e. before the parole system was introduced). It was calculated for each male prisoner from information on 16 predictive factors such as age on first conviction, the offence for which he was imprisoned, and time in his last job. Each factor contributed to a raw score which was then converted into the RPS representing the percentage probability of reconviction within two years of discharge, as estimated for the data for 1965 (see Chapter 11).

The score was revalidated by Denis Ward in 1987 (Ward 1987) using a sample drawn from those discharged during the years 1977–9). He concluded that the RPS still provided a useful discriminator between those with low and high probabilities of reconviction. Interestingly, however, he found that by then (i.e. some 12 years after it had been originally developed), the score seemed to over-estimate the risk of reconviction for both groups (i.e. the paroled and unparoled) by an average of some 8–11 per cent for those paroled and by 4 per cent for those not paroled.[5]

Three main purposes were seen for the RPS:

(1) a means of measuring the effectiveness of parole in reducing re-offending;

(2) an administrative measure; and

(3) a means of selecting cases for the Parole Board.

The effectiveness of parole

As noted above, the thinking behind parole was essentially rehabilitative and some system was needed to see if early supervised release into the community had any effect on prisoners' propensity to reoffend.

Nuttall *et al.* (1977) concluded that there was no evidence that parole served to reduce the rate of reconviction within two years of release. However, an analysis at six months from release (the average time on licence) showed that parolees did better than expected. This could imply that parole did have an effect in reducing reconviction during the currency of the licence. But, as non-parolees did worse than expected, this was also consistent with a selection effect, i.e. parole authorities were taking into account factors not included in the predictor, for example the prisoner's plans on release.

Ward (1987) also found that paroled offenders performed better – and non-paroled offenders worse – than their prediction scores. His study of 3554 males serving more than 12 months showed that 34 per cent of those granted parole had been reconvicted within two years as against 58 per cent of those refused parole. He concluded that this difference could indicate that other factors, not included in the RPS but taken into account by the LRCs, the Parole Unit, and the Parole Board, reduced the risk of reconviction. Similarly the action of granting parole itself might have reduced (either by changes of attitude or by supervision) the risk of reconviction. Whatever the reason, the prediction score seemed to be over-estimating the risk of reconviction in the late 1970s.

---

[5] Ward suggested that the differences might arise from:

(1) a genuine drop in reconviction rates since 1972;
(2) an effect of parole in reducing reconviction rates;
(3) a possible change in the pattern of the prison population itself towards longer sentences (which tend to have lower reconviction rates);
(4) the varying sample fractions in the strata of the reconviction samples.

Administrative uses

The system was also intended to be used for administrative purposes, in particular as a means of ensuring rough parity of parole decisions for people with similar risks of reconviction released from different prisons. It was known that LRCs tended to gauge an individual's risk of reconviction in terms of the 'average' risk of reconviction for the 'average' offender from that particular prison. Since the 'average' offender varied greatly from establishment to establishment, this meant that comparable offenders were being recommended for early release in some establishments but not in others. Consequently, the administrative system was intended to ensure that offenders with low prediction scores (less than 45: i.e. less than a 45 per cent chance of reconviction) who had been judged unsuitable for release by an LRC, had their cases adjudicated by the Parole Board.[6]

Parole selection

The other use for the score – as an aid to parole selection – was never really pursued. At the individual case level, the prediction score used to be shown on all parole dossiers for determinate sentence male prisoners but it very rarely featured in the deliberations of the board. After 1986, the score was not even calculated (and thus not entered on to the Parole Index) except for those cases mentioned above where the 'equity procedure' required it. Thus the significance of the predictor for individual parole decisions has been virtually non-existent.

Nevertheless, the Carlisle Committee recommended that the Parole Board should take into account statistical prediction techniques which would give it guidance on the question of risk (Carlisle 1988, paragraph 330). In particular, it recognized that the existing reconviction prediction score (RPS), developed in 1977, would no longer be suitable for its purposes. There were a number of reasons for this:

1. Under the new system, prisoners were to be subject to supervision until the three-quarter point of their sentence and then be subject to recall until the end of their sentence; consequently, the focus of attention under the new scheme needed to be the likelihood of reoffending between the point of release and the 100 per cent point of sentence (which would vary from offender to offender), and not (as under the old scheme) the point of release and a fixed time period of two years.

2. In addition, the score was to be concerned with the length of time it took to *commit* the new offence, and not the length of time it took to commit and be *convicted* of a new offence. This was because the latter could be affected too easily by delays in the detection of the offence and/or in the prosecution being completed.

3. The score needed to be able to predict the risk of serious reoffending as well as just *any* reoffending. There were two reasons for this:

---

[6] In 1988, 8185 prisoners were found suitable and 7366 unsuitable by LRCs (and hence had their RPSs calculated). Of the latter, 2776 were referred to the Parole Board because of their low RPSs, that is, a probability of 45 per cent or less. (Altogether 4590 had a higher figure).

(a) firstly, it was considered that a small risk of a serious offence (for example an offence involving drugs or violence) posed a greater threat to society than a larger risk of a minor offence (for example a property offence); and

(b) secondly, it was known that most reoffending tended to be of a minor nature. Prediction scores which were concerned only to predict *any* kind of re-offending were therefore biased towards minor reoffending. (It was decided that a 'serious' offence would be one which resulted in a custodial sentence.)

4. Changes in society and in the prison population since 1977 may well have brought about changes in the type and relative importance of factors affecting reoffending. It was decided to attempt to collect a wider range of information, to try to improve the predictive power of the score.

These requirements led to the adoption of a statistical technique known as 'survival analysis' to develop the new scores. This is a technique which makes it possible to predict the probability of reoffending at any point in time, i.e. the length of time a prisoner will 'survive' without reoffending. For any period of time following release, the technique enables a prediction to be made of the probability that the offender will have committed a new offence within that time period. Professor Copas of Warwick University, a recognized authority in this field, undertook the statistical analyses necessary to develop the new scores.[7] (A fuller description is given in Chapter 11.)

A sample of around 1500 prisoners serving sentences of four years and over who had been discharged in 1987 (about 60 per cent of the total) was analysed. Data were taken from four separate sources – the Prison Index, parole files, the Offenders' Index, and Criminal Records Office (CRO). Demographic, social, and criminological information was extracted from the parole files and records of conviction histories were taken from the Offenders' Index for analysis. Prisoners with convictions recorded after discharge were followed up at CRO in order to locate the date(s) of their offence(s). These dates were then added to the data set and the time from release to the commission of the offence became the dependent variable.

Although a wide range of information had been collected, it was finally decided to base the new 'risk of reconviction' score (the 'ROR' as it became known) on the following five items of information, all of which are available at the time the current sentence is imposed:[8]

---

[7] While the principal function of the new predictor was to advise the parole decision, a further use was identified by the Home Office Carlisle Working Group. It was proposed that a similar – if not the same – indicator should be used to help target supervision for those inmates falling within the automatic conditional release (ACR) scheme (i.e. those serving one year but less than four). This score would identify those inmates who, other things being equal, might be most likely to commit a further offence between release and end of sentence, rendering them liable to recall to custody. This would help probation officers to focus their attention on those clients who were most in need of supervision.

This predictor was developed at the same time as the discretionary release predictor. It is thus very similar to that predictor (and different from current predictors used by the service) in that it predicts reoffending (which eventually results in a conviction) within any time period, for the two categories of reoffending – serious and any reoffending. It has yet to be taken up by the Probation Service.

[8] This approach (of basing the score on purely criminological variables) also had the advantages of (1) being easy to understand, and (2) of providing a simple 'base-line' expectation of reoffending against which the efficacy of later interventions could be judged.

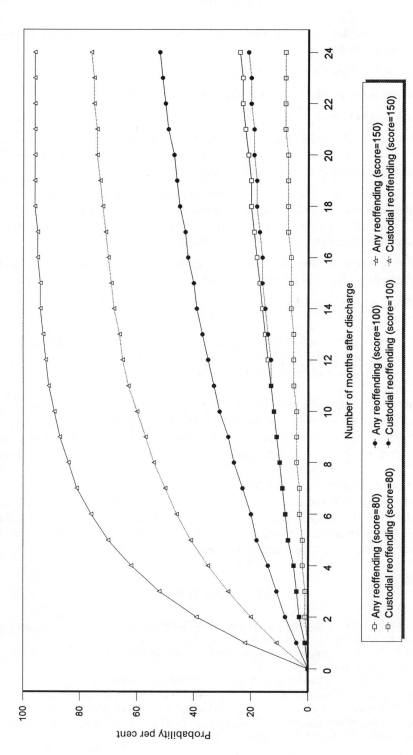

Fig. 7.1. Probability of reoffending during a specified period (based on risk of reconviction score).

(1)   age at conviction (the conviction for which the prospective parolee is currently serving his sentence);

(2)   the number of previous custodial sentences while aged under 21;

(3)   the number of previous custodial sentences as an adult (aged 21 or over);

(4)   the number of previous convictions, and

(5)   the type of offence for which the offender was serving the current sentence, in five broad categories: offences of violence; sex offences; theft, burglary, fraud and forgery; drugs offences; and other offences.

Combining these five variables with appropriate weights results in a 'score' from which the ROR can be calculated, for lengths of parole varying from one to 24 months. In accordance with the Carlisle criteria above, these calculations have been carried out to provide two versions of the ROR for:

(1) any re-offending resulting in reconviction, apart from most summary offences and in particular minor motoring offences; and

(2) 'serious' reoffending, which is taken as offending resulting in a further custodial sentence.

Figure 7.1 gives some examples of 'probability curves' (i.e. the probability of reoffending during any specified period after discharge) for offenders with different scores, both for any reoffending and custodial reoffending. (See also figure 11.6 below, for the curve for all offenders).

The ROR was estimated from the information available only for the men in the sample. Too few women were sentenced for a detailed calculation to be made separately. Instead, it is intended that an approximate ROR will be calculated for women, adjusting that for men by using the approximate relationship between female and male reoffending amongst those released in 1987. Inevitably, the ROR for women will provide only a very rough guide to the risk.

A computer programme has been developed which will enable the Parole Board secretariat to calculate the ROR for each parole-eligible prisoner, and it is intended that for all prisoners sentenced to four years or more since 1 October 1991 a page will be included in the dossier, disclosed to the prisoner, setting out his ROR.

REFERENCES

Carlisle, Rt Hon. Lord, of Bucklow (1988). *The Parole System in England and Wales. Report of the Review Committee*. HMSO, London.

Cavadino, P., Hinton, N., and Mackey, S. (undated) *Parole: the Case for Changes*. Barry Rose, Chichester and London.

Home Office (1965). *The Adult Offender*. Cmnd. 2852, HMSO, London.

Home Office (1990). *Crime, Justice and Protecting the Public*. HMSO, London.

Nuttall, C. P., Barnard, E. E., Fowles, A. J., Frost A., Hammond, W. H., Mayhew, P., Pease, K., Tarling R., and Weatheritt, M. J. (1977). *Parole in England and Wales*. Home Office Research Study No. 38. HMSO, London.

Pascoe, S. (1985). *Prison Service Journal*, October 1985. 10–13. Prison Service.

Parole Board (various). *Annual Report*. HMSO, London.

Ward, D. (1987). *The Validity of the Reconviction Prediction Score*. Home Office Research Study No. 94. HMSO, London.

8 Homicide

PHILIP WHITE

INTRODUCTION

The term 'homicide' includes murder, manslaughter, and infanticide. In England and Wales in 1991 there were about 570 000 deaths, but only 726 were initially recorded as homicide in the Home Office statistics. Thus, while public concern over the incidence of homicide is great (and rightly so), it remains a relatively unusual event, amounting to 13.0 homicides per million population during 1991 (*Criminal Statistics 1991* Chapter 4).

The simple question of how many homicides take place in a year cannot be answered simply. When a death occurs it is not always possible to determine immediately whether that death was unlawful. In the case of Beverly Allitt, found guilty in 1993 of murdering four children, it was necessary for the deaths of those children first to be established as unlawful, and for a time it was a matter of contention as to whether or not they died of natural causes. It follows that even if only a small proportion of all deaths regarded as natural were homicides, then the number of offences currently recorded as homicide would be an under-estimate. It is, however, generally accepted that the police come to know about a very high proportion of homicides (see Lewis, 1992).

Similarly, court decisions show that some offences initially recorded as homicide were never in fact homicides. By September 1992, of the 726 offences initially recorded as homicide during 1991, 51 were no longer regarded to be homicide, with 204 cases still pending on that date. On average, about 85 per cent of deaths initially recorded as homicide are still regarded as homicide after all court proceedings are completed. In recent years it has been estimated that around 20 per cent of the incidents no longer recorded as homicide are dealt with as a lesser offence, 15 per cent are acquittals on the grounds of self-defence, and 32 per cent are adjudged to be accidents. Reliable information is not available for the remainder.

Some offences connected with a death are not conventionally classified as homicide – offences of causing death by reckless driving, for example. Usually separate statistics are available, however, for these offences. In 1991 there were 416 offences of causing death by reckless driving recorded by the police (HOSB 9/93). This illustrates how the terms 'homicide' and 'unlawful killing' are not synonymous.

Another simple question, different but related, is the number of murders which have taken place. This is a question which is truly impossible to answer. For an offence to have been unambiguously decided to be murder, a suspect or suspects must have been identified and apprehended, and a court must make a decision as to whether there was an offence of murder. Because of the small numbers in any one year, Table 8.1 gives the outcomes for offences initially recorded as homicide as a yearly average over the period 1989–91. In the period 1989–91, of an average of 580 offences still regarded as homicide by August 1993, 436 had been decided at court to be homicide, with 21 cases pending. Murder verdicts had been returned in 183 cases, on average. In 47 cases no suspect had been charged, in 24 cases all suspects had been acquitted, and proceedings had not been initiated or had been concluded without convictions in 52 cases. The figures in Table 8.1 refer to the outcomes for each offence (i.e. per victim) rather than to defendants or suspects.

The court will decide, where there is a conviction, whether the offence was murder, manslaughter, or infanticide.

Murder and manslaughter are common law offences. Manslaughter is the unlawful killing of another without any malice either expressed or implied. The Homicide Act, 1957 (section 2) allowed for the defence of diminished responsibility. The Infanticide Act of 1922 (amended 1938) created the offence of infanticide in the case of a woman who caused the death of a child under 12 months while 'the balance of her mind was disturbed by reason of her not having fully recovered from the effects of giving birth to the child or by reason of the effect of lactation consequent upon the birth of the child'.

In summary, the courts have to decide whether a homicide took place, and whether it was murder or some other type of homicide. When a verdict of not guilty is returned, it may be that the court is not convinced that the suspect brought before the court committed the offence, or it may be that the circumstances of the death were such that there was no offence of homicide. For example, where the reason for acquittal was self-defence, or if the death was decided to be accidental, there would have been no homicide.

Table 8.1. Offences initially recorded as homicide by outcome, England and Wales, average 1989–91

Outcome	Number
Offences initially recorded as homicide	671
Offences currently recorded as homicide (August 1993)	580
Of which:	
decided at court to be	
homicide:	
Murder	183
Manslaughter	250
Infanticide	3
Total	436
Court decision pending	21
Proceedings not initiated or concluded without conviction[a]	52
No suspect charged	47
All suspects acquitted[b]	24

[a] Includes where suspect has died or committed suicide.
[b] For cases still regarded as homicide.
Source: *Criminal Statistics*.

Thus, to answer the question of how many murders and other homicides have taken place, we have to put together a patchwork of information relating to offences initially recorded, information about offences no longer regarded as homicide, suspects identified, suspects brought to trial, and court decisions. Because of trials pending, and other new information which comes to light, the numbers are not fixed, but vary depending on the time at which a count is made.

Many of these considerations apply to other offences as well, in particular the difficulty of determining whether a crime has taken place, the initial classification of the offence, and the effect of court decisions on the classification of the offence. Only because of the importance of the topic does the Home Office expend the extra resources needed to provide more information on homicide than is available for most other crimes.

The Home Office has the main sources for information on homicide in England and Wales. The statistics on recorded offences and the court proceedings data are important sources for information on homicide. The Home Office has tackled the issues raised in this introduction, however, by the creation of the Homicide Index.

An account of the statistics of homicide, based on the Homicide Index, is published every year in *Criminal Statistics* Chapter 4.

RECORDED OFFENCES

The way in which the number of crimes is initially recorded by the police is described in Chapter 2. Home Office statistics on recorded crime (HOSB 9/93) give combined figures for murder, manslaughter, and infanticide. A summary table, covering the more serious offences, is provided here as Table 8.2. Between 1989 and 1991, an average of 678 offences were initially recorded by the police as murder, manslaughter, or infanticide. No distinction is made between murder and manslaughter at this stage because to do so would anticipate the outcome of court proceedings. The clear-up rate, at 93 per cent, is among the highest for the different categories of notifiable offences.

Table 8.2. Notifiable offences recorded by the police by offence for more serious offences, England and Wales, average 1989–91

Offence	Number	percentage cleared up[a] (1991)
Murder, manslaughter, infanticide	678	93
Attempted murder	469	92
Threat or conspiracy to murder	4 151	77
Causing death by reckless driving	409	99
Wounding or other act endangering life	9 086	80
Total more serious offences[b]	14 803	80

[a] See Chapter 2 above.
[b] Includes offences of child destruction (average 1 per year) and endangering railway passengers (average 9).
Source: *Criminal Statistics*.

This table shows the category of causing death by reckless driving, not conventionally treated as homicide. In 1992 a new offence category, causing death by aggravated vehicle taking, was introduced. Nineteen offences were recorded during 1992.

A feature of this table is the distinction which is made between homicide offences, attempted murder, and threat or conspiracy to murder. For most other offences, attempts and threats or conspiracies are included under the main category. The number of attempts and threats recorded was more than six times the number of homicides reported in 1989–91. (See p. 14 for a discussion of these offences.)

COURT PROCEEDINGS

Table S 2.1(A) (*CS, ST 1991*, Vol. 2) gives the number of defendants tried and/or sentenced at the Crown Court by offence, including the categories of homicide (manslaughter due to diminished responsibility, other manslaughter, murder, and infanticide separately) as well as causing death by reckless driving. A summary table for the more serious offences is given here as Table 8.3, presented as averages for 1989–91. All proceedings for homicide offences must be tried in the Crown Court, although some of the other offences in this table can be passed through from magistrates' courts for sentence.

During 1989–91, an average of 254 defendants were tried at the Crown Court for murder, 282 for manslaughter, and 4 for infanticide. The court proceedings statistics also include details on sentencing, which are included in the table. Persons aged 18 and over who are found guilty of murder are sentenced to immediate custody for life, younger offenders must be sentenced to 'detention during Her Majesty's pleasure' (Section 53, Children and Young Persons Act, 1933).

A wide range of sentences are given for manslaughter, from immediate custody to probation in 1991. Apart from those found guilty of manslaughter due to diminished responsibility, 71 per cent of men found guilty of manslaughter in 1989–91 were given immediate custody, and 32 per cent of women. Many of the women convicted of infanticide were given probation orders.

Apart from the type of sentence and the gender of the defendant, the tables in Volume 2 of the *Criminal Statistics* Supplementary Tables also give information on age group of defendant and length of sentence.

When comparing the statistics on recorded offences and those on court proceedings, it is important to note that the former refer to offences reported to the police in the year. The latter refer to trials completed, and for any particular offence the trial often takes place in a subsequent year.

THE HOMICIDE INDEX

The Homicide Index is a comprehensive record of homicide offences in recent years and contains the most detail, not only on offences but on victims and offenders.

If the police suspect that an offence of homicide has taken place, they are required to make a special return to the Home Office. This return includes more detail than

Table 8.3. Defendants tried and/or sentenced at the Crown Court by offence for selected serious offences, sex and result. England and Wales, average 1989–91.

Offence		Number tried	Number sentenced[a]	Immediate custody[b]	Suspended sentence	Hospital order[c]	Other orders[d]	Fine	Otherwise dealt with[e]
Murder	M	236	181	181					1
	F	18	9	9					0
Attempted murder	M	75	58	47	1	5	5	0	1
	F	7	6	2	0	1	3	0	0
Threat or conspiracy to murder	M	354	236	102	71	7	41	2	12
	F	17	13	5	2	0	4	1	0
Manslaughter (diminished responsibility)	M	25	24	11	0	11	2	0	0
	F	4	4	1	0	3	1	0	0
Manslaughter (other)	M	222	195	157	10	18	9	0	1
	F	31	28	10	4	2	12	0	0
Infanticide	F	4	4	1	0	0	4	0	0
Causing death by reckless driving	M	346	311	220	31	1	26	32	1
	F	10	8	5	1	0	2	1	0
Wounding or other act endangering life	M	2 363	1 507	1 206	132	34	105	9	23
	F	161	87	40	16	3	26	0	3
Total	M	3 561	2 511	1 922	245	76	188	43	38
	F	253	159	72	22	8	51	2	3

[a] Including a small number convicted in magistrates' courts.
[b] Immediate custody includes detention under section 53 of the Children and Young Persons Act, 1933. In 1991, 17 persons were so detained on conviction for homicide.
[c] Hospital orders under the Mental Health Act, 1983.
[d] Probation orders, community service orders, attendance centre orders and care orders.
[e] Includes conditional and absolute discharges.
Source: *Criminal Statistics, Supplementary Tables*, Vol. 2, Table S2.1 (A).

would otherwise be available on the offence, the victim, and any identified suspects. The Homicide Index began to be maintained in 1967, initially as a paper-based system on index cards. The present index consists of a computerized database on homicides reported since 1982 and is continuously updated as information becomes available.

An important task is to ensure that the index is a complete record of all offences believed to be homicide. The number of homicides initially recorded in any year should be broadly similar to the recorded offence figures, but they will not match exactly, even though the two sources are cross-checked to ensure that the same information is available to both. For example, in the recorded offence statistics, offences reported to the Home Office as 'no-crime' are subtracted from the total for the current year. Thus if a homicide is reported in one year, but reported as no-crime in a subsequent year, it will be the total for the subsequent year that is reduced. ('No-crime' in this context means that the police have decided that an offence initially recorded as homicide was not a homicide.) It is a principle of the Homicide Index that all statistics relate to the year in which the incident was originally recorded (which, in turn, is not necessarily the year in which the incident took place). Thus offences recorded in one year, but decided in subsequent years to be 'no-crime' are subtracted from the total for the initial year. Offences such as wounding offences, which may be later recorded as homicide if death results, are added to the Homicide Index when the police first record the offence as homicide.

The difference between the recorded offence statistics and the Homicide Index, can be illustrated by comparing Tables 8.1 and 8.2. During 1989–91 the Homicide Index has an average of 671 offences of homicide initially recorded, compared with 678 from the recorded offence statistics.

The police are required to make a further return when a suspect is committed for trial, and again when the case against a suspect is concluded. These returns give the offence for which the suspects were charged or indicted, and the results of proceedings. A suspect is defined as a person who has been arrested in respect of an offence initially classified as homicide and has been charged with homicide, or as a person who is suspected by the police of having committed the offence but is known to have died or committed suicide. More than one suspect can be tried for one offence and, of course, sometimes no suspect is ever brought to trial. The number of suspects is not the same as the number of offences. Each victim of homicide is counted as a separate offence. For example, the Hungerford incident in 1987 counts as 16 homicides.

Much of the information provided is unstructured, which reflects the different circumstances surrounding each offence, but the police are specifically asked to give information on motive and the circumstances leading up to the offence.

Further information about each proceeding is requested from the Crown Prosecution Service and from Home Office bodies dealing with life sentence prisoners. This information is used to supplement that obtained in the police returns.

From all this information the Homicide Index is compiled. The index is believed to be complete as regards the offences notified to the police and the outcomes in court.

The current version of the Homicide Index contains the following information:

For victims: Surname and initials
                        Initial classification (murder, manslaughter, infanticide)
                        Final outcome
                        Date recorded
                        Date of offence
                        Age
                        Sex
                        Police force area
                        Relationship to suspect (if known)
                        Country of birth
                        Circumstances (quarrels, theft, or gain, etc.)
                        Occupation
                        Method of killing
                        Court disposal (of principal suspect)

For suspects: Surname and initials
                        Initial classification
                        Final outcome
                        Age
                        Sex
                        Court disposal , duration
                        Relationship to victim (if known)
                        Country of birth
                        Indictment
                        Committal proceedings

While every effort is made to keep the information as complete as possible, it may be missing from the record. For example, information on circumstances or motive may not be known to the police.

Information on the types of manslaughter verdicts is partly coded. Section 2 manslaughter is recorded, for example, and section 4 (suicide pacts, where the suspect has *survived*) but other grounds for a manslaughter verdict are not routinely recorded. These omissions can sometimes be made good by examination of the original documents, but these are often found to be incomplete. A similar analysis can be performed on the reasons for acquittals but, again, this information is not always available, if only because juries are not required to give reasons for their decisions. It has to be inferred from information supplied about the defence case.

Apart from the published statistics, information from the Homicide Index is sometimes made available to bona fide researchers, provided the researcher conforms to certain conditions (for example, that the information should be used for statistical purposes only and not published in ways that would identify individuals), and that resources are available to provide the information. The information dating from 1982 is most readily accessible.

THE STATISTICS

This section gives some selected statistics to illustrate both what is available and the nature of the statistics.

Trends

Given the alternative sources of data which do exist, and the complex relationship between them, already described, the choice of any indicator of trends in homicide is an important one. It has been shown that the offences of homicide initially recorded can be misleading, because these figures do not take into account offences subsequently determined not to be homicide. Also, they do not distinguish between murder and manslaughter.

The Homicide Index is more detailed than the other sources, and can supply information on outcomes where there was no trial. It is, however, deficient for the purpose of following trends, because it is not able to supply any statistics before 1968. It can be used to supply information on offences of homicide currently recorded and on indictments for homicide and on indictments for murder.

The court proceedings statistics give convictions for murder and manslaughter, but take no account of unsolved crimes, or offences where no one was brought to trial perhaps because the suspect died or committed suicide. There is also the statistical complication that more than one person may be proceeded against for one incident.

In practice, the number of offences initially recorded as homicide and the number of offences currently recorded have followed much the same trend since about 1969. It is suggested, therefore, that the count of offences initially recorded as homicide is a good guide to trends, and has the great advantage of being available for a long run of years.

Also available over a long period are the court proceedings data on findings of guilt for murder and manslaughter. Figure 8.1 presents trends since 1947 for offences of homicide initially recorded, and convictions for murder and manslaughter. Also included is the trend for offences of homicide currently recorded, available from the Homicide Index for the years 1969 on. Figure 8.1 gives three-year moving averages.

The number of offences initially recorded as homicide tended to be in decline from immediately after the Second World War up to about 1959. Thereafter the rate has increased fairly steadily so that, around 1990, the number of offences initially recorded as homicide was more than double the number recorded in 1959.

The number of persons found guilty of homicide has also been increasing since about 1955. From that date the number of convictions for murder increased at a steady rate, up until about 1988, but may not now be increasing so quickly. There has been no trend for any increase in the number of convictions for manslaughter since about 1975.

While the number of homicides initially recorded has increased steadily, the rate of increase is much lower than the rate of increase for violent crime generally. The total number of offences initially recorded as homicide in England and Wales in the ten-year period 1982 to 1991 was 18 per cent higher than the total in the period 1972 to

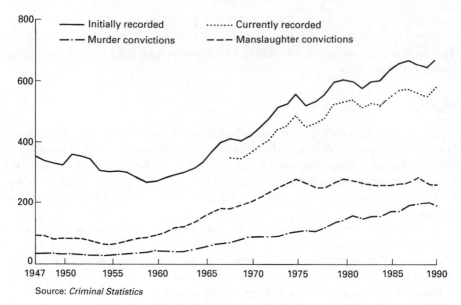

Source: *Criminal Statistics*

Fig. 8.1. Homicide offences initially and currently recorded and convictions for murder and manslaughter by year (three-year moving average).

1981. Over the same period the total number of offences of violence against the person increased by over 80 per cent.

One reason for analysing trends over this period is to shed some light on whether there is any evidence for the effect of the abolition of capital punishment on the incidence of homicide and murder. Three pieces of legislation are significant. The Homicide Act, 1957 restricted capital punishment to murder in the course or furtherance of theft, murder by shooting or causing an explosion, murder in the course of resisting arrest or escaping from custody, and murder of a police or prison officer. The Abolition of the Death Penalty Act, 1965 removed the option of the death penalty for the offence of murder for five years, which provision was made permanent by the affirmative resolution of parliament in 1969.

The statistics cannot answer the question unambiguously, however. At the same time as each piece of legislation was enacted, there would have been many other changes taking place, all of which could contribute to changes in the incidence of homicide. Demographic changes, changes in the economic sphere, and even social changes could all have made a contributory impact.

Nevertheless, an examination of the trends around 1957, 1965, and 1969 is interesting. The decline in the number of offences of homicide initially recorded which was seen after the Second World War continued until around 1959, two years after the initial legislation was enacted but increased thereafter. After 1957 the proportion of recorded offences leading to a conviction also increased, with findings of guilt for murder and manslaughter increasing even though the number of offences recorded was initially in decline. The increase in the number of findings of guilt for manslaughter may have been related to the introduction of section 2 of the 1957 Homicide Act, which provided for the defence of diminished responsibility.

By 1965 the number of recorded offences of homicide had been increasing steadily since about 1960. There was no marked acceleration in the rate of increase after 1965 or 1969. Morris and Blom-Cooper (1979) have remarked on 'sharp rises' which occured in 1966 and 1970, but have noted that the effect was not sustained.

Victims

Figure 8.2 provides information on the victims of homicide. Children under one year of age are by far the most likely to be victims of homicide. Among children under one year, boys are more likely than girls to be victims. Marks and Kumar (1993) in a special analysis of Homicide Index data for 1982–8 showed not only that over this period male babies under one year were more likely to be victims of infant homicide than female babies of the same age (61 per cent of the victims under one year were male), but that male babies were at greatest risk during their first three months. By about four months of age there was no difference between male and female babies. The suspects were nearly always one or other (or both) of the parents. Of 77 suspects of homicide of infants aged four weeks or less, 73 were parents (including step-parents, but few of the suspects were not natural parents).

Those least likely to be victims are aged from 5 up to 15. The ages between 16 and 49 are more likely to yield victims of homicide, men predominate as victims in these age groups.

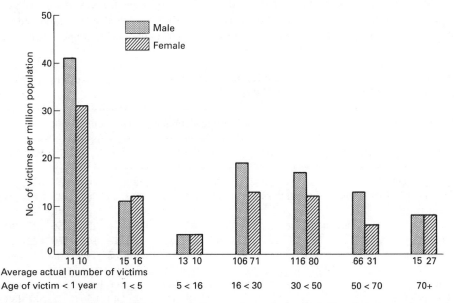

Fig. 8.2. Offences per million population and numbers of victims by age and sex of victim, average 1989–91.

Table 8.4 provides information on the relationship between the victim and the principal suspect, if one or more suspects have been identified. The table shows that most victims were killed by persons known to them, only one in five were killed by strangers in 1989–91. (Suspects had been identified in 89 per cent of recorded homicides but not all of these will have led to court convictions.)

Ten per cent of homicides, where a suspect had been identified, were of children by their parents. If these homicides and those for which there was no suspect identified are excluded, more than half of the women were killed by current or former partners (spouses and lovers). Male victims of homicide (apart from children) were most likely to have been killed by a friend, acquaintance, or other associate. Among victims, men were twice as likely as women to be killed by strangers (36 per cent of male victims were killed by strangers, compared with 16 per cent of women). There were, however, almost three times as many men as women killed by strangers (95 male victims compared with 31 female victims on average per year).

Only 7 per cent of homicides in 1989–91 were carried out in furtherance of theft or gain. Most (55 per cent) were the result of quarrels, revenge or loss of temper. More detailed figures are given in Table 8.5.

Male homicide victims were most likely to have been killed by a sharp instrument (38 per cent), followed by hitting or kicking, etc. (21 per cent), and blunt instruments (11 per cent). Women homicide victims were also most likely to have been killed by a sharp instrument (28 per cent), followed by strangulation (26 per cent) (see Fig. 8.3).

Suspects

Table 8.6 shows that among suspects indicted for homicide offences, most (87 per cent) were indicted for murder. Three-quarters of those indicted were convicted of homicide. Among those convicted, most (57 per cent) were found guilty of

Table 8.4. Victims of homicide by sex and relationship to suspect, England and Wales, average 1989–91

Relationship	Male victims			Female victims			Total		
	No.	%	%	No.	%	%	No.	%	%
Son or daughter	29	9	–	28	12	–	57	10	–
Current or former spouse, cohabitant or lover	28	8	11	109	45	56	137	24	30
Other family	24	7	9	16	7	8	40	7	9
Friend, acquaintance, or other associate	117	35	44	39	16	20	156	27	34
Stranger	95	28	36	31	13	16	126	22	27
No suspect	46	14	–	19	8	–	65	11	–
Total	338	100	100	242	100	100	581	100	100
Base (=100%)		338	264		242	195		581	459

Source: Homicide Index.

Table 8.5. Offences recorded as homicide by apparent circumstances, England and Wales, average 1989–91

Apparent circumstances	Number	%
Quarrel revenge, or loss of temper	317	55
In furtherance of theft or gain	43	7
Attributed to act of terrorism	5	1
While resisting or avoiding arrest	1	–
Attributed to gang warfare, feud, or faction fighting	6	1
Result of arson	6	1
Other circumstances[a]	51	9
Not known:		
suspect committed suicide	38	7
suspect mentally disturbed	26	4
other[b]	87	15
Total	580	100

[a] Offences committed in the course of a sexual attack cannot be accurately identified separately as there is often insufficient information available to determine whether any sexual contact was with the consent of the victim.
[b] Where no suspect has been identified, it is not always possible to establish the circumstances in which a homicide was committed.
Source: Homicide Index.

manslaughter. Table 8.6 also shows that over the five-year period 1987–91 women indicted for homicide were slightly less likely than men to be convicted (72 per cent compared with 76 per cent) as well as being much less likely to be convicted of murder (19 per cent compared with 45 per cent). See also the discussion of domestic homicide in Chapter 9.

Reoffending

Only a very few suspects convicted of homicide have previous homicide convictions – less than five a year in most years between 1981–1991. Over the period 1981–91, a total of 37 suspects were convicted of a second homicide, including 9 who were guilty of a second murder.

Another source of information maintained in the Home Office, the Offenders' Index (see also Chapter 2), can be used to obtain information on reconviction rates for those convicted of homicide. For example, the Home Office Statistical Bulletin 'Life Licensees and Restricted Offenders Reconvictions' (HOSB 3/93) showed that life licensees originally convicted of homicide were less likely to be reconvicted than other life licensees. Nine per cent of persons released on life licence between 1972 and 1985 who had originally been sentenced for an offence of homicide were reconvicted of a standard list offence within two years of release and 20 per cent within five years, compared with 19 per cent and 30 per cent respectively for other life licensees. If we limit reconvictions to 'grave offences' (i.e. mainly homicide, serious wounding, rape, buggery, robbery, aggravated burglary, and arson, all of which

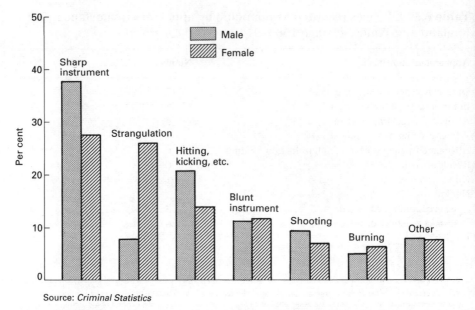

Source: *Criminal Statistics*

Fig. 8.3. Offences recorded as homicide by apparent method of killing and sex of victim, England and Wales, average percentage 1989–91.

Table 8.6. Suspects, indicted for homicide by outcome of proceedings England and Wales, average 1987–91

Indictment and outcome	Male suspects		Female suspects		Total	
	No.	%	No.	%	No.	%
Indictment:						
Murder	497	87	62	86	559	87
Manslaughter	72	13	8	11	80	12
Infanticide	–	–	2	3	2	–
Total	569	100	72	100	641	100
Outcome:						
Not convicted of homicide	139	24	20	28	158	25
Convicted of homicide	430	76	52	72	482	75
Total	569	100	72	100	641	100
Type of conviction:						
Murder	193	45	10	19	203	42
Section 2 manslaughter	60	14	14	27	74	15
Other manslaughter	177	41	25	47	202	42
Infanticide	–	–	4	7	4	1
Total	430	100	52	100	482	100

Source: Homicide Index.

attract a maximum sentence of life imprisonment) then 1 per cent of those originally sentenced for an offence of homicide were reconvicted within two years and 3 per cent within five years, compared with 4 and 7 per cent respectively for other life licensees.

THE WIDER PERSPECTIVE

All the statistics referred to so far in this chapter were collected by the Home Office and refer to England and Wales only. The Scottish Office can provide similar information to that available from the Homicide Index (see Scottish Office 1993).

Information from Northern Ireland is collected by the Northern Ireland Office (Northern Ireland Office 1993).

In making comparisons between different countries it is important to take account of differences in definitions between countries in the way the statistics are collected. In turn, these differences can be rooted in the legal systems operating in different countries. Some of these can be quite profound. For example, in many countries the homicide statistics include attempted murder. Other countries may include deaths through traffic accidents as culpable homicide, or exclude deaths which occur as a result of another serious crime (e.g. robbery, rape, or assault). Even comparisons between Scotland, England and Wales, and Northern Ireland can be difficult. For example, the Home Office England and Wales figures count one for each victim of homicide, but the Scottish practice is to count each incident as one event, even if there is more than one victim. It is also necessary to take into account the different population sizes of each country, if comparisons are to be made.

It is possible to consult the published statistics for different countries and attempt to draw comparisons, but the difficulties of interpretation and definition, mentioned above, make it a very difficult task. The approach which has been adopted by the United Nations is to ask individual countries to supply information according to a common specification supplied by the UN. These can then be more easily compared.

Table 8.7 gives some figures for selected countries in Europe and North America of the number of 'intentional homicides' and the rate of homicide per 100 000 population, as revealed by the third United Nations Survey of Crime Trends (Pease and Hukkila 1990). The figures appear to include attempted murder as well as homicide, for England and Wales[1], and probably most other countries. The authors comment that no direct comparisons should be made between countries on the basis of these figures, because of differences in the definition of offences and their classifications for statistical purposes. The very high rate attributed to the Netherlands looks suspect, for example.

Although these figures were published in 1990, they refer to 1986. This would not be so much of a problem if there had not been so much change in Eastern Europe since that date. Some of these countries no longer exist in the form that they did in 1986, whilst others may produce quite different results for more recent years.

---

[1] But see p. 14, Chapter 2.

Table 8.7. Numbers of homicides recorded in selected countries in Europe and North America and rates per 100 000 population, 1986

Country	No. of homicides	Rate per 100 000 population
Austria	182	2
Bulgaria	313	3
Canada	525	2
Cyprus	8	1
Czechoslovakia	131	1
Denmark	298	6
Federal Republic of Germany	2 728	5
Finland	143	3
France	2 413	4
German Democratic Republic	112	1
Greece	153	2
Hungary	456	4
Italy	2 483	4
Malta	6	2
Netherlands	1 693	12
Norway	37	1
Poland	538	2
Portugal	475	5
Spain	858	2
Switzerland	136	2
Turkey	4 353[a]	9
USSR	14 848	5
United Kingdom		
England and Wales	820	2
Scotland	65	1
Northern Ireland	85	5
United States	20 610	9

Source: Third United Nations Survey of Crime Trends.
[a] Number of persons convicted in court for offence.

REFERENCES

Lewis, C. (1992). Crime statistics: their use and misuse. In *Social Trends* No. 22. Central Statistical Office, HMSO, London.

Marks, M.N. and Kumar, R. (1993). Infanticide in England and Wales. *Medicine, Science and the Law* **33**, pt 4, 329–390.

Morris, T. and Blom-Cooper, L. (1979). Murder in England and Wales since 1957. Published by the *Observer*.

Northern Ireland Office (1993). *A Commentary on Northern Ireland Crime Statistics 1992*, HMSO, London.

Pease, K. and Hukkila, K. (1990). *Criminal Justice Systems in Europe and North America*. Helsinki Institute for Crime Prevention and Control, Report 17. Helsinki, Finland.

Scottish Office (1993). *Homicide in Scotland 1983–92*. Scottish Office Statistical Bulletin CrJ/1993/5, Scottish Office.

9   Gender, crime, and the criminal justice system

CAROL HEDDERMAN

INTRODUCTION

This chapter discusses gender differences in overall offending rates and criminal careers, in types of offending, in cautions and convictions, in the proportions going to the magistrates' courts and the Crown Court for trial and in the sentences handed out at either venue. Detailed consideration is then given to two forms of gender-related offences: rape and domestic homicide. The discussion is based primarily on a consideration of the information contained in *Criminal Statistics* and *Prison Statistics* which are published annually by the Home Office. However, some research material is also referred to where this helps to explain the statistical picture.

The chapter concludes with a consideration of whether there is any research or statistical evidence to support the view that women and girls are discriminated against in the criminal justice system.

OFFENDING RATES AND CRIMINAL CAREERS

Official statistics, across time and across different cultures, show that an overwhelming majority of those caught, convicted, and sentenced for criminal acts are males[1] (see, for example, Harvey *et al.* 1992). This suggests that crime is a mainly male activity. However, it is important to bear in mind that such statistics are as much a measure of reactions to crime as its commission, as they are based on cases in which the perpetrator is reported to, or apprehended by, the police. For example, Skogan (1990) found from the British Crime Survey that males were twice as likely as females to be stopped by the police because they thought an offence had been committed; and Farrington and Burrows (1993) found that almost half of the shoplifters apprehended in their own 1990 survey, and in a previous one covering 1985, were female, but females made up only 40 per cent of recorded shoplifters in both years. Thus, official statistics are an unreliable source of information about the *extent* of gender differences in offending (although the fact that there is an overall gender difference has not been seriously disputed).

That said, the consistency with which the sex ratio in known offending is maintained is remarkable. For example, Table 9.1 shows that the overall ratio between

---

[1] The terms *male* and *female* are used when all age groups are being discussed, *men* and *women* are used only when those under discussion are aged 21 or over.

Table 9.1. Numbers of males and females found guilty or cautioned for indictable offences/100 000 population by age-group 1982 and 1992

Age	1982			1992		
	M	F	M/F	M	F	M/F
10–13	2 920	983	3.0	1 927	706	2.7
14–16	7 646	1 722	4.5	6 333	2 231	2.8
17–20	7 231	988	7.3	7 558	1 491	5.1
21+	1 349	264	5.1	1 368	272	5.0
All ages	2 314	440	5.2	2 029	442	4.6

This table is based on figures from Table 5.22 of *Criminal Statistics 1992*.

males and females cautioned or convicted for indictable offences[2] remained very similar between 1982 and 1992 at around 5 to 1, although there are signs that the ratio is narrowing slightly each year. Also, the ratio for convictions only increased from 6.6 in 1982 to 7.5 in 1992 (see Table 9.2). The difference reflects the fact that females were more likely to be cautioned than males, and the cautioning rate increased more for females than for males.

Longitudinal studies of cohorts born in 1953, 1958, and 1963 based on data held on the Offenders' Index,[3] estimated that 1 in 3 of the male population in England and Wales will have a conviction for a serious offence by the age of 31 compared with only 7 per cent of females – a ratio of 4.7 to 1 (HOSB 32/89). The difference between this ratio and that for overall male/female convictions (6.9:1 in 1984) is explained by the fact that the latter includes repeat offending and that males are more likely than females to be reconvicted (see, for example, Phillpotts and Lancucki 1979). The average length of male criminal careers is also longer than that for females (Tarling 1993).

Interestingly, although there are many fewer active female than male offenders, their average offending rate is the same, at about three crimes per year (Tarling 1993).

Table 9.2. Numbers of males and females found guilty for indictable offences/100 000 population by age: 1982 and 1992

Age	1982			1992		
	M	F	M/F	M	F	M/F
All ages	1 940	294	6.6	1 311	175	7.5

This table is based on figures from Tables 5.22 and 5.25 of *Criminal Statistics 1992*.

---

[2] See Chapter 2.
[3] The Offenders' Index data refer to convictions for standard list offences, a slightly wider group than indictable offences (see Chapter 2).

An alternative source of information to *Criminal Statistics* about differences in male and female offending are self-report studies, in which samples are asked about the extent to which they have committed offences. Although some such studies have been carried out in this country (for example, Riley and Shaw 1985; Mayhew and Elliott 1990), few of these have been conducted recently and most have concentrated on male offending; for the most part they have also been based on small samples and include admissions to questions about 'trivial' offences, such as smashing bottles in the street.

Those self-report studies which have examined the sex ratio in offending tend to suggest that the discrepancy between males and females is less than official figures suggest. For example, Riley and Shaw's (1985) self-report study of juvenile delinquency by 14 and 15 year olds suggests that for those ages, at least, the male/female offending ratio may be less than 2:1. A similar finding has recently been reported by Bowling *et al.* (1994) in their study of 14 to 21 year olds, although this study – and that by Rutter and Giller (1983) – also showed that the sex ratio increases with offence seriousness.

One clear difference between males and females is in the age at which they most frequently offend. Between 1972 and 1987 the peak age of known offending for both sexes was 15. This has remained the peak age for females, but the peak age for males rose to 18 in 1988 and has maintained that level for the last four years. The increase in the peak age of offending for males was explained by Barclay (1990) as resulting from a reduction in the annual number of offenders cautioned or convicted for shoplifting. However, a survey of 7873 retail outlets suggests that this decrease was in the numbers being dealt with formally, rather than in actual levels of offending (Farrington and Burrows 1993).

The male/female ratio in offending is at its greatest in the late teens and early 20s. As Tarling (1993) has pointed, out this is not because females commit the same offences as males but at a later age, but because they are much less likely to commit the sorts of offences committed by younger people, such as burglary, and theft from or of motor vehicles (see below).

TYPES OF OFFENDING

Indictable offences

Table 9.3 shows that although there has been a rise in the proportion of females who are being dealt with for violence and for drug offences over the last ten years, the majority are still dealt with for theft and handling, whereas this is true of less than half of the males.

Differences in the sorts of offences females and males commit are also remarkably consistent across different age groups, with a higher proportion of male offenders being cautioned or convicted for offences such as burglary, drugs, and criminal damage and a higher proportion of females being dealt with for theft and handling and for fraud and forgery (see Table 9.4).

Table 9.3. Percentage of males and females found guilty or cautioned for indictable offences (excluding motoring): 1982 and 1992

	1982		1992	
Offences	M	F	M	F
Violence	11	6	13	10
Sexual	2	<1	2	<1
Burglary	18	4	13	2
Robbery	1	<1	1	<1
Theft and handling	54	80	43	71
Fraud and forgery	5	6	5	7
Criminal damage	3	1	3	1
Drugs	3	2	11	5
Other non-motoring	4	1	9	3
Number (000s) = 100%	457.5	98.0	428.7	100.7

This table is based on figures from Table 5.11 of *Criminal Statistics 1992*.

Table 9.4. Percentage of males and females convicted or cautioned for indictable offences (excluding motoring) by age: 1992

	10–16		17–20		21+	
Offences	M	F	M	F	M	F
Violence	11	12	11	9	15	9
Sexual	2	–	1	–	2	<1
Burglary	19	4	16	3	10	1
Robbery	2	<1	1	<1	1	<1
Theft and handling	57	79	41	69	40	67
Fraud and forgery	1	1	3	7	7	10
Criminal damage	4	1	3	1	3	1
Drugs	3	1	14	6	11	6
Other non-motoring	2	<1	8	4	10	5
Number (000s) = 100%	82.4	27.7	107.9	20.5	237.2	52.5

This table is based on figures from Table 5.12 of *Criminal Statistics 1992*.

Summary offences

Table 9.5 shows the numbers of young adult and adult offenders convicted of summary offences in 1992. It can be seen from this that the two summary offences for which young adult male offenders were most commonly convicted were taking and driving away a motor vehicle (TDA) and contravening the Public Order Act (POA)

Table 9.5. Numbers of males and females found guilty of non-motoring summary offences by age (thousands): 1992

	17–20		M:F ratio	21+		M:F ratio
	M	F		M	F	
Criminal damage (under £2000)	5.7	0.3	19	15.9	1.1	14
Public Order Act 1986	7.1	0.4	18	18.1	1.1	16
Offence by prostitute	0.02	1.8	0.01	0.1	7.0	0.01
Drunkenness	4.0	0.2	20	18.1	1.4	13
Common assault	1.0	0.2	5	5.5	0.6	9
Assault on constable	2.0	0.4	5	6.3	1.1	6
TV licence	0.8	2.1	0.4	59.3	107.9	0.5
TDA	6.0	0.2	30	3.6	0.1	36
Other	11.9	1.0	12	145.2	21.6	7
Total	38.5	6.6	6	272.1	141.9	2

This table is based on figures from Tables S1.1(D) and S1.1(E) of *Criminal Statistics 1992*.

1986. For males aged 21 or over failing to have a TV licence and drunkenness and POA 1986 offences were most common, closely followed by criminal damage.

The most common summary offences for which young adult and older female offenders were convicted were failing to have a TV licence and 'offences by prostitutes' (soliciting). Indeed, as the table shows, the overall numbers, as well as the proportions, of females convicted for these two offences far exceeded the numbers of males, with twice as many females as males being convicted of having no TV licence and 100 times as many being convicted for soliciting.

The sex difference in the numbers convicted for having no TV licence probably reflects the fact that TV licence inspectors prosecute whoever answers the door when they visit a household without a licence and that women are more likely to be at home than men (because they are less likely to be in full-time employment).

Sex differences in statistics on offences related to prostitution reflect the fact that males tend to be dealt with under legislation concerning homosexual activities; and that, although an increasing number of men are now being convicted of 'kerb crawling' (889 in 1992), it remains true that a woman found soliciting for the purposes of prostitution is more likely to be arrested and convicted than her (male) client.

Offences related to motoring

Two-thirds of the 7.9 million motoring offences dealt with by official police action in 1992 did not result in court proceedings, but were dealt with by other means (mainly fixed penalty notices). Of the 2.4 million offences which were prosecuted, just under 1.6 million (involving 734 000 offenders) resulted in a conviction. More than 90 per cent of these convictions involved male offenders (HOSB 34/93). While the number of males convicted of motoring offences exceeded that for females across the board and by offence, the extent of the difference did vary by both type of offence and age. For example, the ratio of males to females convicted of reckless driving in 1992 was 72:1 for 17 to 20 year olds but 39:1 for those aged 21 or over. Among those convicted of taking and driving away the ratios were 25:1 and 31:1 for the different age groups.

CAUTIONS AND CONVICTIONS

Cautioning is the main disposal used for female offenders. In 1992, for example, 61 per cent of all females found guilty or cautioned for indictable offences received a caution compared with just over a third of males (36 per cent). The difference held true across all age groups and most offences (the exception being drug offences).

Comparing cautioning rates for all age groups between 1982 and 1992, reveals that while the proportion of females cautioned for indictable offences has increased from 34 to 61 per cent, that for males has only increased from 17 to 36 per cent. However, the cautioning rate for summary offences has increased from 9 to 22 per cent over the same period for males, while the cautioning rate for females has decreased from 15 to only 9 per cent. The decreased use of cautions for female offenders seems to be most marked among adults, falling from 10 per cent in 1982 to 6 per cent in 1992. The low rate for females is partly explained by the fact that three-quarters of those convicted were dealt with for TV licence evasion which is not controlled by the police (and thus an offence for which cautioning is not an option). Further differences between males and females who were cautioned are apparent in the extent to which they have been previously cautioned or convicted.

A special statistical exercise carried out by the Home Office examined the criminal histories of samples of those cautioned for standard list offences in 1985 and 1988. This showed that, while a majority of both sexes had no criminal history, cautioned males were twice as likely as females to have been previously convicted. They were also somewhat more likely to have been cautioned on a previous occasion (HOSB 20/92). The most likely explanation for this difference is that it is simply a consequence of the higher offending rate for males. However, without knowing more about these cases and about cases from the same time periods in which the police took no further action or in which they decided to prosecute the offender, we cannot eliminate the possibility that different standards are being applied when deciding whether to caution males and females. This is clearly something which would benefit from new research.

The number of offenders found guilty of any offence (either summary or indictable) in 1992 was 1.5 million – in 1982 the figure was 2 million. The drop, which mainly occurred in 1987, is largely accounted for by the introduction of fixed penalties for motoring offences. However, there has also been a decrease in the number of convictions for non-motoring indictable offences – from 331 700 in 1990 to 314 200 in 1992.[4] Nearly half of this decrease is attributable to a fall in convictions for violent

---

[4] A number of previously indictable offences were reclassified as summary offences in the Criminal Justice Act, 1988. This makes it impractical to compare figures before and after 1989 (see p. 36).

offences by males, yet we know from the 1992 British Crime Survey that violent crime has continued to rise (Mayhew *et al.* 1993).

Although there was an apparent increase in the number of convictions for summary offences between 1991 and 1992, mainly involving female defendants, this seems to have been a consequence of improved recording procedures by the Metropolitan Police (see paragraph 5.12 of *Criminal Statistics 1992*).

MODE OF TRIAL

Around 95 per cent of those proceeded against each year are dealt with at magistrates' courts. In 1992, this amounted to 2.03 million people.

Only about a fifth of those dealt with at the Crown Court are charged with crimes which are considered so serious that they cannot be dealt with at magistrates' courts (e.g. homicide and rape). The majority (73 800 defendants in 1992) are charged with offences which may be tried either by magistrates or at the Crown Court.

About 60 per cent of triable-either-way cases come to the Crown Court because magistrates have declined jurisdiction. In the remainder, defendants have opted for jury trial (Hedderman and Moxon 1992). It is open to magistrates to try a defendant and then remit for sentence to the Crown Court, if they consider their sentencing powers are insufficient. However, in practice, this happens in less than 1 per cent of cases.

Given that known female offenders tend to commit less serious offences than males, it is not surprising that figures for the last five years (1988–92) show that overall they are less likely to be committed to the Crown Court for trial. In 1992, for example, 14 per cent of the females, aged 17 or over, who were proceeded against for an indictable offence went to the Crown Court for trial compared with 24 per cent of males. Drug offences are the only indictable or triable-either-way category for which the proportion of females going to the Crown Court regularly exceeds that for males (32 per cent versus 27 per cent in 1992).

A recent Home Office study which examined mode of trial decisions for a sample of selected triable-either-way offences at five Crown Court centres found that magistrates declined jurisdiction in most of the cases in which female defendants were committed for trial. It may be that females are even less likely to elect jury trial than males because they are less likely to have previous convictions, and defendants with no previous convictions are more likely to consent to magistrates' court trial (Hedderman and Moxon 1992).

REMANDS AND SENTENCING

Until recently there has been little research into the decision to remand an offender in custody. One of the few studies (Morgan and Pearce 1989) which examined remanding practices at two magistrates' courts and included a consideration of whether men and women were treated differently concluded that part of the reason that fewer women were remanded in custody was because they were less likely to be judged 'high risk' (defined as those who had previously failed to appear after being given court bail, or had been charged with a further offence while on bail, or were of no fixed abode). However, as Morgan and Pearce acknowledge, they were unable to explain why females who fell into the main low risk group in both areas were also less likely to be remanded in custody than their male counterparts.

Prison Statistics shows that about 30 per cent of women who are remanded in custody are subsequently received into prison under sentence, compared with 40 per cent of their male counterparts. According to *Gender and the Criminal Justice System* (Home Office 1992), women on bail are also less likely than men on bail to receive a custodial sentence – about 5 per cent compared with 10 per cent of men. The most obvious interpretation which could be put on these figures is that men and women are being treated differently when *either* the remand *or* the sentencing decision is being made. However, the available statistics are incomplete and may under- or over-estimate the size of the difference.[5] The Home Office is currently carrying out research to investigate the reasons underlying apparent sex differences in remands and sentencing.

Sentencing statistics show large overall differences in the extent to which males and females receive custodial sentences and in the extent to which they are given different community penalties. For example, in 1992, 38 per cent of females convicted of indictable offences were given absolute or conditional discharges, compared with 19 per cent of males, and 17 per cent were given a probation or supervision order compared with 10 per cent of males. Only 5 per cent of female offenders were given a sentence of immediate custody,[6] 5 per cent were given a community service order (CSO) and 26 per cent were fined compared with 16, 10, and 35 per cent of males respectively. As Table 9.6 shows, for adults, these differences persist over time. Similar sentencing differences are found when the sentencing of young adult offenders is compared. However, boys and girl under the age of 17 have quite similar sentencing patterns, the exception being that girls are more likely to be given a discharge and boys to receive an attendance centre order or to be sentenced to a young offender institution (see Table 9.7).

With the exception of drug offences, overall sex differences in sentencing also pertain when individual indictable offences are considered. Among those convicted of drug offences, males and females were equally likely to receive a CSO or an unsuspended custodial sentence (5 per cent and 14 per cent respectively).

As well as being generally less likely to receive a custodial sentence than men, women also tend to receive shorter terms of imprisonment: in 1992 the average length of prison sentences awarded for indictable offences at the Crown Court was 17.7 months for women aged 21 or over and 21.1 months for men. The average length was lower for females convicted of burglary, fraud and forgery, robbery, and theft and handling, but higher for criminal damage and drug offences.

---

[5] Remand trends in both *Criminal Statistics* and *Prison Statistics* were broadly consistent until 1986, when they diverged quite markedly. In Chapter 8 of *Criminal Statistics 1991* this is attributed to the introduction of the CPS. The text also warns that the remand figures should be regarded as '*providing no more than an order of magnitude*' (paragraph 8.3, italicized in the original). *Criminal Statistics 1992* does not include a breakdown of remand data by sex, because of inaccuracies in the data, but the Home Office estimates that approximately 8 per cent of males and 3 per cent of females proceeded against for indictable offences are remanded in custody during magistrates' court proceedings.

[6] Immediate custody here includes being sentenced to a young offender's institution.

Table 9.6. Sentences awarded to males and females aged 21 or over convicted of indictable offences: 1982 and 1992

	1982		1992	
Sentences	M	F	M	F
Absolute/conditional discharge	8	21	17	36
Probation order	6	16	9	16
Fine	47	48	37	27
CSO	6	2	9	5
Suspended sentence	12	7	8	7
Immediate custody	19	5	18	6
Other	1	1	3	2
Number (000s) = 100%	215.5	42.3	190.1	28.5

This table is based on figures from Table 7.13 of *Criminal Statistics 1992*.

Table 9.7. Sentences awarded to males and females convicted of indictable offences by age: 1992

	10–16		17–20		21+	
Sentences	M	F	M	F	M	F
Absolute/conditional discharge	37	55	19	42	17	36
Supervision order	20	20	–	–	–	–
Probation order	–	–	13	19	9	16
Fine	12	10	33	27	37	27
Attendance centre order	17	5	3	–	–	–
CSO	4	2	15	7	9	5
Care order	<1	<1	–	–	–	–
Suspended sentence	–	–	–	–	8	7
Young offenders institution	8	1	15	3	–	–
Immediate custody	–	–	–	–	18	7
Other	2	5	3	3	3	2
Number (000s) = 100%	18.2	2.2	74.3	9.3	190.1	28.5

This table is based on figures from Tables 7.6–7.12 of *Criminal Statistics 1992*.

In the 1970s and 1980s a number of studies attempted to examine the question of why men and women appear to have such different sentencing patterns. Some of these studies (Pearson 1976; Eaton 1983; Edwards 1984) were impressionistic accounts which focused on interactional aspects of the (magistrates') court process. They were not concerned with measuring differences between male and female defendants in terms of factors such as their past or present offending, but in how differences in the way they behaved and how they were perceived affected the decision-making process. On the other hand, studies which did look at such differences (but ignored interaction in the courtroom) came up with somewhat conflicting results (Young 1979; Kapardis and Farrington 1981; Farrington and Morris 1983). For example, Young's study of over 2000 court records and Kapardis and Farrington's small-scale sentencing simulation study both concluded that the defendant's sex had an independent effect on sentence when other factors were controlled, whereas Farrington and Morris's correlational analysis of 400 court records found that it did not.

The recent study by Roger Hood (1992) is one of the few to have compared the sentencing of men and women at the Crown Court using multivariate techniques. He found that women were less likely to be sentenced to custody than men when purely legal factors were taken into account and when socio-demographic factors were controlled.

Hood also succinctly explains why the various authors, such as Seear and Player (1986), Carlen (1988), and NACRO (1991), who have used prison statistics to argue that women are *more likely* to receive custody than men, have misinterpreted the data. He points out that these statistics, which show that the sentenced female prison population contains proportionately more first offenders than the male population, are an inappropriate basis from which to draw conclusions about sentencing as they concern those *in prison* not those being *imprisoned*; and concludes 'a much higher proportion of women than men convicted in the courts are convicted of theft or have no previous convictions. Therefore, even though a smaller proportion of women than men are sentenced to custody for theft or with no previous convictions, they are still over-represented in the prison population in comparison with men' (Hood 1992, p. 169). A similar point is made in the Home Office paper on gender published in 1992.

GENDER-RELATED OFFENCES

The various sweeps of the British Crime Survey, and other victim surveys, have shown that young men are most at risk of most violent crime. They are especially prone to be victims of assault and robbery. However, women are more likely than men to be victims of certain types of crime, including sexual assault, snatch theft, domestic violence, and domestic homicide. This section focuses on two such offences: rape and domestic homicide. The former, along with indecent assault on a female and infanticide, is one of the few crimes for which the legislation is sex-specific. Domestic homicide, on the other hand is an offence which both men and women can and do commit, but for which women are said to be dealt with more severely than men.

Rape

A recently published Home Office study (Grace *et al.* 1992), examined the processing of a sample of 336 cases of the 1842 cases originally recorded by the police as rape in 1985. This showed that there were three key attrition points where most cases failed: first, when the police decided whether to 'no-crime' an incident (i.e. not to record it as an offence), which occurred in a quarter of cases; second, when the police [7] decided whether to proceed to prosecution (13 per cent of cases fell at this stage); and third, when the jury decided whether to convict. Forty per cent of the sample cases did end in a conviction, but in only a quarter of cases was this for rape. Factors which were most closely associated with a case resulting in a conviction involved young, single women who were unacquainted with their attacker and had been physically injured in the attack. Cases in which the offender was known to the victim were least likely to end in conviction. Such cases often hinged on the question of whether the victim consented to intercourse.

An examination of the figures for 1992 shows that while the number of cases being recorded as rape by the police has more than doubled since 1985 to 4142, the proportion resulting in a conviction for rape has decreased to 12 per cent. How far, this reflects a real increase in the attrition and how far it reflects the fact that the police appear more willing to record an offence as rape, remains a question for further research, as does the impact of the Home Secretary's announcement that judges should no longer warn juries against the dangers of accepting uncorroborated evidence about the victim's lack of consent (speech to the Conservative Party Conference at Blackpool, 6 October 1993).

Domestic homicide

The term homicide covers the offences of murder, manslaughter, and infanticide. In 1991, there were 675 such offences (an increase of more than a third on 1981 figures). Excluding cases in which children were killed by their parents and cases in which no suspect had been identified leaves 537 cases. Forty-four per cent of the victims in these cases were female, of whom 53 per cent had been killed by their current or former lover, spouse or, cohabitant. This was true of only 10 per cent of male victims. This represents 122 females and 30 males.

Recent cases, such as those involving Sara Thornton and Karanjit Ahluwalia, have raised questions about whether women who are accused of 'domestic homicide' are treated more harshly than men accused of the same crime. An analysis of the 1016 persons indicted for murder in domestic homicide cases between 1984 and 1992 does not support this view (*CS 1992*). Only 4 per cent of males compared with 23 per cent of females indicted for murder were acquitted on all charges.

Of those found guilty of domestic killing, 80 per cent of the women were found guilty of the lesser charge of manslaughter compared with less than two-thirds (61 per cent) of the men.

Much of the controversy around recent cases has surrounded the use of the provocation defence, which is said to be less easy for women to employ. Yet, of those found guilty of manslaughter, and for whom we have such information, roughly equal proportions used defences of provocation (36 per cent) and diminished responsibility (35 per cent). Other defences – usually no intent to kill – were employed in 28 per cent of cases[8].

---

[7] In 1985 the decision to prosecute was made by the police. Now, of course, it is taken by the Crown Prosecution Service.

[8] Cases resulting in a manslaughter verdict, where the grounds for the defence are not known, have been apportioned pro rata between provocation and 'other' defences. Diminished responsibility defences are believed to be fully accounted for.

Around a third of men (32 per cent) also used the provocation defence, but 48 per cent used diminished responsibility and 19 per cent used other defences. By combining the percentages employing the provocation defence with the percentages of men and women convicted of manslaughter, we can infer that a defence of provocation was accepted in about 29 per cent (or 36 per cent of 80 per cent) of cases involving female defendants compared with only 20 per cent (32 per cent of 61 per cent) of cases involving male defendants.

Claims that women convicted of domestic homicide are routinely sentenced more harshly also do not appear to hold up as, between 1984 and 1992, 71 per cent of men convicted of manslaughter received a prison sentence, compared with 42 per cent of women. Forty seven per cent of women were sentenced to either probation or a suspended sentence compared with 11 per cent of men.

IS THERE EVIDENCE OF DISCRIMINATION?

We know that official statistics are a poor source of information about how great a difference there is in the extent to which males and females commit offences. Unfortunately, the existing self-report data are too limited to provide a more accurate picture. However, they do suggest that the difference is less than the five to one, male/female ratio indicated by the official statistics.

Females are more likely to be cautioned and less likely to receive a custodial sentence than males. However, evidence that there are overall differences in the way males and females are treated by the criminal justice system is not necessarily evidence that one or other group is being unfairly treated. For example, the fact that women appear to receive less severe sentences than men may be a consequence of the police and courts treating them differently or a legitimate reflection of the fact that they generally commit less serious offences, their offending (within a particular offence type) is more minor, and they offend less frequently than males. In the absence of statistical information on all these factors, we cannot say which of these explanations is more likely. The existing research evidence tends to support the latter explanation, but as the discussion above shows, it is equivocal; more large-scale studies which control for a wide range of legal and social factors are required.

REFERENCES

Barclay, G. (1990). The peak age of known offending by males. *Research Bulletin* **28**, 20–3. Home Office Research and Planning Unit, London.

Bowling, B., Graham, J. and Ross, A. (1994). Self-reported offending among young people in England and Wales: methodology and preliminary findings. In *Delinquent Behaviour among young people in the Western World* (ed. J. Junger-Tas, G.J. Terlown, and M. W. Klein. Kluger, Amsterdam/New York.

Carlen P. (1988). *Women, Crime and Poverty*. Open University Press, Milton Keynes.

Eaton, M. (1983). Mitigating circumstances: familiar rhetoric. *International Journal of the Sociology of Law* **11**, 385–400.

Edwards, S. S. M. (1984). *Women on Trial*. Manchester University Press, Manchester.

Farrington, D. P. and Burrows, J. N. (1993). Did shoplifting really increase? *British Journal of Criminology* **33**(1), 57–69.

Farrington, D. P. and Morris, A. M. (1983). 'Sex, sentencing and reconviction'. *British Journal of Criminology* **23**, 229–48.

Grace, S., Lloyd, C., and Smith, L. (1992). *Rape: from Recording to Conviction*. Research and Planning Unit Paper No. 71. Home Office, London.

Harvey, L., Burnham, R. W., Kendall, K., and Pease, K. (1992). Gender differences in criminal justice: an international comparison. *British Journal of Criminology* **32**(2), 208–17.

Hedderman, C. and Moxon, D. (1992). *Magistrates' Court or Crown Court? Mode of Trial Decisions and Sentencing*. Home Office Research Study No. 125. HMSO, London.

Home Office (1992). *Gender and the Criminal Justice System*. Home Office, London.

Hood, R. (1992). *Race and Sentencing: a Study in the Crown Court*. Clarendon Press, Oxford.

Kapardis, A. and Farrington, D. P. (1981). An experimental study of sentencing by magistrates. *Law and Human Behaviour* **5**, 107–121.

Mayhew, P. and Elliott, D. (1990). Self-reported offending, victimisation and the British Crime Survey. *Violence and Victims* **5**(2), 83–96.

Mayhew, P., Aye Maung, N. and Mirrlees-Black, C. (1993). *The 1992 British Crime Survey*. Home Office Research Study No. 132. HMSO, London.

Morgan, P. and Pearce, R. (1989). *Remand Decisions in Brighton and Bournemouth*. Research and Planning Unit Paper No. 53. Home Office, London.

NACRO (1991). *A Fresh Start for Women Prisoners: the Implications of the Woolf Report for Women*. NACRO, London.

Pearson, R. (1976). Women defendants in magistrates' courts. *British Journal of Law and Society* **3**, 265–73.

Phillpotts, G. J. O. and Lancucki, L. B. (1979). *Previous Convictions, Sentence and Reconviction: a Statistical Study of a Sample of 5000 offenders Convicted in January 1971*. Home Office Research Study No. 53. HMSO, London.

Riley, D. and Shaw, M. (1985). *Parental Supervision and Juvenile Delinquency*. Home Office Research Study No. 83. HMSO, London.

Rutter, M. and Giller, H. (1983). *Juvenile Delinquency: Trends and Perspectives*. Penguin, Harmondsworth.

Seear, N. and Player, E. (1986). *Women in the Penal System*. Howard League for Penal Reform, London.

Skogan, W. G. (1990). *The Police and Public in England and Wales: a British Crime Survey Report*. Home Office Research Study No. 117. HMSO, London.

Tarling, R. (1993). *Analysing Offending: Data, Models and Interpretations*. HMSO, London.

Young, W. (1979) *Community Service Orders: the Development and Use of a new Penal Measure*. Cambridge Studies in Criminology No. XLII. Heinemann, London.

10 Ethnic differences

MARIAN FITZGERALD

INTRODUCTION

In the late 1960s Rose *et al.* (1969) recommended:

that the methods of collecting and presenting data be improved to allow accurate assessment of rates of crime and delinquency among ethnic and other minority groups.

The book was seminal in comprehensively raising issues about racial prejudice, discrimination, and disadvantage, a key reference source for groups campaigning for government action on these problems. Yet when official statistics on 'race'[1] and crime began to enter the public domain some ten years later, the response of these groups was ambivalent. The publication[2] in 1982 by the Metropolitan Police Commissioner of figures selected to show an over-representation of black[3] offenders in street crime relative to their presence in the population at large was roundly condemned; yet the same data sources were used by the black-led 'scrap sus'[4] campaign to demonstrate discrimination by the police (Demuth 1978).

Nearly 25 years on, there remains some suspicion of the purposes for which official statistics on ethnic minorities as offenders are collected (Carr-Hill and Drew 1989) and this underlay the large-scale failure, for example, of probation officers to comply with a circular (71/90) from the Home Office on ethnic monitoring. Yet opposition in principle to ethnic monitoring in the field of criminal justice has largely disappeared; and campaigning organizations, including those representing the interests of ethnic minorities, are now actively demanding an extension of the data which are currently available (see, for example, Commission for Racial Equality (CRE) 1992; NACRO 1991).

Partly as a direct response to these pressures and partly because of the momentum generated by existing monitoring, in a climate of increased emphasis on quantifiable measures of the performance of public agencies, the rapid expansion of ethnic data collection in other spheres of public policy, and the important catalytic effect of

---

[1] The term 'race' is not used here in a biological sense but reflects its common usage to refer to social groups distinguished on the basis of skin colour.

[2] Scotland Yard press release, 10 March 1982.

[3] The term 'black' is used here and throughout to refer to people wholly or partly of Caribbean origin. 'Asian' collectively describes those with origins in the Indian subcontinent.

[4] The campaign opposed the disproportionate use against black people of section 4 of the 1824 Vagrancy Act. This gave the police powers to arrest without warrant a person whom they 'reasonably' suspected of 'loitering with intent to commit a felonious offence'.

section 95 of the 1991 Criminal Justice Act,[5] there have recently been signs that the routine collection of data on the ethnic origin of suspects and offenders is about to expand rapidly. It is, therefore, timely to examine two sets of questions. The first concerns the extent to which such data capture ethnicity in a meaningful way; and the second (which is, in part, related to the first) concerns the interpretation of inter-ethnic differences.

Both sets of questions are discussed here by reference primarily to the official criminal statistics which were publicly available at the time of writing. As background to this discussion, though, it is worth pausing to consider the coverage of ethnic minorities in the 1991 census. This not only constitutes the 'benchmark' for measuring and interpreting the extent to which different groups are represented in any criminal statistics; the ways in which it classifies ethnicity raise important conceptual questions which need to be borne in mind in this type of discussion.

THE 1991 CENSUS

For the first time in 1991 the census asked a direct question about the ethnic origin of those enumerated in Great Britain.[6] There had been an attempt to do so ten years previously but it was abandoned at the pilot stage. Respondents in 1991 were asked to classify themselves and other members of their households into one of nine categories (see below). Seven of these categories were 'off-the-peg'; but those who chose the 'black other' or 'other' category were additionally asked to describe themselves.

The tables subsequently produced by the Office of Population Censuses and Surveys (OPCS) expand these categories to ten by splitting the 'other' category into 'other' and 'Asian other', giving the breakdown shown in Table 10.1. Non-white minorities form 5.5 per cent of the total population of Great Britain but 5.9 per cent of the population of England and Wales. People of Indian origin form the largest group and at least one-fifth of all non-whites are classified under one of the three 'other' groups, the smallest of which (the 'black others') is itself as large as the Bangladeshi and Chinese populations.[7]

There has been extensive criticism of the census classification (much of it expressed in letters to the press and concerned with the apparent blurring of ethnic and national origins). However, the question which was finally asked was chosen because, after extensive testing over several years, it was the version which had proved acceptable to the majority of respondents of all ethnic origins (Sillitoe 1987). Certainly the census data provide a more reliable benchmark for checking the results of any ethnic monitoring than the two main sources used hitherto. The 1981 census could only extrapolate

---

[5] Section 95 of the 1991 Criminal Justice Act requires the Secretary of State 'in each year (to) publish such information as he considers expedient for the purpose of … facilitating the performance of (persons engaged in the administration of criminal justice) of their duty to avoid discriminating against any persons on the ground of race.

[6] The ethnic question in the 1991 census was not asked in Northern Ireland.

[7] However, it is important to note that the figures in the three 'other' categories exclude those who had originally ascribed themselves to these groups but were reclassified by OPCS into the seven 'off-the-peg' categories on the basis of a 35-code system devised for this purpose.

Table 10.1. Ethnic group composition of population 1991

	Great Britain %	England and Wales %
White	94.5	94.1
Black Caribbean	0.9	1.0
Black African	0.4	0.4
Black other	0.4	0.4
Indian	1.5	1.7
Pakistani	0.9	0.9
Bangladeshi	0.3	0.3
Chinese	0.3	0.3
Asian other	0.4	0.4
Other	0.5	0.6

Source: 1991 census.

figures on ethnic origin (to varying degrees of accuracy for different groups) from the birthplace of heads of households. The Labour Force Survey (LFS) has provided valuable information since 1981 based, like the 1991 census, on self-classified ethnicity; but because of its sample size it has only been reliable at national and regional level using data aggregated over three years.[8]

For these reasons, there are powerful arguments in favour of standardizing statistical series and other survey data on the census categories and the LFS has already adopted these in place of the classification it had used since 1981. This had also used ten categories. Only five, however, exactly matched those used in the 1991 census (White, Indian Pakistani, Bangladeshi, Chinese and other); the rest were West Indian/Guyanese, African, Arab, and mixed. The latter group – those of 'mixed' ethnic origin – are of particular interest in the context of the discussion which follows. It is a young, rapidly growing, and predominantly British-born population, a large proportion of whom appear to have been of Caribbean/white parentage. By the mid-1980s the 'mixed' group identified by the LFS already outnumbered the population of Caribbean origin in the under-15 age range. For statistical purposes, however, the category was insufficiently discrete to capture the 'mixed' group with accuracy and there is evidence that they were, in fact, under-counted in the LFS (Shaw 1988). In the census, however, they are lost completely between the 'white', 'black Caribbean', 'black other' and 'other' categories.

Despite these discontinuities, the broad picture which emerges from the census confirms the pattern repeatedly shown by the LFS, which is one of marked contrasts not only between the minority ethnic groups and whites but between the minorities themselves. Moreover, the ways in which they differ may significantly affect the likelihood of their becoming involved in the criminal justice process and this should *de*

---

[8] Until it was expanded in 1991 the Labour Force Survey had an annual sample size of 150 000 adult respondents.

facto raise questions about the usefulness of a concept of 'over-representation' which rests on a crude comparison of criminal justice statistics with the overall proportion of different groups in the population at large. All the minority groups, for example, are, on average, younger than whites and their geographic distribution is very uneven. The Pakistanis and Bangladeshis are much more deprived in socio-economic terms, as are the black-Caribbeans (albeit to a slightly lesser extent), whereas the position of the Indians is broadly comparable and, on some measures, actually better than that of whites. (For fuller details see the series of statistical papers on the 1991 census published by the National Ethnic Minority Data Archive at the University of Warwick).

INTERPRETING ETHNIC DIFFERENCES IN CRIMINAL JUSTICE DATA

Prison Statistics

Until 1993 the only criminal justice statistics collected nationally by ethnic origin were those on prisoners in England and Wales. Tables based on these have appeared in the annual *Prison Statistics* since the mid-1980s and have been extensively cited in a polarized political debate with one side claiming that they provide 'proof' of discrimination by the criminal justice system against black people living in Britain while others have taken them to infer 'proof' of inherent criminality among the same group. Important new light will be thrown on this debate by the prison data generated since 1992 when the form of classification was changed and additional measures were introduced to improve their quality, as this section demonstrates. It is, however, salutory to explore the limitations of the statistical basis on which the protagonists to the debate (and, in particular, those making claims of discrimination) have hitherto set such store.

The prisons data have consistently shown a pattern of over-representation of black (but *not* of Asian) prisoners relative to their presence in the population at large which is illustrated in Table 10.2. The pattern is particularly marked in respect of women.

Further analyses of these data have shown the following: different patterns in the offences for which different ethnic groups are imprisoned; a different pattern of distribution between open and closed prisons; and ethnic differences in sentence lengths. These are available in HOSB 17/86, which provides commentary and benchmark data from the Labour Force Survey by age and ethnic origin for the population of England and Wales, and as tables in the annual *Prison Statistics*.

Three key questions hang over the interpretations which have been read into these differences. They concern: the influence of antecedent factors in the criminal justice process; the meanings attached to the ethnic categories shown in the published figures; and the accuracy with which prisoners had been allocated to these categories. Only the first has been fully acknowledged by campaigning organizations and more dispassionate observers alike. The second has tended to be ignored by those intent on making a case of discrimination, although it has been explored (albeit *de facto* inconclusively) in more rigorous academic discussion. But the third has received remarkably little public scrutiny.

Table 10.2. Sentenced prison population by ethnic origin on 30 June 1991 (England and Wales)

	White	West Indian Guyanese African	Indian Pakistani Bangladeshi	Chinese Arab Mixed	Other, not recorded (incl refusals)	All = 100%
Prisons:						
Male	84.1	9.9	2.9	1.9	1.1	33 966
Female	66.8	24.2	2.0	3.7	3.3	1 148
1991 census:						
Age 16–59	93.8	1.9	2.9	[a]	14	[a]	29 274 000
LFS 1989–91:						
All	94.2	1.1	2.5	0.9	[a]	

[a] No equivalent category.
Source: *Prison Statistics 1991.*

Figure 10.1 illustrates the complexity of the first question which concerns the relationship of data at one point of the criminal justice system to decisions reached at other points. It represents the main filters through which offenders may pass before being found guilty and receiving custodial sentences. Only a small proportion enter the system at all and only a small minority of these follow route 'A' which leads directly to prison; most are filtered out into one of the boxes at 'B'. And for those who remain on route 'A' at each of the filter points, the decisions taken about them at that point may in turn influence the likelihood of their being filtered out at a subsequent point (the most obvious example being the offence with which they are charged).

We know nothing about ethnic differences in offending rates or in the likelihood of being reported to the police. And, although the Metropolitan Police hold ethnic data at the point of arrest, such data are not available nationally; nor do the Met use the same ethnic classifications as the Prison Service.[9] So it is impossible to tell whether the pro-

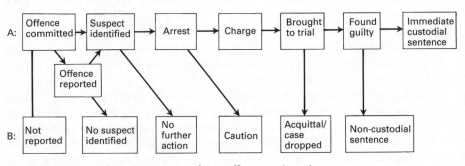

Fig. 10.1. Criminal justice process from offence to imprisonment.

---

[9] The categories used by the Metropolitan Police are: White European; dark European; black; Indian/Pakistani/Bangladeshi; Chinese/Japanese; Arabian/Egyptian; not recorded.

portions in the prison population reflect actual levels of offending or to trace any variations in ethnic ratios at the key filtering points of the criminal justice process shown in Fig. 10.1. Nor is there systematic evidence of the extent to which different decisions taken about different groups at different points within the system account for ethnic differences in rates of imprisonment.

In discussing the second question – the meanings which have been attached to the ethnic categories used in the published prison statistics – clearly the residual 'other, mixed and refused' category is too amorphous to warrant discussion here. The published data on both the 'West Indian, Guyanese, and African' and the 'Indian, Pakistani and Bangladeshi' categories, however, have posed problems of interpretation which have often been overlooked.

The group which has attracted most attention because of its over-representation has been the 'West Indian/African' group. However, the fact of higher levels of criminal activity among young people and the strong correlation between socio-economic status and criminality (that is, criminality as measured by official statistics)[10] should lead us to expect some over-representation among the British-based Caribbean-origin population since we know them to be both younger and more disadvantaged than whites. Nonetheless, the fact is that neither of these considerations seems adequate to explain the full extent of their over-representation in prisons and a polarized but largely inconclusive debate has surrounded the additional factors involved, including the possibilities already referred to of higher rates of criminal activity, on the one hand, and discrimination by the criminal justice system, on the other (see, for example, Jefferson 1988; Reiner 1989; FitzGerald 1993*a*).

What has rarely been called into question is the *basis* on which this over-representation has been calculated. Protagonists in the debate have tended simply to accept the benchmark figures for the population of England and Wales (see Table 10.2) as a valid point of comparison without allowing for three important factors. The first is that we have not known for sure what proportion of this group of prisoners is, in fact, normally resident in the UK. The second concerns problems of categorization under a system which (formally at least) was based on visual assessment by third parties. And the third is that comparisons have rarely adjusted the benchmark figure to eliminate the population below imprisonable age, and still less to take into account other aspects of the different age and socio-economic distributions of the respective ethnic groups.

The implications of these factors are explored more fully below. However, it is worth noting here the improvement brought about by the new system introduced in 1992 and which will provide the basis for the tables on ethnic origin in future publications of *Prison Statistics*. The additional over-representation of women in the 'West Indian, Guyanese, and African' group (see Table 10.2) had often been cited by campaigning groups as evidence of 'double discrimination against black women'. Although it seemed more likely that the figures were simply inflated by a high proportion of African women who were non-residents and who had been imprisoned for drug importation offences, this could not reliably be demonstrated from the data available

---

[10] Self-report studies, on the other hand, tend to show less difference in levels of offending between socio-economic groups (see, for example, Ouston 1984; Anderson *et al.* 1990).

under the old system. The new system is not yet able to distinguish clearly between British residents and non-residents; but it does allow more refined disaggregation between those whose ethnic origins put them in one of the 'black' groups. The figures for June 1993 show that, for black groups overall, the gender differences persist, with black people comprising 11 per cent of the male prison population but 20 per cent of female prisoners. However, there is a marked convergence in the black Caribbean group where the figures are 7 per cent for men and 9 per cent for women. This contrasts with an equally marked divergence in the black African group where men contribute an additional 2 per cent to the black total whereas women account for an extra 7 per cent.

The 'Asians' have received far less attention since, at this level of aggregation, they have until recently appeared not to pose the same problems of over-representation. Yet this category comprises three groups which are by no means homogenous but which is dominated by one – the Indians – who are far more numerous (see Table 10.1) and far less disadvantaged than the other two. As data become available under the new system, however, it will be possible to look at the groups separately; and initial results do, in fact, suggest that there is – as one would have expected – over-representation of Pakistanis even on the basis of very crude benchmark data (although it is still not of the same order as the over-representation of the black groups). At June 1993, 1.5 per cent of male prisoners were recorded as being of Indian origin and the *same* proportion were of Pakistani origin, although there were far more Indians in the population at large (in the ratio of about five to three). (Bangladeshis, on the other hand, remained slightly under-represented at 0.2 per cent; but this will at least in part reflect that in the population at large they fall disproportionately under the age at which offenders are usually eligible to be imprisoned.)

Thirdly, in looking critically at how to interpret the ethnic groupings described hitherto in the annual *Prison Statistics*, we need to bear two factors in mind. One is the question of the accuracy with which prisoners were allocated to these groupings for, under the system which prevailed until relatively recently, prison officers were supposed to ascribe prisoners to ethnic categories at the point of initial reception, that is, in circumstances which are often trying and where they are often having to record a lot of information on relatively large numbers of individuals. The second factor is that the system has produced considerable confusion between prisoners' ethnic origin and their nationality as such (see, for example, Cheney 1993 p. 11). These criticisms were raised in the course of internal reviews on behalf of the Prison Service and it is largely for this reason that the present system of self-classification was introduced in 1992.

Certainly, under the previous system, which was based mainly on visual assessment, the classification of prisoners between the Indian, Pakistani and Bangladeshi categories is likely to have been inaccurate.[11] Similarly, the Prison Service reviews suggested that a large proportion of prisoners of mixed Caribbean – white origin may have been classified as 'West Indian' (rather than 'mixed'). From the earlier discussion of this group in the population at large, it would appear that to calculate the extent

---

[11] It seems likely that officers may have asked Asian prisoners to self-classify for this reason; but it is not known how extensively this occurred.

of over-representation in this group the denominator should have been higher than that shown in Table 10.2.[12]

Police statistics

Many of the problems of capturing ethnicity referred to so far in this chapter have now been obviated, at least at the end point of the criminal justice system, by the new system of collecting information on the ethnic origin of prisoners. This will, in future, provide data which are both more refined and more accurate and which will continue to show over-representation of certain minorities in relation to data for the England and Wales population at large. Problems will still persist, however, in interpreting that over-representation. If it were possible to remove non-residents from the prison statistics *and* to take full account of age and socio-economic factors, it seems likely that there would still be over-representation but that the picture might look less dramatic than the one which has attracted so much political and academic attention. Even so, it has already been pointed out that the prison statistics could only satisfactorily be interpreted in the context of reliable and systematic information on decisions made on the different groups at earlier stages in the criminal justice process and, indeed, of some empirical understandings about offending and reporting rates. It is, therefore, of particular interest to examine further the interpretation of ethnic differences by reference to information which is beginning to become available at an early stage in the process.

Sample surveys over many years have consistently shown that black men are disproportionately involved in stops and searches by the police[13] and this issue has regularly been raised as a source of concern by campaigning groups. From April 1993, Her Majesty's Inspectorate of Constabulary (HMIC) have required all forces to record the ethnic origin of those members of the public they stop/search (albeit initially *only* on the basis of whether they are white or not). Prior to the introduction of this national requirement, however, a number of forces had begun their own monitoring.

One of these pioneers was the Holborn division of the Metropolitan Police. On 23 February 1993 it presented a report to the local community and Police Consultative Group on all stop/searches, arrests, and disposals in the six month from April to September 1992, broken down by ethnic group. In all, there were 2155 stop/searches and 2736 people were held in custody. Ethnic origin was recorded by the police on the basis of appearance and the report gave the breakdown shown in Table 10.3.

However, as the report points out, comparing the two sets of figures is not straightforward for three main reasons. In the first place, the ethnic breakdown of stop/searches relates to only 77 per cent of the total since information was missing in

---

[12] The new system shows a 7:1 over-representation of black men, compared with 9:1 under the previous system. For women the ratio reduces to 13:1 but this is largely driven by the over-representation of African women referred to earlier. (A crude adjustment by excluding all drug offenders, for example, would reduce the ratio for women to 9:1.)

[13] Chief among these are Smith's large-scale survey of Londoners conducted in the early 1980s (Smith 1983) and Skogan's analysis of policing questions in the 1988 British Crime Survey which included an over-sample of respondents from ethnic minorities (Skogan 1990).

Table 10.3. Holborn division Metropolitan Police
stop/searches and those held in custody, 6 months
April–September 1992

	Stop/search	Held in custody
White	67%	75%
Black	27%	16%
Asian	4%	4%
Other	2%	4%

Source: Report to Community and Police Consultative Group, 23 February 1993.

23 per cent of cases. Secondly, the custody records double-count those bailed to return who did so within the six-month period. A higher proportion of blacks (12 per cent) than whites (10 per cent) or Asians (9 per cent) were bailed; but there is no record of the proportions who ended up being double-counted for this reason. And thirdly, the report emphasizes that those in custody include members of the public who technically have been arrested but are not suspected of having committed a crime (such as those taken into care).

Although the two groups represented in Table 10.3 cannot be treated as directly comparable populations for the reasons given above, two further sets of comparisons appear at first sight to be worth pursuing. One is the most basic of all comparisons – to look at both populations in relation to the population at large; and the other is to look at what subsequently happens to different groups in the custody population.

Benchmark data for comparing the two populations with the population at large should do two things. Obviously, they should show the ethnic make-up of the populations from which these samples are drawn; but they should additionally be able to indicate whether the stop/search and custody populations are atypical of that wider population in respects *other* than their ethnic composition (for example, because they are on average younger, or more likely to be unemployed).

With regard to the first of these criteria, at least two studies (Tuck and Southgate 1981; Walker *et al.* 1990) have suggested that ethnic differences shown in most studies of 'race' and policing might disappear (or even be reversed) if the area base for comparison is drawn sufficiently tightly. Holborn falls within the borough of Camden whose minority ethnic population as a whole was 18 per cent in 1991, with considerable variation between different wards. However, the choice of appropriate benchmark data is problematic in this case since the police division in question deals with a largely transient population rather than with local residents: the report points out that only one in seven of those in custody actually lived in the borough at all, and this will almost certainly be reflected, if not amplified, in the stop/search population.

On the second criterion for benchmark data, it has already been noted that people caught up in the criminal justice process are systematically atypical of the population at large. The main differences are in terms of age, gender, and socio-economic characteristics. There are now few differences between white and minority ethnic groups in the ratio of men to women, but previous sections of this paper have drawn attention not only to important variations in their age structure but also in their socio-economic characteristics. Thus, even if the Camden data were based on a population drawn from a more clearly defined area, significant obstacles would still beset interpreting the ethnic differences they show on a basis of comparing like with like.

— The figures are based on visual assessment by police officers whereas the census was based on self-classification, so there is already bound to be some degree of mismatch. Moreover, visual assessment inevitably groups people into very broad ethnic categories. This makes it impossible to know the proportions of, for example, black Caribbeans relative to black 'others' or Indians relative to Pakistanis. As earlier sections of this chapter have shown, these groups differ in their probability of appearing in the criminal justice statistics for reasons which have nothing to do with their ethnicity. If they were over-represented – whether for these reasons or as a result of discrimination – this might not be apparent: rather it might be masked in an average figure which included the results for other, larger groups who were not over-represented.

— No information is provided on the gender or age composition of the two groups covered by the police statistics; and, although this may be available (at least in the case of the custody sample) it is highly unlikely that relevant information also exists on their socio-economic characteristics.

There are, then, major difficulties in making inferences about 'over-representation' relative to the population at large. However, one would expect at least to be able to make comparisons *within* the custody population of the treatment meted out to different ethnic groups. The Holborn report allows for the problems of double-counting and of non-suspects in custody by excluding from Table 10.4 those who were bailed to return as well as those disposed of by 'other action'. Together these categories had accounted for over 30 per cent of whites in the original custody population, over 40 per cent of blacks and over 50 per cent of both 'Asians' and 'others'.

The table appears to show quite starkly that black people in custody are much less likely than any other group to be cautioned, with nearly two-thirds sent on to appear in court compared with under half of those in other groups. It also suggests that *all* minority ethnic groups are markedly more likely than whites to have been brought

Table 10.4. Holborn division Metropolitan Police disposals of those held in custody[a] April–September 1992

	Charge/Summons	Caution	No further action	Total
White	49	36	16	100%
Black	65	9	26	100%
Asian	49	22	29	100%
Other	41	31	28	100%

[a] Excluding those at Table 10.3 who were bailed to return or who had no further action taken against them.
Source: Report to Community and Police Consultative Group, 23 February 1993.

into custody on suspicion of an offence only to be subsequently released without further action being taken against them.

However, at least two factors need to be taken into consideration before any inference of discrimination can be drawn. One is that cautions are almost never available to those suspected of indictable only offences (e.g. robbery) and that they are given only to those who admit their offence. There is evidence that black people are more likely to be charged with indictable only offences (Walker 1988; 1989; Hood 1992) and they appear less likely to admit the offences they are accused of. Thus, a recent pilot study of juvenile cautioning found that once those who did not admit to the offence were excluded, prima facie ethnic differences disappeared (CRE 1992). The Camden data, however, provide no information on either of these essential points.

The second problem of interpretation arises when looking at the figures in the 'no further action' column. It is an obvious cause for concern that over a quarter of the black custody population covered in this sub-sample were detained at a police station when no further action was to be taken against them. But it is dangerous to assume that, because the proportions are similar, the same grounds exist for concern about the other two minority groups. The table reproduced here does not give base numbers; but these can be calculated from the original custody sample. Contrary to the impression of parity given by the percentage figures, the actual numbers involved are strikingly different. No further action was taken against 69 black suspects but only 7 Asians and 4 'others'. While a comparison with the 221 whites in this category shows a statistically significant difference from blacks, with such small numbers, no conclusions can safely be drawn in respect of the other two groups.

Finally, before turning to a more general discussion of the implications of these limitations for the development of ethnic monitoring, it is worth noting that the comparable figures in the vast majority of police divisions nationally are likely to be very small indeed. If we take the 'catchment' area for Holborn at its widest we are talking about a minority ethnic population of 20.2 per cent in Greater London as a whole, rising to 25.6 per cent in Inner London. This is over three times as high as the average of 5.9 per cent in England and Wales – a figure which is, itself, only attained in 6 of the 53 local authorities outside London.

DISCUSSION

Rose *et al.* were writing at a time when allegations of racism by the police on the one hand and of minority ethnic criminality on the other, were based on anecdotal rather than statistical evidence. Today the situation seems little clearer. The over-representation of black people in the criminal justice system is now well established by both empirical studies and official data series; yet the media, various sections of the public, and academics themselves (Reiner 1989; Smith 1993) continue to wrangle over how to interpret this fact. The momentum behind generating this type of data has apparently become unstoppable; but remarkably little a priori thought seems to have been given to their precise purpose and still less to their limitations. Three key questions need to be addressed:

1. What ideally, should we be able to learn from ethnic data in the criminal justice system?

2. How far does what is available match up to this ideal?

3. What are the implications of the gap between (1) and (2)?

These will now be discussed in turn by reference to the material in the preceeding sections.

The ideal is that ethnic data in the criminal justice system should be able to show not only whether there are ethnic differences which are at variance with those in the population at large; they should also be able to demonstrate whether any such disparities are due to:

(1) ethnically different rates and patterns of offending;

(2) socio-economic or demographic differences between ethnic groups;

(3) discrimination in the criminal justice process;

(4) any combination of these factors (and the relative weight of each).

Moreover the data should additionally be able to pinpoint where and how any discrimination is occurring. They should also be able to identify whether the problem is changing over time (and the reasons for this).

Viewed in the context of this ideal, the available data are very limited. While they strongly indicate that one particular ethnic minority is disproportionately involved in crime, the crude categories they use may mask important differences between other sub-groups. Questions also arise, on the one hand, about both the quality of the data and its completeness (especially where they are compiled on the basis of third-party assessment) and, on the other, about the choice of benchmark data against which to estimate the rate of over-representation. Beyond this, there is the absence of essential data on actual offending rates. Nor do we know for sure whether either reporting or detection rates vary according to the ethnic origin of suspects.

The effects of important socio-economic and demographic differences between ethnic groups on the probability of their appearing in the criminal statistics have not – with one notable but now rather dated exception (Ouston 1984) – been systematically examined even in the academic literature. And statistical data generated by criminal justice agencies provide no information on the socio-economic characteristics of the whites who serve as the main comparison group, thus making it impossible even to infer expected rates for the minorities and still less to make direct comparisons of like with like.

Partly because these unknowns already hang over the existing data, it is difficult to get a handle on the central question of discrimination. Moreover, the concept itself is slippery. It can take direct and indirect forms. It might occur systematically; but Dr Hood's important study of sentencing at several Crown Court centres in the West Midlands (Hood 1992) confirms that it is more likely that it does not. (For a fuller discussion of the implications in this study for ways in which discrimination can occur in the criminal justice system, see FitzGerald 1993*b*.) In the context of the present discussion, however, Hood stands out precisely because it is exceptional. It contrasts with other empirical studies and data series because it provides relevant information on the social and criminal justice background to a data set large enough to withstand rigorous statistical analysis. Similarly, it scores over most other sources because – albeit to a limited degree – it is also able to do the following: make links between what happened at one stage of the criminal justice process with what had happened at others; estimate the relative influence of ethnic and non-ethnic factors in accounting for prima facie ethnic differences; and identify the points at which discrimination was most likely to occur. Yet, on its own account, the study still has many limitations and there are key questions which fell outside its remit. It suffers from inadequate benchmark data; it is unable to disaggregate within the 'Asian' group; and it cannot establish whether or not discrimination has occurred in individual cases. Invaluable as its insights are, then, they are the limited insights of a single study confined primarily to one point of the criminal system, in a single area, at one moment in time.

For the present, there are two main possibilities for establishing trends over time. In principle, comparisons could be made of the findings of empirical studies at each single decision-making point in the criminal justice process. However, many of these studies suffer from inherent weaknesses and even the best are often mutually incompatible for methodological reasons (FitzGerald 1993a) and few are capable of making adequate links between decisions made at each of the key stages.

The other main sources for establishing trends are the two large data series referred to earlier. The Metropolitan Police statistics cover arrests but they ceased to include information about the disposal of those arrested in 1987 and they pose two related problems. Their information on ethnicity is based on visual assessment and the categories used[14] have never been directly comparable with those used in any available benchmark data. It is arguable that visual assessment has the advantage that it might be more revealing of direct discrimination than self-categorization. That is, direct discrimination is based on what someone looks like rather than on how they see themselves. On the other hand, we would lose one of the main early warning signs of discrimination without criminal justice data which can be matched to population data. The inherent problems of the prison statistics available since 1985 were discussed earlier in this chapter although reference was also made to the changes introduced in 1992 to try to overcome these. It should, however, be noted that these changes also introduced new categories to make the data compatible with the census, and thereby sacrificed strict continuity.

Moreover, while such large-scale data sets may be invaluable in suggesting whether discrimination may be occurring, they are unlikely to be able to pick up where and how this is occurring with sufficient precision for appropriate action to be taken. If, indeed, discrimination is unsystematic, this is probably best done through local monitoring. The problem at this level, however, is that small numbers will usually make it unsafe to interpret year-on-year figures as 'trends'; and, even where numbers are relatively large, a single major incident in one year (for example, in connection with a pop concert or a demonstration) would often be enough seriously to distort any emerging pattern.

---

[14] See footnote 9 above.

So finally, can these problems be overcome? To what extent can the gulf realistically be bridged between what is currently available and the ideal? And to what extent would the remaining gaps mean that even new, improved, and more comprehensive data would still be open to conflicting interpretations? Using as a framework criteria based on the ideals specified in (1) above, the following answers emerge.

Data quality

There is clearly scope for improving the accuracy and completeness of the data which are presently available. The agencies concerned have already been taking steps to this end and the new prison data cited here already show that these may produce quite dramatic improvements. The new system of self-classification provided the breakdown of the prison population at June 1993 found in Table 10.5. In any case, both accuracy and completeness have been found to improve with time and experience where managers are committed to the exercise and those responsible for its implementation understand the reasons for it.

Table 10.5. Breakdown of the prison population at June 1993 (%)

	White	Black Caribbean	Black African	Black other	Indian	Pakistani	Bangladeshi	Chinese	Asian other	other	Not recorded	Total
M	83.7	6.9	2.0	2.0	1.5	1.5	0.2	0.1	0.5	1.5	–	100%
F	73.3	8.7	6.9	4.4	a	a	a	0.1	0.2	4.9	–	100%

a Because of small numbers only an aggregated 'Asian' figure of 1.4 per cent can be provided these three groups.
Source: *Prisons Statistic 1993*

The categories used, on the other hand, are likely to remain very crude. At their self-classifying best they will reflect the limitations of the census data; and it is unrealistic in many circumstances (e.g. police stops) to expect more than the very broadbrush data based on visual assessment by criminal justice personnel. For the reasons already rehearsed, the value of third-party assessment in relation to direct discrimination may have been insufficiently recognized. However, it is not entirely satisfactory for the purpose of matching criminal justice data with population data and its potential is extremely limited for explaining any mismatch.

Actual patterns of offending/ethnic filtering at the point of entry into the criminal justice system

An estimate of *actual* rates of offending by different ethnic groups will not come from monitoring data. It could only come from a major survey of self-reported offending which contained a sufficiently large and representative sub-sample of minority ethnic respondents and, even then, any findings of ethnic difference might not be totally reliable, given the limitations of such studies (see, for example, Bowling 1990).

The introduction nationally of monitoring of stop/searches and local initiatives in monitoring arrests are clearly an important move towards providing a picture of what happens at the point of entry to the system. However, it should be borne in mind both that stops account for only a small proportion of those brought into the criminal justice process and that the disproportionate representation of a particular group in either set of data does not *de facto* prove that the group is disproportionately involved in crime, only that they are more likely to be picked up by the police. Among several possible reasons for this, a number of studies (of which Hood is the latest) have suggested that black people are more likely to come into the system as a result of pro-active policing. Obviously the extension of monitoring to cover a fuller range of points of entry to the system would be a way of checking this; but additional, more qualitative approaches, including direct observation of the processes at work would probably be needed to interpret the findings.

The significance of socio-economic and demographic differences

Individual studies – including large-scale surveys of which the National Prison Survey is a good example (see Chapter 6) – can and should routinely capture background information on the socio-economic and demographic characteristics of their subjects. However, to expect large-scale data series to include all such relevant variables is utopian. The scope for doing so in either the long or the short term is limited for a number of reasons, from perennial resource constraints to the absence of spare fields for recording the information in the systems currently in use.

Background data from the 1991 census will become increasingly less useful over the decade, undermining the scope for accurately interpreting local monitoring data (although the LFS is capable of filling the gap at national and regional level). The census data do, however, offer the potential for modelling likely crime rates for different age cohorts in different ethnic groups using the known socio-economic and demographic correlates of offending.

Discrimination in the criminal justice system

Ethnic monitoring data need to do three things if they are to address concerns about possible discrimination in the criminal justice system and to evaluate the impact of the many steps being taken throughout the system to safeguard against this possibility. They should be able to identify patterns of decision making at each of the key points of the criminal justice process; they should also be able to identify the interaction between decisions taken at different points; and they must be capable of describing trends in both over time. This will require generating data which are based on a common core set of classifications across the whole criminal justice system. The obvious way to do this would be to allocate a standard ethnic marker (based on the census categories) to each individual entering the system which would form part of the documentation which accompanies them through it.

Currently, however, most criminal justice agencies undertake only patchy monitoring and (with the exception of pilot and one-off studies) the courts have not yet started. Different forms of ethnic classification have been used, even within the same agency, and only the Prison Service has so far adopted census-based categories. Even if agreement can be reached in principle for a more coordinated approach, it is likely to be some time before the practicalities of implementation can be smoothed out.

Meanwhile, if local monitoring is to realize its potential for testing for discrimination, it too will need to improve the material it has to work on. In particular, if it is to uncover *direct* discrimination, it will need to grasp the nettle of generating data on individual suspects and offenders (anonymized as appropriate) which can also identify the individual criminal justice personnel involved in the case and the decisions they took. This may create technical problems (including issues of data protection) and meet resistance from the personnel involved. However, as long as the available data only provide group averages, all offenders in the group affected, however properly they may have been treated, may claim to be victims of discrimination; and all criminal justice personnel, however scrupulous their behaviour, will be suspected of discrimination.

Finally – and crucially – if discrimination is occurring, the ability to take appropriate remedial action will depend on understanding the ways in which the system makes this possible. This understanding is unlikely to derive primarily from large-scale data collection exercises but will depend on observational and other qualitative approaches.

In sum, then, ethnic data are not the *sine qua non* of tackling discrimination in the criminal justice system. They are invaluable as a guide to whether and where such discrimination may be occurring; but if their usefulness is to be fully realized, two things are needed. On the one hand, it will require a more comprehensive and systematic approach to ethnic monitoring throughout the criminal justice process, as well as better contextualized analyses of the data this produces. On the other, the data will be most useful when their limitations are more fully acknowledged. Complementary research methods are needed both to compensate for those limitations and to generate well-grounded propositions about the likelihood of and the reasons for ethnic differences in the criminal justice process. Ethnic data provide a tool for testing such propositions and for measuring the impact of policy interventions. Even with the major improvements suggested here it would remain crude; but it is nonetheless an essential tool and one for which there simply is no obvious substitute.

REFERENCES

Anderson, S., Kinsey, R., Loader, I., and Smith, C. (1990). *Cautionary Tales: A Study of Young People and Crime in Edinburgh*. Centre for Criminology, University of Edinburgh.

Bowling, B. (1990). Conceptual and methodological problems in measuring 'race' differences in delinquency. *British Journal of Criminology* **30** (4), 483–92.

Carr-Hill, R. and Drew, D. (1989). Blacks, police and crime. In *Britain's Black Population – a New Perspective* (eds. A. Bhat et al.). Gower, Aldershot.

Cheney, D. (1993). *Into the Dark Tunnel: Foreign Prisoners in the British Prison System*. Prison Reform Trust, London.

Commission for Racial Equality (CRE) (1992). *Juvenile Cautioning – Ethnic Monitoring in Practice*. CRE, London.

Demuth, C. (1978). *'Sus': a report on the Vagrancy Act 1824*. Runnymede Trust, London.

FitzGerald, M. (1993a). *Ethnic Minorities and the Criminal Justice System*. Research Study No. 20, The Royal Commission on Criminal Justice. HMSO, London.

FitzGerald, M. (1993*b*). Racial discrimination in the criminal justice system. *Research Bulletin* **34**, 43–7. Home Office Research and Statistics Department, London.

Home Office (1990). *Ethnic Monitoring*. Circular 71/90.

Hood, R. (1992). *Race and Sentencing*. Clarendon Press, Oxford.

Jefferson, T. (1988). Race, crime and policing. *International Journal of the Sociology of Law* **16**, 521–39.

Ouston, J. (1984). Delinquency, family background and educational attainment. *British Journal of Criminology* **24** (1), 2–26.

Owen, D. (1993). *1991 Census Statistical Papers*. National Ethnic Minority Data Archive, Centre for Research in Ethnic Relations, University of Warwick.

National Association for the Care and Resettlement of Offenders (NACRO) (1991). *Race and Criminal Justice*. NACRO, London.

Reiner, R. (1989). Race and Criminal Justice. *New Community 16* (1), 5–21.

Rose, E. J. B., Deakin, N., Abrams, M., Jackson, V., Peston, M., Vanags, A. H., Cohen, B., Gaitskell, J., and Ward, P. (1969). *Colour and Citizenship*. Oxford University Press.

Shaw, C. (1988). Latest estimates of ethnic minority populations. In *Population Trends* No. 51 OPCS, London.

Sillitoe, K. (1987). Questions on race/ethnicity and related topics for the census. In *Population Trends* No. 49. OPCS, London.

Skogan, W. (1990). *The Police and Public in England and Wales: a British Crime Survey Report*. Home Office Research Study No. 117, HMSO, London.

Smith, D. (1983). *Police and People in London: I. A Survey of Londoners*. Policy Studies Institute, London.

Smith, D. (1993) Race, crime and criminal justice. In *The Oxford Handbook of Criminology* (eds. M. Maguire, R. Morgan, and R. Reiner), Oxford University Press.

Tuck, M. and Southgate, P. (1981). *Ethnic Minorities, Crime and Policing: a Survey of the Experiences of West Indians and Whites*. Home Office Research Study No. 70, HMSO, London.

Walker, M. A. (1988). The court disposal of young males, by race, in London in 1983. *British Journal of Criminology* **28** (4), 441–60.

Walker, M. A. (1989). The court disposal and remands of white, Afro-Caribbean and Asian men (London) 1983. *British Journal of Criminology* **29** (4), 353–67.

Walker, M. A., Jefferson, T., and Seneviratne, M. (1990). *Ethnic Minorities, Young People and the Criminal Justice System*. Centre for Criminological and Socio-legal Studies, University of Sheffield.

Walmsley, R., Howard, L., and White, S. (1992). *The National Prison Survey 1991: Main Findings*. Home Office Research Study No. 128, HMSO, London.

11 On using crime statistics for prediction

JOHN COPAS

INTRODUCTION

The uses of statistics on crime can perhaps be grouped into three somewhat overlapping categories – description, administration, and research. The first is the most important: rational discussion of crime needs to be informed by accurate statistics on the present state of the criminal justice system and how it is evolving over time. In administration, statistics are needed for the allocation of resources, for decision-making, and in consideration of issues of policy. In research we aim to understand, and to pose (if not answer) 'what if' questions. The overlaps are obvious: good administration needs both description and the results of research on policy changes and evaluation. Some applications of statistics involve prediction, uses covering both administration (decision-making) and research (policy evaluation). A classic example of the former is decision-making in parole, where it can be useful to summarize background information on a prisoner in the form of a prediction score for the risk that the subject will reoffend. An example of the latter is when a prediction score is used to stratify subjects into risk groups for the purpose of monitoring some policy development. It is the use of statistics in the construction and validation of prediction scores which forms the subject of this chapter.

In England and Wales the 1991 Criminal Justice Act has quite a lot to say about the assessment of risk and so, also, indirectly, about the importance of statistical analysis of data on offending. An example is in Chapter 6 of the White Paper 'Crime, Justice and Protecting the Public' on which the Act is based. This section describes the criteria for the granting of parole, and states: 'the decision whether to allow parole should be based first and foremost on considerations of the risk of serious harm to the public and only then on the likely benefits to the public and the prisoner of a longer period under supervision' (paragraph 6.21). In making their decision the Parole Board 'would need to take into account the prisoner's offence and criminal history, his record in prison … and any other available indicator of the likelihood of his re-offending'. The Carlisle Committee, whose recommendations led to this section of the White Paper, recognized that this is essentially a matter of statistical prediction, and wrote: 'the (Parole) Board should be under a duty to take into account statistical prediction techniques'. An early example of a statistical prediction technique of this kind was provided by the noted study of Nuttall *et al.* (1977), whose reconviction prediction score (RPS) was used, with varying degrees of enthusiasm, by the Parole Board during the period up to the 1991 Act. The methodology of the RPS has been copied in several later studies – for instance the scores for use in probation developed by Humphrey *et al.* (1991) and Fitzmaurice *et al.* (1991). These score are derived by the method of 'point scoring', a simple approach to binary regression using the covariates analysed one at a time. Although the method has some advantages (Copas 1993) it has obvious statistical deficiencies, and surprisingly few prediction techniques have been based on 'mainstream' statistical methods of the kind which would be considered commonplace in other areas of applied statistics.

Our aim in this chapter is to discuss some of the statistical questions arising in the fitting of statistical models for use in prediction. In the first part of the chapter we consider the choice of statistical model and methods of inference and validation. Then in the second part we illustrate some of these issues by presenting an extended example of a recent prediction score for use in the management of probation.

STATISTICAL MODELLING FOR PREDICTION SCORES

Introduction

Most problems of interest can be expressed in the following form: we wish to estimate the probability that, for an individual described by covariates $x = (x_1, x_2, ..., x_m)$, an event E will happen in a time period of length t,

$$p(x, t) = P(E \text{ at least once in time } t \mid t, x).$$

Each of these terms needs to be carefully defined, and clarifying what is meant here is an important and non-trivial task. The time t has to be measured from a defined origin, such as the date of conviction or of release from prison. The definition of E highlights a major dilemma – usually it is the occurrence of an offence that is of interest but in practice one can only work with data on arrests or convictions. Many studies take E to be a conviction for one or more of the offences in a predefined list of sufficiently serious offences. Sometimes E is taken as the offence which is cited in a subsequent conviction.

Next, the meaning of 'probability' in this context needs to be clarified. Various interpretations are possible. On the one hand this can be thought of as a stochastic model with independent random outcomes and, on the other hand, a weaker interpretation in terms of labelling 'risk groups' by the value of $p(x, t)$. Taking this interpretation, we imagine that a conceptually infinite population of subjects is divided into risk groups by the different possible levels of $p(x, t)$, for some fixed t. The actual value of $p(x, t)$ is assumed to be calibrated to be equal to the proportion of subjects in the appropriate risk group for whom E happens within time t. The values of these labels $p(x, t)$ are then estimated by statistical analysis. It can be thought of as 'prediction' in the sense that the calculated $p(x, t)$ is a prediction of the future behaviour of individuals arising in that risk group. This interpretation is discussed further in Copas (1994).

Finally, the choice of covariates to include in the vector x is always a difficult problem. Substantive knowledge is obviously important, but inevitably some empirical choices will be made on the basis of the data. Some technical aspects of empirical covariate selection will be addressed below.

Models for fixed time

Most prediction scores have used a single fixed value of t, and so are essentially binary regression models. The RPS (Nuttall *et al.* 1977) chose $t = 2$ years, a value which has become conventional in several similar studies. The great advantage here is in ease of data collection. All that is needed is to follow up a sample of subjects for the chosen time t and to note in each case whether or not E has occurred, thus resolving problems of how to deal with multiple offences of different degrees of severity that arise when more complex models are fitted. The major statistical techniques used in this case are point scoring and logistic regression.

Point scoring

Criminological applications of point scoring are usually attributed to Burgess (1928) and to Glueck and Glueck (1950), and several variations are possible including the one used in constructing the RPS. The methods seem to rest more on intuition and a quest for simplicity than on any specifically statistical considerations. The basic idea is to find an additive score

$$S(x) = \sum_{i=1}^{m} g_i(x_i) \tag{1}$$

where the functions g_i depend only on the *marginal* association between x_i and the incidence of E. Let the ith covariate x_i take the possible values $v_{i1}, v_{i2}, \ldots, v_{ik_i}$, which are observed to occur $n_{i1}, n_{i2}, \ldots, n_{ik_i}$ times in a sample of size

$$n = \sum_{j=1}^{k_i} n_{ij} \quad i = 1, 2, \ldots, m.$$

Suppose that, of these n_{ij} subjects with $x_i = v_{ij}$, E is observed to occur within time t for f_{ij} subjects and observed not to occur for $n_{ij} - f_{ij}$ subjects. The total number of subjects with E observed is

$$f = \sum_{j=1}^{k_i} f_{ij} \quad i = 1, 2, \ldots, m,$$

and the chi-squared statistic for the association of x_i with E is

$$\chi_i^2 = \frac{n^2}{f(n-f)} \left[\sum_{j=1}^{k_i} \frac{f_{ij}^2}{n_{ij}} - \frac{f^2}{n} \right]. \tag{2}$$

Then the Glueck method, essentially that used in the RPS, is given by

$$g_i(x_i) = \begin{cases} \dfrac{f_{ij}}{n_{ij}} - \dfrac{f}{n} & \text{if } x_i = v_{ij} \text{ and } \chi_i^2 \geq c_i, \\ & j = 1, 2, \ldots, k_i \\ 0 & \text{if } \chi_i^2 < c_i \end{cases} \tag{3}$$

where c_i is the 95th percentage point of the chi-squared distribution on $k_i - 1$ degrees of freedom. Thus, apart from an additive constant, the score is a sum of increments calculated over the 'significant' covariates, each increment being derived from the overall rate of occurrence of E at the observed level of that covariate.

Apart from some rounding in the components of the score, this is the method used by Nuttall *et al.* (1977) in constructing the RPS. Seventeen covariates were found to be significantly associated with reconviction within 2 years for a sample of 2276 male prisoners discharged from prison in 1965. The increments for 'age of offence', for example, are

Under 21	+5
21 to 24	+1
25 to 39	0
40 to 49	−1
50 and over	−2

As these weights for age depend only on the marginal cross-classification of age with reconviction, it is a trivial matter to try different groupings of age categories. Here we have a non-linear dependence on age with particular weight on the under 21s.

As pointed out by Copas and Tarling (1986), the above point scoring technique is very similar to what has been called the 'independence Bayes method'. Here, instead of modelling the conditional probability of E given x (the 'predictive paradigm') we model the conditional distributions of x given E and given E^c, the complement of E (the 'sampling paradigm'). The two approaches are linked by Bayes' theorem giving

$$\frac{P(E \mid x)}{P(E^c \mid x)} = \frac{P(E)}{P(E^c)} \cdot \frac{P(x \mid E)}{P(x \mid E^c)}. \tag{4}$$

If we make the very strong assumption that the covariates are conditionally independent given E, and also conditionally independent given E^c, then the fraction to the right of (4) splits into a product over the individual covariates, which, after taking logarithms gives

$$\text{logit}\,(P(E \mid x = v)) = \log \frac{P(E)}{P(E^c)} + \sum_i \log \frac{P(x_i = v_{ij_i} \mid E)}{P(x_i = v_{ij_i} \mid E^c)} \tag{5}$$

where v is a vector of covariate levels $(v_{1j_1}, v_{2j_2}, \ldots, v_{mj_m})$ and 'logit' stands for the logistic transformation defined by

$$\text{logit}\,(p) = \log \frac{p}{1-p}.$$

The probabilities in the right-hand side of (5) can be estimated directly from the observed frequencies detailed earlier, giving

$$\log \frac{f}{n-f} + \sum_i \log \left(\frac{f_{ij_i}}{f} \cdot \frac{n-f}{n_{ij_i} - f_{ij_i}} \right). \tag{6}$$

Note that this is of the form of a point scoring rule (1). If we now suppose that none of the covariates plays a dominant role in prediction in the sense that f_{ij_i}/n_{ij_i} does not differ greatly from f/n, then (6) is approximately

$$\log \frac{f}{n-f} + \frac{n^2}{f(n-f)} \sum_i \left(\frac{f_{ij_i}}{n_{ij_i}} - \frac{f}{n} \right). \tag{7}$$

This is simply a linear transformation of the Glueck score (3), provided the covariates are first screened to retain only those which are significantly associated with the incidence of E. Since, in practice, point scoring rules are recalibrated on the data (see below), such a linear transformation is irrelevant.

It has become a tradition in some research areas in psychology to dichotomize data to redefine each covariate to take just one of two possible levels. Although this simplifies the notation in the above formulae, there is nothing in the point scoring method which precludes multiple levels. In fact dichotomizing data simply loses information, and sometimes substantially so. Assuming dichotomized data, however, Burgess (1928) proposed an even simpler version of point scoring in which

$$g_i(x_i) = \begin{cases} 1 & \text{if } x_i = v_{ij}, \dfrac{f_{ij}}{n_{ij}} > \dfrac{f}{n} \text{ and } \chi_i^2 > 3.84, \\ & j = 1, 2 \\ 0 & \text{otherwise.} \end{cases} \tag{8}$$

The score (1) is then just counting how many of the covariates take the level which is more indicative of the occurrence of E, leaving out any of the covariates which do not have any statistically significant association with E.

The object of these methods is to find a score measuring propensity to E, rather than the actual rate of occurrence of E. The required probabilities of E are found by calibrating S against the data. In practice this has been done by grouping values of S into adjacent class intervals or risk groups, and then plotting the relative frequency of E observed in each risk group against the mid-point of that group. The RPS, and several other studies, have simply fitted a straight line to the resulting points, giving a linear calibration. Some truncation is obviously needed to keep the estimated probability within the range of 0 to 1: the calibration line for the RPS passes through 0 at $S = -31$ and 1 at $S = +31$, and so RPS is defined to be 0 if $S < -30$ and 1 if $S > +30$. Linear calibration does not seem very satisfactory, and examples suggest that calibration by a logistic curve would be more sensible; in other words we find coefficients a and b such that

$$\text{logit } P(E \mid x) \simeq a + bS.$$

Copas (1993) follows Farrington and West (1990) by fitting a Burgess score (8) to data from the Cambridge Study of Delinquent Development. Here E is taken to be one or more criminal convictions by age 30 years, and the covariates relate to social background and behavioural measures in childhood. Eight covariates are significantly associated with the occurrence of E, giving an 8-point scale, the 9 possible values of this score giving the calibration plot in Fig. 11.1. Lines giving a linear and a logistic calibration are shown, the latter being closer to the observed data.

Despite the rather crude nature of these methods, and of the assumption of independence on which they implicitly rely, point scoring has been found to work quite well in practice. Requiring that $g_i(x_i)$ in (Fig. 11.1) depends only on the marginal association of x_i and E ensures that the contribution of each covariate is intuitively sensible, the contribution of age to the RPS, for example, corresponding to observed experience of the dependence of reconviction rates on age. Regression methods do not have this property, and can give coefficients on the covariates which have the 'wrong' sign. Although regression methods will usually be better in terms of conventional statistical criteria (such as maximum likelihood), purely statistical considerations may not be sufficient to overcome scepticism on the part of practitioners in accepting a prediction score which they see as counter-intuitive.

In attempting to explain the perhaps surprising success of point scoring in practice, three points are worth mentioning. Firstly, the independence made explicit in the 'Independence Bayes' approach is *conditional* on the occurrence of E (or E^c), not *marginal*. What is important is the correlation between covariates amongst those who reoffend, and amongst those who do not, and we would expect these conditional correlations to be much less than the corresponding marginal correlation. Secondly, any systematic over- or under-prediction caused by the duplication of the contributions of

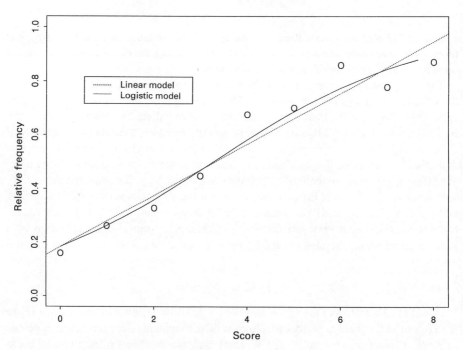

Fig. 11.1. Linear and logistic calibration.

closely related covariates is automatically allowed for in the calibration stage. And thirdly, in criminological applications the predictive power of any individual covariate is typically modest, the effectiveness of the score relying on combining together the effects of several such covariates. A change in the weight on one covariate can often be compensated by a complementary change in the weight on another, suggesting that precision in the individual weights is not important.

Logistic regression

Although point scoring has some merits, as indicated, its development is limited in that it is not based on any explicit model for the way the probability of E depends on x. Only with a model is it possible to develop statistical procedures which have desired optimal properties, and is it possible to develop diagnostic measures to assess whether an assumed model gives a good representation of the data.

The most widely used model for relating a dichotomous outcome (E or E^c) to covariates x is logistic regression, where we assume

$$\text{logit } P(E \mid x) = \beta_0 + \sum_{i=1}^{m} \beta_i x_i. \tag{9}$$

This means that if we hold all but one of the covariates fixed, say those x_js with $j \neq i$, then logit $P(E|x)$ depends on x_i in a linear way with a slope (β_i) that does not depend on the fixed values chosen. Because the covariates will in general be correlated with each other, the coefficient β_i does not directly reflect the marginal dependence of E on x_i.

Given n subjects in the sample, let $p_k(\beta)$ be the value of $P(E|x)$ in (9) with x taken to be the covariate vector observed in the kth subject, and let the outcome for this kth subject be $y_k = 1$ if E occurs and $y_k = 0$ if E does not occur. Then the probability that we would observe the outcome y_k for the kth subject is

$$[p_k(\beta)]^{y_k} [1 - p_k(\beta)]^{1 - y_k}.$$

Assuming independent outcomes between subjects gives the logarithm of the probability of observing all n outcomes to be

$$L(\beta) = \sum_{k=1}^{n} [y_k \log p_k(\beta) + (1 - y_k) \log (1 - p_k(\beta))]. \tag{10}$$

This is the likelihood function, and the standard way of estimating the model parameters is to find the value of β which maximizes (10). The theory of models of this kind is explored in detail in McCullagh and Nelder (1989), who show how the estimation of β can be carried out by a sequence of weighted least squares analyses. Such calculations are easy to implement in the computer package GLIM (Baker and Nelder 1978) or in other packages such as GENSTAT (Payne 1987) or S-PLUS (Statistical Sciences Inc. 1983). Practical aspects of data analysis using this (and other) models are discussed in Aitkin *et al.* (1989). In particular, the value of (10) at the estimated parameter values can be used for comparing different models. For example, the significance of the contribution of a further covariate is assessed by calculating how much (10) increases when the new covariate is added to the current model. Twice this increase is compared to a chi-squared distribution on one degree of freedom.

The model (9) gives a direct estimate of the probability of E as a function of x, and fitting the model does not involve the calibration step used in point scoring. However it is still useful to plot the observed relative frequencies of E against risk groups formed by class intervals on the fitted probabilities, both for testing the fit of the model and for demonstrating the extent to which the model differentiates between cases with high and low risk. This and other aspects of logistic regression are illustrated in the case study later in this chapter.

Models for varying time (survival models)

Although most prediction scores have used a fixed time horizon, there is now considerable interest in survival models which consider the dependence of risk on both x and t. A useful review is Schmidt and Witte (1988). The need for survival models is in fact made explicit in the Criminal Justice Act 1991. The section on parole, quoted earlier, goes on to say that the parole decision 'should be based upon an evaluation of the risk to the public of the person committing a further serious offence *at a time when he would otherwise be in prison*' (my italics). The time of potential parole is not fixed, but varies with sentence length and may be shortened by earlier parole refusals or procedural delays.

To fit a survival model, we need to know for a sample of subjects the actual times at which E occurs for the first time. In practice it is only possible to follow through a subject's criminal record for a limited period, and so for a subject for whom E has never been observed it is always possible that E may occur at some time in the future. It is the ability to analyse *censored* data of this kind which is the special feature of survival techniques.

A survival model specifies a mathematical form for the probability $p(x, t)$, and will depend on unknown parameters, say

$$p_\theta(x, t).$$

This is the probability of E occurring for the first time before time t, and so the probability density function of the time of first occurrence is

$$f_\theta(x,t) = \frac{d}{dt} p_\theta(x, t).$$

Suppose that the kth subject in the study sample has covariate vector x_k and is followed up for a time T_k. Define $y_k = 1$ if E occurs by time T_k, in which case define t_k to be time of the actual first occurrence. Define $y_k = 0$ otherwise. Then the logarithm of the probability of the observed outcomes for n subjects is

$$L(\theta) = \sum_{k=1}^{n} [y_k \log f_\theta(x_k, t_k) + (1 - y_k) \log (1 - p_\theta(x_k, T_k))]. \tag{11}$$

This is the likelihood function, analogous to (10) in the case of logistic regression, and the standard procedure for fitting the survival model is to find the estimate of θ which maximizes (11).

A variety of mathematical models for $p(x, t)$ have been proposed in the literature, and the choice has to be guided by the observed pattern of reoffending. If the follow-up times T_i all exceed some minimum time T^*, then an empirical estimate of $p(x, t)$ for values of t less than T^* is simply given by the observed proportion of subjects with a given value of x who are reconvicted by time t. Figure 11.2 shows an example giving the times to the first reconviction for a large sample of prisoners in England and Wales released in 1987 and followed up to 1990. Here the dependence on x is ignored, and so the whole sample is used. The top row of dots corresponds to the time of first reconviction for any (sufficiently serious) type of offence, the lower row of dots corresponding to reconvictions which subsequently led to a further prison sentence. To extend these plots beyond T^* an allowance for censoring is needed, and the Kaplan-Meir estimate is usually used – see Aitkin *et al.* (1989) or any standard textbook on survival analysis such as Cox and Oakes (1984). Note that in more familiar applications of survival analysis (medical statistics and actuarial science), modelling is conventionally done in terms of the survival curve which is simply one minus the above function $p(x, t)$. (The survival curve at t is then the probability of surviving up to time t without an occurrence of E).

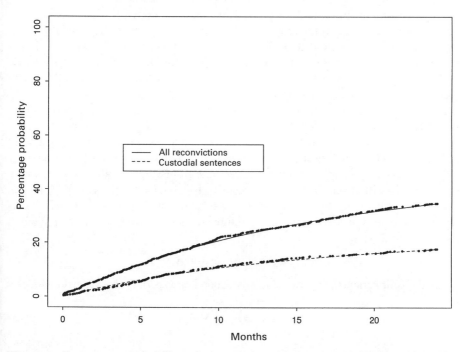

Fig. 11.2. Percentage probability of reconviction. (Crown copyright. Reproduced by permission of the Controller of HMSO).

It is helpful to think of the modelling of $p(x, t)$ in two stages. Firstly we need to model the dependence on t for a fixed x. This will typically involve intermediate parameters η_x, say. Secondly we need to model how the individual covariates enter into η_x. One of the simplest, but reasonably flexible, models is based on the assumption that the time of first occurrence of E has a Weibull distribution, implying that

$$p(x,t) = 1 - \exp(-\lambda_x t^{\alpha_x}). \tag{12}$$

Hence η_x consists of the pair (λ_x, α_x), λ_x controlling the rate of incidence of E and α_x controlling the shape of the dependence on t. The usual second stage model is to postulate

$$\alpha_x = \alpha \quad \text{for all } x$$

$$\log \lambda_x = \beta_0 + \sum_{i=1}^{m} \beta_i x_i, \tag{13}$$

a constant shape parameter and a log-linear model for the rate parameter. Of special interest is the case $\alpha = 1$, when a particularly simple interpretation is possible. The time to first occurrence of E then has an exponential distribution, corresponding to a completely random process with a constant average rate of λ_x occurrences of E per unit time (the exponential model).

The Weibull model (12) and (13) is fitted by forming the likelihood (11), and maximizing over the parameters $\theta = (\alpha, \beta)$. This can be done using a package such as GLIM, as explained in Aitkin et al. (1989). In criminological applications it is often found that α is fairly close to 1. Tarling (1993) reports examples where α is not significantly different from 1 once proper allowance for important covariates is made in the log-linear part of (13). Weibull models fitted to the curves in Fig. 11.2, where there are no covariates, give α around 0.9.

An unattractive feature of (12) is that as t increases to infinity $p(x, t)$ tends to one, implying that for every subject E is bound to occur eventually. From the point of view of statistical modelling of data this may be irrelevant, as the values of t needed to make $p(x, t)$ close to 1 will usually be far greater than any values of t_i actually observed. But in principle we should have some positive probability, say γ_x, that a given subject will never reoffend. This leads to the so-called split population model, where we assume that a conventional survival model applies only to those subjects who will reoffend at some time in the future. If these reoffences follow a Weibull model, we now have

$$p(x,t) = (1 - \gamma_x)(1 - \exp(-\lambda_x t^{\alpha_x})), \tag{14}$$

where the split parameter γ_x will generally depend on x, perhaps by a logistic model

$$\text{logit } \gamma_x = \delta_0 + \sum_{i=1}^{m} \delta_i x_i. \tag{15}$$

Although it is straightforward to formulate the likelihood (11) corresponding to (14) and (15), the model can be very difficult to fit in practice. The reason is that if the follow-up is not sufficiently long to make the exponential term in (14) close to zero, the model finds it difficult to differentiate between decreasing γ_x (making more people potential reoffenders) and increasing λ_x (making those who are in the reoffending group offend more quickly). Substantial constraints can then be placed on the parameters without materially affecting the goodness of fit of the model.

Without covariates, the model gives an extremely good fit to the curves in Fig. 11.2, as shown by the sold line (all reoffending) and the dotted line (reoffending leading to custody). With covariates, successful models are found by constraining γ_x in (15) to be constant for all subjects or, with a slightly better fit, by constraining the right-hand side of (15) to be a linear function of the right-hand side of (13). This second constraint recognizes that those covariates x which give a high chance of being in the offending group (low γ_x) tend also to be those which give a high offending rate (high λ_x), and vice versa. Explicitly the model is (13) together with

$$\text{logit } \gamma_x = a + b\log\lambda_x$$

Figure 11.3 illustrates the excellent fit of this model to the data used in Fig. 11.2. Here the fitted values of λ_x are ranked across subjects in the study, and the subjects divided into thirds (high λ_x, medium λ_x, low λ_x). The data for all reoffences are represented by the dots, and the fitted model by the curves, separately for each of the three sub-samples. See also Fig. 7.1, p. 127.

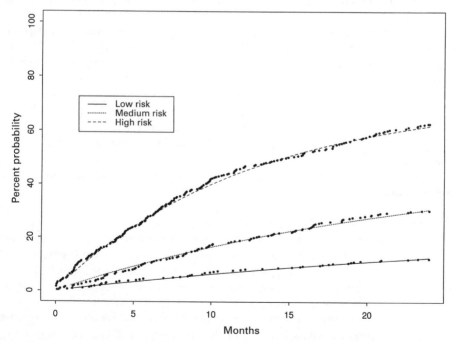

Fig. 11.3. Percentage probability of any reconviction, by risk group. (Crown copyright. Reproduced by permission of the Controller of HMSO).

These models are fully parametric in that they postulate a mathematical form for the dependence of $p(x, t)$ on both x and t. A completely different model, now widely used in medical studies, is that proposed by Cox (1972). Cox's model, or the 'Cox proportional hazards model' as it is usually known, is semi-parametric in that it specifies a log-linear model for the role of x but leaves the dependence on t to be empirically determined by the data. Details can be found in Cox's original paper or in many other references, and computational aspects are spelt out in Aitken *et al.* (1989). Applications to criminological data include Barton and Turnbull (1979, 1981) and Schmidt and Witte (1988). However, Cox's model seems less appropriate for problems of prediction, the concern of this chapter. Here we are interested in estimating $p(x, t)$ for all x and t, details of the dependence on individual covariates being of secondary concern. In the Cox model, on the other hand, the primary interest is in the role of the covariates, the dependence on t being a secondary consideration. In medical applications, for example, the covariates may include treatment variables, the main concern being to evaluate the evidence that choice of treatment does have an effect on survival.

Choice of covariates

The choice of covariates can be the most difficult part of statistical modelling, and it is impossible to be prescriptive about how this should be done. It has to involve a blend of common sense, experience in the application area, and purely statistical considerations. The choice of covariates (and choice of model itself) is inevitably a somewhat subjective process: it is unlikely that two statisticians working independently, but on the same set of data, would arrive at exactly the same model, although hopefully their two models would give similar predictions for the subjects observed in the study.

The notation $x_1, x_2, \ldots, x_m$ used in the above models does not imply that the x_is are a list of the covariates which are measured in the data, and in the form in which they happen to have been coded. Transformations and recoding of covariates will nearly always be needed, as will the selection of a relatively small number of them for the final model.

The following comments concerning specific issues arising in covariate choice seem worth making.

Transformation of quantitative covariates
For simplicity nearly all parametric models assume that covariates act in a linear fashion, such as in (9), (13) or (15). Linear dependence on x_i taken as a single covariate by itself is no guarantee of linear dependence when other covariates are included, or vice versa, but an examination of the association between the incidence of E and values of x_i provides a rough guide, and can be done as a routine part of the preliminary analysis of the data. A simple method is to choose a suitable fixed t (if not already fixed) and plot the logit of the relative frequency of the occurrence of E against values of x_i, grouping values of x_i into class intervals if necessary. In the notation of the section on point scoring, this amounts to plotting, for each i,

$$\log \frac{f_{ij}}{n_{ij} - f_{ij}} \text{ versus } v_{ij} \quad j = 1, 2, \ldots, k_i.$$

A computer programme which divides the sample values of x_i into approximate deciles, and then produces this plot automatically, is useful. Non-linearity in the plot suggests that a transformation might be helpful. If x_i is the number of previous convictions, for example, the logit may rise roughly linearly for most values but level off once x_i reaches about 20. This suggests transforming x_i into x_i^* where $x_i^* = x_i$ if $x_i < 20$ and $x_i^* = 20$ if $x_i \geq 20$. A smoother concave plot might be straightened by a logarithmic transformation.

Recoding of qualitative covariates

The conventional way of modelling qualitative covariates is to use dummy variables which estimate the effect of each level separately. If x_i has three levels coded 1, 2, and 3, for example, x_i is split into two new covariates $x_i^{(1)} = 1, 0, -1$ and $x_i^{(2)} = 0, 1, -1$ when $x_i = 1, 2$, and 3 respectively. The difficulty is that too many dummy variables are usually needed to model all the levels of several qualitative covariates. One practical alternative is to recode x_i into a new set of codes which reflect a subjective view of the 'severity' of the various levels, then treat the recorded x_i as a quantitative covariate before refining the codes using the plot suggested in the previous section. A second alternative is to amalgamate the levels of x_i into a smaller number of groups and define dummy variables for the resulting categories. The latter seems the only feasible way of modelling 'type of offence' which is usually coded in some detail – the model has to rely on a rather crude list of broad categories of crime.

Combinations of covariates

Common sense may suggest that groups of covariates can be summarized by one or two combined scores. For example, dates of previous convictions might be summarized by the number of convictions and the rate of convictions (number divided by total time), or lengths of previous prison sentences might be reduced to the average length. Often it is found that once summary scores are included in the model the individual covariates on which they are based are found to contribute little further, and can be omitted.

Significance of covariates, and predictive measures

The usual statistical measure of the importance of a covariate is the statistical significance of the coefficient of that covariate in the model. A conventional procedure is to fit several covariates together, retain those which are statistically significant at some nominal level (such as 5 per cent) and discard those which are not. The first difficulty is that, as discussed in Copas (1985), significance of a covariate is only indirectly linked to its effectiveness in prediction, and so judging covariates by their statistical significance can only be taken as a very rough guide. In small samples a covariate may play a useful role in prediction and yet only attain a modest level of significance. In large samples covariates may be highly significant and yet contribute little to prediction, suggesting that quite stringent significance levels could be used in screening covariates. The second difficulty, common to all regression models involving multiple covariates, is that the statistical significance of any one covariate may depend on which other covariates are included. A covariate may seem important when taken on its own, but unimportant when taken along with another covariate. Conversely, two covariates may seem unimportant when taken singly, but highly significant when taken together. Problems arise when covariates are highly correlated with each other, and again common sense is needed to avoid closely overlapping variables and to suggest suitable transformations. For example, if in a sample of prisoners x_1 is age at first conviction and x_2 is age at first custodial sentence, then x_1 and x_2 are likely to be highly correlated; it would be better to take x_1 as it is and replace x_2 by $x_2 - x_1$. These and other aspects of choosing subsets of covariates are reviewed in the monograph by Miller (1990).

An alternative approach to using significance levels is to compare different choices of covariates by a direct measure of predictive accuracy. Unfortunately none of the measures proposed in the literature seems entirely satisfactory. A simple but crude measure which is often used is the 'percentage correctly classified (PCC)'. Here, a prediction score S is compared with a threshold k, often chosen such that the proportion of cases with $S \geq k$ matches the overall incidence of E (within some suitable time t). Then PCC is simply the percentage of cases in which either $S \geq k$ and E occurs, or $S < k$ and E does not occur. A sequence of models can be fitted in which covariates are added in one at a time, and the value of PCC calculated at each stage. Typically PCC will increase sharply when the first few covariates are added but then level off. The model suggested by this approach is the one for which further increases in PCC are too small to be of practical importance (even though further covariates may be statistically significant). In the example later in this chapter, a PCC of 67 per cent is reached with only six covariates. The PCC for the RPS (Nuttall *et al.* 1977), which is based on 17 covariates, is 69 per cent. In interpreting these percentages it is worth noting that if a predictor gives probabilities of E uniformly distributed from 0 to 1, and is perfectly calibrated, then the PCC is 75 per cent. For PCC to be higher than this the distribution of predicted probabilities needs to be bimodal, which seems unlikely in practice. Obvious inadequacies of PCC as a measure of predictive performance are that it is based on an artificial binary decision criterion which is unlikely to correspond to how the score is to be used in practice, and that it is completely insensitive to the accuracy of calibration. Attempts to overcome some of these difficulties have suggested modified measures as reviewed in Copas and Tarling (1986).

Interactions and non-linear effects

All of the models reviewed earlier assume that the covariates are additive: the effect of changing one covariate does not depend on the values taken by the others. This will rarely be so exactly, and sometimes interactions between pairs of covariates need to be modelled explicitly. The logistic regression score proposed in Copas and Whiteley (1976) allows for an interaction between recidivism (whether there has been more than one criminal conviction) and psychiatric admission (whether the subject has ever been admitted to a psychiatric institution). The formal way of modelling interactions is to add cross-product terms into the model. For example, if there are two covariates x_1 and x_2 with means $\bar{x}_1$ and $\bar{x}_2$, then the new covariate would be $x_3 = (x_1 - \bar{x}_1)(x_2 - \bar{x}_2)$. The sample means are subtracted from the variables before multiplication in order to reduce the correlations between x_3 and x_1 and x_2. Some statistical packages use a short-hand code for including such interactions. The significance of an individual interaction is then judged by the fitted coefficient of the corresponding cross-product, and the significance of the interactions as a whole is judged by comparing the fit of the model with and without these cross-product terms.

An informal way of checking interactions, and one which aids interpretation, is to calculate the relative frequency of the occurrence of E (within some fixed time t) within each cell of the cross-classification of the levels of x_i with the levels of x_j. Often grouping of adjacent levels will be needed to ensure that there are a reasonable number of cases in each cell. A simple approach (which can usefully be automated in a statistical package) is to split x_i and x_j by their medians, and then calculate the relative frequency of E in each cell of the resulting 2×2 table. An interaction is indicated if the ratio of the two relative frequencies in the left-hand column is substantially different from the ratio in the right-hand column, or equivalently for rows. A graphical representation of the same idea is to choose one covariate, x_i say, and carry out of the plot suggested on p. 186 but separately for each level of another covariate x_j. The absence of an interaction between x_i and x_j corresponds to these plots being parallel.

Non-linearity in the effect of the covariates can be approached in a similar way. Although approximate linearity in the effect of x_i by itself may have been achieved by transformation as suggested above, this linearity may be upset by the presence of other covariates in the model. The formal procedure is to add squares $(x_i - \bar{x}_i)^2$ into the model and to judge their significances in the same way as for cross-products. Higher order polynomials can be added, but these are not usually very useful, especially if any marked non-linearities in the dependence on the covariates taken one at a time have already been removed. An informal graphical procedure is to look for non-linearities in the plots suggested in the last paragraph.

Simplification and recalibration

In the models discussed earlier it is useful to distinguish between a raw score, say S, and the final estimate of risk which is a function of S. In logistic regression, for example, S is the linear function of the covariates in (9), and the final prediction is the solution of

$$\text{logit } P(E|x) = S$$

namely

$$P(E \mid x) = \frac{e^s}{1 + e^s}.$$

If the procedure is to be acceptable to practitioners then, ideally, S should be easy to calculate. For this, S not only needs to involve a small number of covariates, but the coefficients need to rounded to simple numbers. This can be done by taking the score S

arising from fitting the model, and then finding a factor c such that the coefficient in cS are reasonably close to small integers. Negative values of cS are avoided by adding a suitable constant onto the intercept term. This leads to a simplified score S^* which can then be recalibrated by fitting the same model as before but with S^* taken as a single covariate. In logistic regression this amounts to fitting

$$\text{logit } P(E|x) = a + bS^*$$

giving

$$P(E \mid x) = \frac{e^{a+bS^*}}{1 + e^{a+bS^*}}. \tag{16}$$

In practice S^* is calculated as a simple weighted sum of covariates, and then $P(E|x)$ is read from a table or graph of the function (16). It is usually found that severe rounding of cS can be done without materially altering the fit of the final model. The same procedure can be used in survival models, with (13) or (15) being replaced by $a + bS^*$ and then (12) or (14) being refitted as the recalibration step.

A recalibration of this kind can also be useful in other circumstances. Ward (1987) used data on prison discharges in 1977–9 to monitor the effectiveness of the RPS (Nuttall *et al*. 1977) which had been constructed from a much earlier sample of prisoners in 1965. Bearing in mind that parole had been introduced during the intervening years, the RPS was found to remain remarkably effective, although there had inevitably been some drift in reconviction rates. Ward proposed that the RPS should be scaled by multiplying by a factor of 0.84 in order to give a better fit to the more recent data. This amounts to a linear recalibration. Ward's scaling factor was found by an informal graphical procedure; a slightly better fit could have been obtained by the logistic recalibration suggested here.

Updating by recalibration is simple to carry out, since only actual outcomes and predictions need be recorded, and is effective provided there are no major changes in the role of the covariates. If the coefficients of covariates are likely to change substantially, then a complete refitting of the prediction score is needed, based, of course, on data on all the covariates as well as follow-up data on the incidence of E.

Validation and shrinkage

In developing statistical predictors it is important to distinguish between retrospective fit (how well the predictions fit the data on which the model is fitted) and prospective fit (how well the predictions will fit the observed incidence of E in a completely independent set of data). Since the choice of covariates and estimated coefficients will reflect statistical features of the original data, prospective fit will inevitably be worse than retrospective fit. Clearly it is prospective fit that is important for prediction; retrospective fit will be biased and tend to give too optimistic a picture of the likely performance of the prediction score in practice. The extent of this bias is described as shrinkage.

Shrinkage can be very substantial, as illustrated in one of the earliest prediction studies – Simon (1971). Simon studied data on about 500 young adult males who were given probation in 1958. About 60 covariates were available, and in this case E was taken to be reconviction within 3 years from the beginning of the probation order. Using alternate allocation from an alphabetical list, Simon divided the sample into two sub-samples, using the first data set (the construction sample) for fitting the predictor, and the second data set (the validation sample) to provide an estimate of prospective fit. Each of the two sub-samples can itself be divided into two risk groups, those with predicted probability greater than 1/2 and those with predicted probability less than 1/2. The observed incidence of E within each of the four groups of subjects is shown in Table 11.1. A crude measure of the effectiveness of the predictor is the difference between the actual percentages of E for the high and low risk groups. This difference of 32 per cent for the construction data (retrospective fit) shrinks to 20 per cent for the validation data (prospective fit). Simon (1971), and later Tarling and Perry (1985), fitted a number of different statistical predictors to the same data, and found that the extent of shrinkage was about the same for all of the methods tried.

Of course shrinkage in the sense being used here refers only to the statistical deterioration of fit inherent in all statistical estimation methods, and assumes that other factors remain stable. The future performance of a predictor may be deflated for many other reasons, such as a change in the criminal justice system or a demographic change in the population to which the predictor is applied. Such changes were evident in the validation of the RPS reported in Ward (1987).

Shrinkage depends most critically on the sample size and the number of covariates which are either included in the model or were potential candidates for inclusion. The example above shrinks very substantially because the number of potential covariates (62) is quite large relative to the sample size (270). Nuttall *et al.* (1977) maintained that the RPS suffers little or no shrinkage. The sample size for the RPS was considerably larger (2276), and shrinkage is not usually a problem for studies with such large data sets, as confirmed in the example later in this chapter.

Simon's method of splitting the data into two halves for fitting and for validation has become a tradition adopted in several subsequent studies. To discard half the data when estimating the parameters of a model, however, does not seem very satisfactory, particularly if the total sample size is not large. In the related area of discriminant analysis, the problem of shrinkage is often handled by using cross-validation or the 'hold-one-out method'. Here the model is fitted to data on all subjects except the kth, with the predictor then being applied to the covariates of that kth subject. This is repeated n times for k from 1 to n. Validation consists of comparing the n predictions with the n actual outcomes. For large sample sizes the whole procedure can be computationally demanding, but for linear models (e.g. discriminant analysis) efficient algorithms have been worked out and are implemented in most statistical packages.

Table 11.1. Percentages reconvicted for Simon's data

	Construction sample	Validation sample
High risk	64%	53%
Low risk	32%	33%

Table 11.1 suggests how shrinkage can be thought of in terms of calibration. Although retrospective calibration may appear satisfactory, the validation sample shows that high predicted probabilities tend to be too high and low predicted probabilities tend to be too low. A completely different approach is to use the model as fitted to the whole data to estimate how much the calibration will be biased in future samples. The idea is then to adjust the fitted model so that the predictors are, in some approximate sense, likely to be correctly calibrated when used in practice.

Copas (1983, 1987, 1993) develops techniques for such shrinkage corrections. In simple cases with a linear score S, defined as a linear function of covariates, the idea is to replace S by

$$\bar{S} + b(S - \bar{S}) \tag{17}$$

where $\bar{S}$ is the overall average score and b is a 'shrinkage factor' less than one. This has the effect of scaling down the predictors towards an overall average. For point scoring Copas (1993) proposes a formula for b which is fairly easy to calculate with the aid of the table given in that paper. Copas (1993) gives an example of a small study with eight binary covariates and a sample size of $n = 77$. Dividing the sample into two risk groups according to the value of the point score S gives retrospect reconviction rates of 25 per cent in a low risk group and 51 per cent in the high risk group. The shrinkage factor is estimated as $b = 0.79$, leading to adjusted rates of 28 per cent and 49 per cent respectively.

Shrinkage in logistic regression models is considered in Copas (1983). Suppose there are m covariates, and that a sequence of models is tried leading to a chosen subset of covariates. Let S be the logistic score based on this sub-set. Then Copas (1983) suggests that b is estimated as

$$b = \max \left(0, 1 - \frac{m - 2}{\chi^2} \right) \tag{18}$$

where χ^2 is the chi-squared statistic (or deviance) used for testing the significance of the contribution of the complete set of covariates. For a small number of effective covariates b will be close to 1 (little shrinkage); for a large number of weak covariates b will be small (substantial shrinkage). The formula is based on a number of simplifying assumption as discussed in Copas (1983). These assumptions are unlikely to hold exactly, but examples suggest that (18) works reasonably well in practice. An important feature of (18) is that it depends on the statistical fit of the logistic model with *all* the covariates, and not just those covariates which are selected for use in the final prediction score. This reflects the fact that when covariates are selected on the basis of statistical significance, it will be those with large coefficients which will be selected, and so covariates whose coefficients in the fitted model are, by chance, over-estimated are more likely to be selected than covariates whose coefficients happen to be underestimated. The sizes of the coefficients of the selected covariates will therefore be positively biased and hence differences $(S - \bar{S})$ in (17) will tend to be too large. This selection bias is a major cause of shrinkage and also suggests that the shrinkage factor b in (17) needs to be less than one.

Copas (1983) discusses an example of logistic regression with a sample of 500 borstal trainees admitted to open borstals in 1977–8, E being absconding during sentence. Here $m = 22$, but only four covariates were selected. Formula (18) gave $b = 0.60$, and an independent validation sample confirmed the accuracy of prospective calibration using the adjusted score in (17). This large shrinkage is almost entirely due to the selection bias of choosing 4 out of 22 covariates; the shrinkage would have been much less had the chosen variables been identified in advance or chosen on the basis of an independent study.

The need to consider shrinkage of predictions from survival models is just as great as it is for point scoring or logistic regression, although no theory for shrinkage correction seems to be available. Informal methods, however, are still useful. If the sample is split into two sub-samples, empirical plots of the survival times can be drawn for groups of subjects defined by appropriate ranges of a prediction score, and compared with model predictions on the lines of Fig. 11.3. This is done twice, for the construction sample (retrospective fit) and the validation sample (prospective fit). Shrinkage is seen in the extent to which the fit of the model is worse in the second plot than the first. An alternative approach is to fix t at some convenient value, and use the survival model to predict the probability that E will occur by time t. Comparing these probabilities with the observations on whether E does in fact occur by time t, leads to ways of assessing shrinkage appropriate to the fixed-t models already considered in this section.

CASE STUDY: A RISK OF RECONVICTION PREDICTOR

Background

In the final part of this chapter we illustrate many of the points discussed above by presenting a case study in the development of a national reconviction prediction score for use by probation officers. There are already several statistical scores which have been suggested or are in use in connection with probation, including Merrington (1990), Humphrey et al. (1991) and, in a slightly different context, Fitzmaurice (1991). These, however, are mostly based on local studies, use locally available data and differ considerably in the choice of covariates and the way the covariates enter into the predictor. They tend to follow the point scoring approach of Nuttall et al. (1977). The aim of this study is to estimate a national reconviction scale using a large sample covering a cross-section of recent convictions with covariates extracted in a systematic way from the Home Office's Offenders' Index. All the information on the index concerns convictions related to standard list offences (see Chapter 2). The immediate application envisaged for the proposed predictor is to aid probation officers in their recommendations to the courts as to the type of supervision required for particular offenders. Other important uses of a national predictor would be to allow different administrative areas to monitor the type of offenders supervised by their Probation Service, and to help in assessing the effectiveness of particular interventions by the availability of an agreed stratification of subjects into different risk groups.

Ideally a predictor should provide predictions conditional on sentence, and measure risk specific to different types of reoffence. Survival analysis could be used to monitor changes in risk over time. In this study, however, the need for the predictor to be straightforward and easy to use was judged to be of paramount importance, and so we focus on the more limited objective of estimating risk of reconviction for any standard list offence within a fixed period of $t = 2$ years.

The sample

The total sample size is 13 711, made up of four sub-samples as follows:

(1) Sub-sample 1: a sample of subjects given probation orders (without 4A/4B conditions) in 1987 (3466 cases);

(2) Sub-sample 2: a sample of subjects given community service orders (CSO) in 1987 (3322 cases);

(3) Sub-sample 3: a sample of subjects given probation orders with 4A/4B conditions in 1987 (4413 cases) (see Chapter 5);

(4) Sub-sample 4: a stratified sample of subjects released from prison in 1987. The stratification was used to over-sample young offenders, cases with longer sentences, female offenders and ethnic minorities (2510 cases).

The year 1987 was chosen to enable each subject to be followed up for at least two years from the date of conviction, for the non-custodial sentences, or from the date of release from prison for the custodial sentences. The time 'at risk' is taken to be the two-year period starting from conviction, but discounting any period spent in prison.

The overall sample is, of course, not intended to be representative of all convictions, and community penalties are heavily over-represented in the data. It can be argued, however, that these are the cases where the predictor is most likely to be useful and where reliability is particularly important. The approach in the analysis is to study the sample as a whole, but to carry 'sub-sample type' as a factor at the modelling phase. Including this factor as a main effect, plus interactions between this factor and the other variables in the model, is equivalent to fitting separate models to each sub-sample. In this way differences between the sub-samples as far as the prediction equation is concerned can be systematically monitored.

Data were missing from the sample in a substantial minority of cases, and this was of some concern in the analysis. In each sample the data were drawn from two sources: the Prison/Probation Index, and the accumulative Home Office database on convictions, the Offenders' Index. In order to combine the information from the two sources, offender entries in both databases had to be matched. A satisfactory match could not be found in up to 20 per cent of cases.

Although many variables were recorded in the source files for the cases selected in the sample, a relatively small number of covariates were chosen as being of potential use in the predictor. Again considerations of simplicity were involved: to be easy to use in practice a statistical score should involve only covariates which are readily available and which are likely to be accurately measured, and preferably only a few of them. The chosen covariates concentrate on criminal history, although social variables may be important they are much more difficult to measure in an unambiguous and systematic way. The criminal history covariates considered were:

(1) age at target conviction;

(2) first conviction (age, offence, disposal, severity of sentence);

(3) target conviction (similar details);

(4) total numbers of
     (a) court appearances at which there was a conviction;
     (b) previous convictions;
     (c) previous custodial sentences under age 21;
     (d) previous custodial sentences age 21 and over;

(5) time between target and most recent previous conviction.

The data for analysis also included sex and sub-sample type (1 to 4 above), and the binary outcome noting any reconvictions within two years.

Preliminary data analysis

Before attempting formal statistical modelling, a useful, and arguably more important, step is to study the sample using simple descriptive statistics. Simple measures such as frequency distributions, histograms, scatter plots, or frequencies of missing data codes are invaluable in identifying errors and ambiguities, and in gaining an understanding of the nature and limitations of the data. Close collaboration with colleagues involved in the sampling and in the substantive area is particularly important here so that problems can be discussed and resolved. Often this is the most time consuming part of statistical work and the present study proved no exception.

An immediate problem arises in the analysis of offence type. For administrative purposes type of offence is usually coded in some detail, but a much simpler coding is needed if it is to be a useful covariate. Codes for offence type for both first and target convictions were grouped into nine broad categories covering offences of violence, sexual offences, burglary, theft and handling, fraud and forgery, motor theft, criminal and malicious damage, drugs, and other offences.

As well as studying the covariates as presented, various transformed and combined covariates can also be useful, as stressed earlier in the chapter. No single covariate relates directly to a rate of offending or the rate of appearing in court, suggesting the new covariate

$$\text{Court appearance rate} = \frac{\text{Total number of court appearances}}{1 + \text{Number of years from first to target convictions}}$$

Defining a rate of court appearances when the target conviction is in fact at the first court appearance is somewhat arbitrary. The variable here then takes the value 1 but other versions are of course possible. This particular variable was chosen after several alternatives had been tried.

The substantial presence of missing data due to unmatched cases has already been mentioned. For covariates affected by such missing data, attempts were made to relate the probability of missing values to the values of other covariates. This was to assess whether the incidence of missing values could safely be assumed random, in which case missing data can be omitted without risk of bias. No significant relationships were found, and hence the main modelling of the data was confined to cases with complete data on the relevant covariates. However this procedure is not entirely satisfactory since the incidence of missing data could be related to unobserved factors which are not adequately represented by the other variables in the data. Missing values on some covariates were 'structural'; for example the time between the target and the most recent previous conviction cannot be defined if the target conviction is for a first offence. In this case a missing value is informative and needs to be explicitly allowed for at the modelling stage.

The covariates were studied at some length to see which are likely to be useful for prediction, and to see where recording or redefinition would be helpful. The main aim here was to guide the choice of covariates to be used in the main analysis but brief comments on the main covariates are given as follows. Percentages given without qualification refer to the overall percentages of cases within the relevant categories which have one or more reconvictions within two years of conviction or release.

Sub-sample type (defined above):

	1	2	3	4
%	50	55	65	53

Sex: 59 per cent for males, 41 per cent for females.

Age: 75 per cent for age under 18, decreasing steadily to 35 per cent for age over 36.

Time from first to target convictions:
44 per cent for 1 year or less, about 60 per cent for 1 to 7 years, about 55 per cent for 8 year or more.

Target offence type:
34 per cent for sex or drugs, 59 per cent for property offences, 51 per cent for the others.

First offence type: similar to target offence type.

Length of sentence or order from target conviction: modest decreasing trend within both community and prison cases.

Previous convictions: 40 per cent at zero, rising steadily to 70 per cent for 30 or more.

Youth custody: 51 per cent at zero, rising to about 85 per cent for 3 or more.

Adult custody: 56 per cent at zero, rising to 65 per cent for 2 or more.

Time between target and most recent previous conviction: about 70 per cent for short times, decreasing steadily to about 30 per cent for ten years or more.

Court appearances: steady rise from 40 per cent for first appearance to about 70 per cent for 10 or more.

Court appearance rate: increases from about 30 per cent for 0.3 appearances per year or less, to about 80 per cent for two appearances per year or more.

Logistic models

The main analysis was carried out on a 50 per cent random sample of the available data. This enables some validation checks along the lines of p. 191 to be carried out, and also reduces the substantial computational burden of fitting non-linear models to such large sample sizes.

Sex and age are obvious covariates for the model, both being strongly associated with reconviction. Figure 11.4 shows the way in which the rate of reconviction decreases with age. Because the variables relating to criminal history are correlated with each other, there is no obvious choice of the 'best' set of such covariates to use. Timescale of offending history is best taken account of by the rate of court appearances defined above, this being the strongest individual predictor of reoffending (see Fig. 11.5). The outlying point in this graph corresponds to the subjects with no previous court appearances, for whom the definition of the rate variable is rather arbitrary. These subjects however can be identified by including the number of court appearances as an

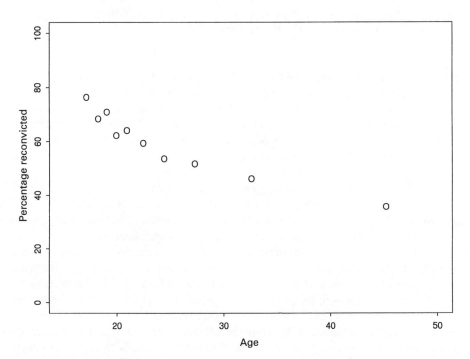

Fig. 11.4. Reconviction rate vs. age. (Crown copyright. Reproduced by permission of the Controller of HMSO).

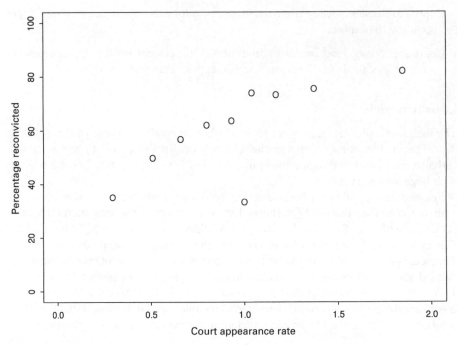

Fig. 11.5. Reconviction rate vs. court appearance rate. (Crown copyright. Reproduced by permission of the Controller of HMSO).

additional variable. Both Fig. 11.4 and Fig. 11.5 are reasonably close to logistic curves, as can be checked by replotting using a logistic scale, suggesting that these variables are suitable as covariates as they stand. With the rate variable it is sensible to include factors relating to the 'size' of criminal history and to specifically custodial aspects. After experimenting with several models, the number of court appearances seemed marginally preferable to the number of previous convictions, and the number of youth custodial convictions adequately represented the custodial dimension.

A satisfactory predictor was now obtained using just five variables: sex, age, rate, court appearances, and youth custody. Expanding the model to include polynomial and cross-product terms provides a systematic way of assessing non-linear effects and interactions, but none of these extra terms is statistically significant.

As mentioned above there are substantial differences in reconviction rates between the offence types relating to the target conviction. However, offence type is clearly related to previous criminal history, and so some of these differences may be explained by differences in the profiles of background variables. Table 11.2 gives the raw reconviction rates for each category of offence type, and also 'adjusted rates' after correcting for the differences between the offence types on sex, age, rate, court appearances, and youth custody. The range in percentages falls from 37 percentage points before adjustment to 19 percentage points after adjustment. The residual effect of offence type is incorporated into the model by adding offence code as a factor with

Table 11.2. Percentage reconvicted in two years, by offence type. (Crown Copyright. Reproduced by permission of the Controller of HMSO)

Offence type	Raw %	Adjusted %	% of cases
Violence	51	50	13
Sex	28	42	2
Burglary	69	61	23
Theft	58	59	31
Fraud	44	50	6
Motor	65	56	13
Criminal damage	64	60	7
Drugs	37	45	3
Other	50	45	2

9 levels, and the improvement thereby to the fit of the model is highly significant (chi-squared = 56 on 8 degrees of freedom).

The resulting logistic model is described in Table 11.3. For offences type, the usual convention for factor coefficients is adopted: only 8 are given corresponding to the 8 degrees of freedom for a factor with 9 levels. A coefficient for the 9th level can be calculated using the fact that the coefficients over all 9 levels must add up to zero. Including this factor as a crossed rather than an additive term monitors interactions with the earlier variable, but none seemed important. Several more complicated models were investigated, but they were at best only marginally superior to the simple fit

Table 11.3. Coefficients in logistic regression of reconviction rates on covariates

Covariate	Coefficient	Coefficient/standard error
Constant	0.916	5.0
Sex (M = 1, F = 2)	−0.501	−5.3
Age (in years)	−0.058	−12.1
Number of youth custodial sentences	0.224	4.1
Number of court appearances	0.111	13.9
Court appearances rate	0.617	7.3
Offence type factor level for:		
violence	−0.094	−1.1
sex	−0.503	−2.2
burglary	0.396	5.3
theft	0.315	4.6
fraud	−0.057	−0.5
motor	0.165	1.9
criminal damage	0.369	3.3
drugs	−0.289	−1.8

of Table 11.3. Detail of first offence contributed little over and above the variables already included.

Validation

The coefficients in Table 11.3 define a score which can be converted to a predicted probability of reconviction using the logistic transformation. Grouping the resulting predicted probabilities into class intervals using the deciles of the distribution leads to Fig. 11.6, which plots the actual percentage reconvicted in each interval against the average predicted percentage in that interval. The theoretical model is represented by the straight line, showing a very satisfactory retrospective fit for the construction data. A genuine (prospective) test of the model is to calculate the scores on the validation sample and compare with actual reconviction rates in the same way. The corresponding validation results are also shown on Fig. 11.6, and are virtually indistinguishable from the construction values, but with a hint (as expected) of a slightly shallower calibration line. Shrinkage appears not to be a problem.

As a further check on the stability of the predictor, exactly the same model was refitted using the validation data, and compared with the construction fit. The differences between the corresponding coefficients of the logistic models were small relative to the standard errors of the respective fits.

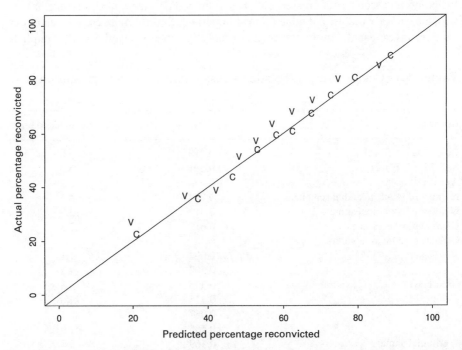

Fig. 11.6. Construction (C) and validation (V) fit of predictor. (Crown copyright. Reproduced by permission of the Controller of HMSO).

A further check on shrinkage is to calculate the shrinkage factor for logistic regression given in (18) above. Here the significance of some of the covariates is extremely high, and this, coupled with the very large value of n and modest value of m, makes (18) extremely close to 1. This confirms the lack of shrinkage already suggested by Fig. 11.6.

The value of the PCC measure discussed above is 67.4 per cent for the construction data, falling to 66.6 per cent for the validation data. This is comparable to the value obtained by Nuttall *et al.* (1977) and in several other studies, most of which also use social as well as criminal history variables.

A simplified score

Most of the coefficients in Table 11.3 are reasonably close to integer multiples of 0.55. Dividing through by this figure, recording sex to take value 0 for male and 1 for female, rounding to integers, and finally adjusting the intercept term, gives the simplified score in Table 11.4. This score nearly always gives a value between 0 and 100 (see the distribution in Fig. 11.7). Very little precision is lost by this rounding – Fig. 11.8 shows that the simplified score is close to being an exact linear function of the optimum logistic score. The new score is recalibrated along the lines described above by fitting a further logistic regression taking the score as a single explanatory variable. This gives the calibration

$$\text{logit}(p) = -2.8668 + 0.0564 \times \text{score},$$

shown as the smooth curve in Fig. 11.9.

The curve in Fig. 11.9 shows how the score is transformed into a probability of reconviction. The dotted diagonal line would correspond to taking the score at its face

Table 11.4. The simplified score

Start with 57
If female subtract 9
Subtract age in years
Add 4 times number of youth custodial sentences
Add 2 times total number of court appearances
Add 11 times court appearance rate[a]
If offence group is:

violence	subtract 2
sex	subtract 9
burglary	add 7
theft	add 6
fraud	subtract 1
motor	add 3
criminal damage	add 7
drugs	subtract 5
others	subtract 5

---

[a] Defined as: total number of court appearances divided by 1 plus the number of years since first conviction.

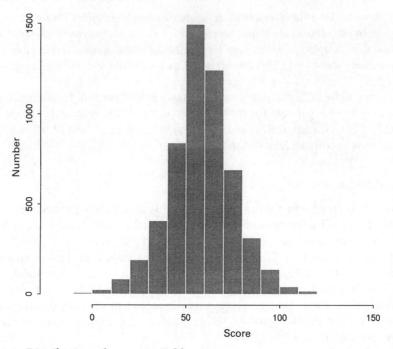

Fig. 11.7. Distribution of scores in Table 11.4.

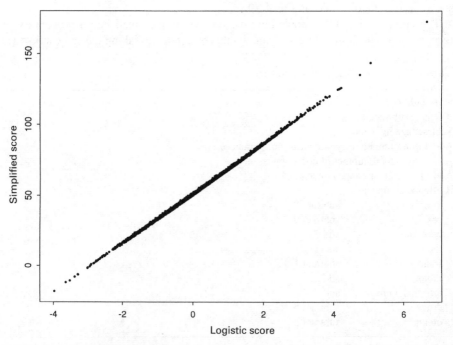

Fig. 11.8. Simplified score vs. logistic score. (Crown copyright. Reproduced by permission of the Controller of HMSO).

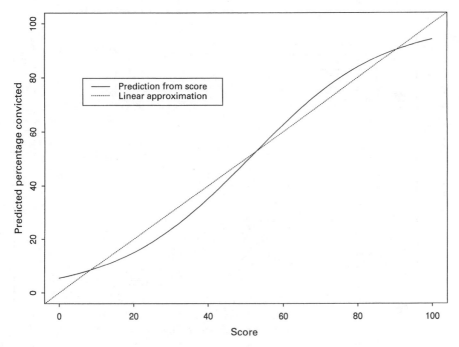

Fig. 11.9. Predicted percentage reconvicted by score. (Crown copyright. Reproduced by permission of the Controller of HMSO).

value without transformation. Clearly some error is involved, but the discrepancy between the two is never more than about 6 per cent. It is worth considering whether use of the untransformed score may be adequate for practical purposes.

Comparison of sub-samples

As mentioned earlier, the predictors have been fitted to a random sub-set of the sample as a whole, with the differences between sub-samples being monitored by taking sample type as a factor (with interactions when appropriate). The raw reconviction rates for the four sub-sample types are 50 per cent (probation), 55 per cent (CSO), 65 per cent (4A and 4B) and 53 per cent (prison). These rates narrow to adjusted rates of 57 per cent, 58 per cent, 60 per cent, and 54 per cent respectively when differences in the prediction score are taken into account. There are clearly differences between the sub-samples which are not fully explained by the variables used in the score, and the sample type factor gives a highly significant contribution when added to the logistic regression (chi-squared of 24 on 3 degrees of freedom). Adding severity of sentence (nested within disposal type) fails to make a significant improvement in overall fit, although is of some importance within the prison sample, with longer sentences tending to have lower reconviction rates.

Fig. 11.10 shows the calibration of the predictor on the construction data separated into the four sub-samples. For a given value of the score, the 4A/AB cases reconvict

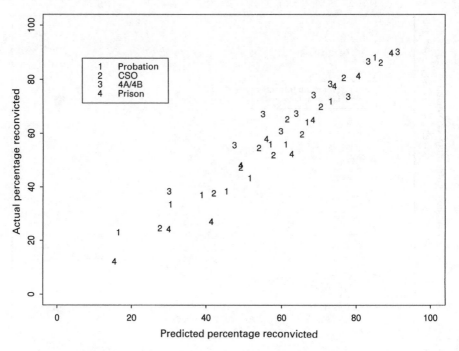

Fig. 11.10. Calibration of prediction by sub-sample type. (Crown copyright. Reproduced by permission of the Controller of HMSO).

rather more often than predicted, the prison sample rather less often, although the differences are not great. Fitting the calibration curve of Fig. 11.9, but for the different sub-samples, gives Fig. 11.11. The greatest differences arise at moderately low scores. For a score of 30, for instance, the rate ranges from 34 per cent for the 4A/4B cases down to only 18 per cent for the prison cases.

As disposal will not (typically) be known at the time the prediction score is applied, it is simplest to just ignore these intersample differences. A more careful approach might be to weight the predictions according to the prevalence of each disposal type in the population of cases for which the predictions will be required.

A cautionary note

An obvious comment is that analyses such as these are based on observational data, and caution is needed in attempting any causal interpretation. A minimal interpretation of the score is in terms of likening a future individual to groups observed in the past. A prediction of 30 per cent, for example, is identifying the individual with a similar group of subjects in the past of whom 30 per cent had a reconviction within two years. In particular, the four probabilies conditional on sub-sample type cannot be used at their face value in indicating whether risk for a *particular individual* would increase or decrease if the disposal were to be changed.

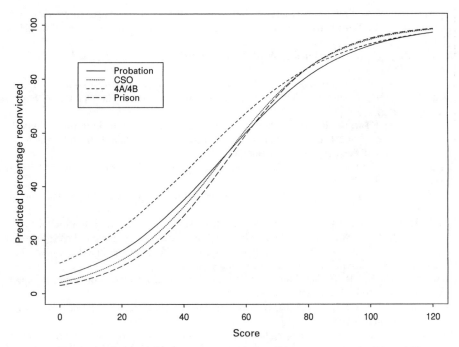

Fig. 11.11. Predicted percentage reconvicted by sub-sample type. (Crown copyright. Reproduced by permission of the Controller of HMSO).

Acknowledgement

The author is grateful for the support and collaboration of staff in the Research and Planning Unit of the Home Office in developing the case study reported in this chapter.

REFERENCES

Aitkin, M., Anderson, D., Francis, B., and Hinde, J. (1989). *Statistical Modelling in GLIM* Oxford University Press.

Baker, R. J. and Nelder J. A. (1978). *The GLIM System, Release 3, Generalized Linear Interactive Modelling.* Numerical Algorithms Group, Oxford.

Barton, R. R. and Turnbull, B. W. (1979). Failure rate regression models for evaluation of recidivism data. *Evaluation Quarterly* 3, 629–41.

Barton, R. R. and Turnbull, B. W. (1981). A failure rate regression model for the study of recidivism. In *Models in Quantitative Criminology* (ed. J. A. Fox), Academic Press, New York.

Burgess, E. W. (1928). Factors determining success or failure on parole. In *The Workings of the Intermediate-sentence Law and the Parole System in Illinois* (ed. A. A. Bruce, A. J. Harno, E. W. Burgess and J. Landesco). Illinois State Board of Parole, Springfield, Ill.

Copas, J. B. (1983). Regression, prediction and shrinkage (with discussion). *J. Roy. Statist. Soc.* **B, 45**, 311–354.

Copas, J. B. (1985). Prediction equations, statistical analysis and shrinkage. In *Prediction in Criminology* (ed. D. P. Farrington and R. Tarling). State University of New York Press, New York.

Copas, J. B. (1987). Cross-validation shrinkage of regression predictors. *J. Roy. Statist. Soc.* **B, 49**, 175–183.

Copas, J. B. (1993). The shrinkage of point-scoring methods. *Applied Statistics* **42**, 315–31.

Copas, J. B. (1994). Criminal prediction scores and survival analysis. *DCLP Occasional Papers* (Forthcoming).

Copas, J. B. and Tarling, R. (1986). Some methodological issues in making predictions. In *Criminal Careers and 'Career Criminals'* (ed. A. Blumstein, J. Cohen, J. A. Roth, and C. A. Visher). National Academy Press, Washington, DC.

Copas, J. B. and Whiteley, S. (1976). Predicting success in the treatment of psychopaths. *Brit. J. Psychiatry* **129**, 388–92.

Cox, D. R. (1972). Regression models and life tables (with discussion). *J. Roy. Statist. Soc.* **B, 34**, 187–220.

Cox, D. R. and Oakes, D. (1984). *Analysis of Survival Data*. Chapman and Hall, London.

Farrington, D. P. and West, D. J. (1990). The Cambridge study in delinquent development: a long-term follow-up of 411 London males. In *Criminality: Personality, Behaviour, Life History* (ed. G. Kaiser and H. J. Kerner). Springer, Heidelberg.

Fitzmaurice, C., Biddle, F., and Stanby, P. (1991). SPS: sentence prediction scale. Research Report, Staffordshire Probation Service.

Glueck, S. and Glueck, E. T. (1950). *Unravelling Juvenile Delinquency*. Harvard University Press, Cambridge, Mass.

Humphrey, C., Carter, P., and Pease, K. (1991). A reconviction predictor for probationers. Research Report, Department of Accounting and Social Policy, University of Manchester.

McCullagh, P. and Nelder, J. A. (1989). *Generalized Linear Models* (2nd edition). Chapman and Hall, London.

Merrington, S. (1990). The Cambridgeshire risk of reconviction scale. Research Report, Cambridgeshire Probation Service.

Miller, A. J. (1990). *Subset Selection in Regression*. Chapman and Hall, London.

Nuttall, C. P., Barnard, E. E., Fowles, A. J., Frost, A., Hammond, W. H., Mayhew, P., Pease, K., Tarling, R., and Weatheritt, M. J. (1977). *Parole in England and Wales*. Home Office Research Study No. 38. HMSO, London.

Payne, R. W. (1987). *Genstat 5 Reference Manual*. Oxford University Press.

Schmidt, P. and Witte, A. D. (1988). *Predicting Recidivism using Survival Models*. Springer, New York.

Simon, F. H. (1971). *Prediction Methods in Criminology*. Home Office Research Study No. 7. HMSO, London.

Statistical Sciences Inc. (1983). *S-PLUS Programmer's Manual, version 3.1*. Statistical Sciences Inc., Seattle, Wash.

Tarling, R. (1993). *Analysing Offending: Data, Models and Interpretation*. HMSO, London.

Tarling, R. and Perry, J. A. (1985). Statistical methods in criminological prediction. In *Prediction in Criminology* (ed. D. P. Farrington and R. Tarling). State University of New York Press, New York.

Ward, D. (1987). *The Validity of the Reconviction Prediction Score*. Home Office Research Study No. 94. HMSO, London.

12 Survey design and interpretation of the British Crime Survey

NATALIE AYE MAUNG

INTRODUCTION

For most of this century, the only source of information on levels of crime has been statistics of offences recorded by the police. However, in the last 20 years an alternative has emerged: surveys of the victims of crime themselves. The origins of victim surveys lie in the USA with the 1967 United States President's Commission on Crime, which recommended the collection of information on experiences of crime from representative samples of the population. As a result, the National Crime Victimization Survey (NCVS), covering individuals in private households, was established in 1972, and continues today.

The first victim survey in the United Kingdom was conducted in London (see Sparks *et al.* 1977). After a small number of other local surveys, the first British Crime Survey (BCS) went into the field in 1982. Subsequent sweeps have been carried out in 1984, 1988, and 1992, and the survey will be repeated biennially from 1992 onwards. Scotland took part in the BCS in 1982 and 1988, but set up its own 1993 Scottish Crime Survey. The establishment of a national survey for England and Wales has coincided with similar developments in other countries, such as Canada, Australia, the Netherlands, and Switzerland. Most victim surveys have been launched as separate free-standing studies, although questions on victimization have sometimes been added to other surveys.

Many other *local* victim surveys have taken place throughout England and Wales since the early 1980s: for example, studies in Islington (Jones *et al.* 1986; Crawford *et al.* 1990) and Nottinghamshire (Farrington and Dowds 1985). This chapter will not deal with local surveys in any detail, although many of the issues addressed below are relevant to them.

Victim surveys belong to the larger family of sample surveys. They collect information from a set of respondents who are representative of some wider population of interest, allowing measures relating to this population to be estimated. As with other surveys, victim surveys aim for *valid* and *reliable* measures: valid in the sense that the questions are meaningful and measure relevant concepts; and reliable in that results are stable (subject to as little error as possible). The reliability issue is particularly important for the BCS as a repeated survey measuring trends in crime.

The problems which arise in designing victim surveys and interpreting their results are, in the main, problems of the survey genre. Sample selection, the level of non-response, and the degree of error attached to survey estimates will be familiar to survey researchers in any field. However, the aim of measuring victimization puts a particular spin on these issues, and they will be considered in that context. The chapter will describe the main features of the British Crime Survey and discuss how aspects of the survey's design affect interpretation of its results. There is discussion of the scope of the survey in terms of the types of people it interviews and crimes it covers. The chapter next turns to issues of sampling error, response errors, and interviewer effects, and then considers how questionnaire design and offence coding may affect the survey results. Finally, it looks at issues of measurement across time and the degree to which the survey statistics can be compared with other sources of information described elsewhere in this book.

MAIN FEATURES OF THE BRITISH CRIME SURVEY

Each BCS to date has questioned a large, random sample of around 10 000 individuals aged 16 and over about offences they have experienced in the last year. Its main purposes are fourfold:

(1)   to provide an alternative measure of crime to statistics of offences recorded by the police, by asking about offences which may or may not have been reported to the police;

(2)   to provide a picture of the *nature* of crime from detailed information on the crimes reported in the interview;

(3)   to provide information on how risks of crime vary for different groups; and

(4)   to take up other crime-related issues.

Results from the latest (1992) survey are reported in Mayhew *et al.* (1993) and technical details of this sweep are described in Hales (1993). In terms of levels of crime, the 1992 BCS showed that for those offence categories which can be compared with recorded offences, the BCS estimate of offences is between three and four times higher than police statistics, although the proportion of unrecorded crime (the 'dark figure') varies across offence types. In terms of trends in crime, and again for those crime categories which can be compared, the BCS suggests a rise in crime of about 50 per cent between 1981 and 1991, as against a doubling of recorded offences. Recorded crime shows a larger rise than the BCS mainly because of increased reporting to the police.

Three survey companies have been involved in the design and fieldwork of the BCS in the four sweeps to date. Social and Community Planning Research (SCPR) did the fieldwork in the first survey; NOP Market Research in the second, and a consortium of both companies in the third. For the latest survey, fieldwork was carried out by a consortium of SCPR and British Market Research Bureau (BMRB) who were heavily involved in the design of the survey.[1] The response rate in 1992 was 77 per cent, the same as in 1988 and 1984, but slightly lower than in 1982 (81 per cent).

---

[1] OPCS carried out the fieldwork for the 1994 sweep of the survey.

The 1992 sample was similar in size to that of earlier surveys, covering a nationally representative sample of 10 059 households in England and Wales.[2] Multi-stage sampling was used (see Hales 1993, for a full description of the sampling procedures).[3] All constituences were designated as inner city or non-inner city (see footnote 3 for the survey definition of inner city); inner city constituencies were subsequently over-sampled by a factor of about 2. All constituencies were listed in the following order: by standard region; population density; and percentage of households in socio-economic groups professional and managerial, other non-manual, and skilled manual. Two hundred and eighty-eight constituencies (70 inner city and 218 non-inner city constituencies) were then chosen at random. (The ordering of the constituencies ensured the sample contained a relatively even spread on the variables used for listing.) Within the selected constituencies, two postcode sectors were selected at random. The chosen postcode sectors were each split into four equal sized notional segments, one 'quarter sector' selected at random, and addresses selected at random within this 'quarter sector'.

In each responding household, one adult was selected at random to be interviewed. All of them answered a *main questionnaire*. This included some attitudinal questions, and then 'screened' people to see if they or their household had been the victim of crime. To maintain consistency, the questions about victimization have remained largely the same in each BCS sweep. Anyone giving a positive answer completed a supplementary questionnaire about the incident, on the basis of which an offence classification was made. Respondents were asked about their own experience and that of others in the household for *household crimes*: burglary, thefts of and from vehicles, bicycle theft, vandalism, and theft from the home. They were asked only about their own experience with respect to *personal crimes*: assaults, robberies, thefts from the person, other personal thefts, and threats. This distinction reflects the fact that for some crimes, such as burglary, the household is a natural unit of analysis, whereas for others the individual is a better choice. The victim survey is therefore in the unusual position of having to provide two different 'samples': one of individuals and one of households.[4]

---

[2] The 1988 and 1992 surveys carried an additional 'booster' sample of Afro-Caribbeans (West Indians and Africans) and Asians (Indians, Pakistanis, and Bangladeshis); 1654 were interviewed in the 1992 sweep. The data reported here refer only to the main sample.

[3] Selecting particular areas (e.g. postal sectors) in which to conduct interviews (rather than selecting addresses at the first stage so that the sample is scattered across England and Wales) keeps down interviewers' travelling time between selected addresses, making workloads more manageable and reducing field-work costs. For the 1992 sample, the following definition of inner city constituencies was used: *either* their population exceeded 50 persons per hectare *or* fewer than 54 per cent of households were owner-occupiers *or* fewer than 1 per cent of household heads were classified as professional or managerial (see Hales 1993, for a fuller description). Because inner city areas are over-sampled, the resulting sample contains too high a proportion of such areas compared to the population. In presenting national estimates, the sample is *weighted* to correct for this imbalance (see also footnote 4).

[4] The 1992 sample was selected from the PAF. Broadly speaking, this gives an equal probability sample of *households*. However, as only one individual is chosen from a household, the sample of *adults* is chosen with probability inversely related to the number of adults in the household (if a household contains one adult, that person is selected for interview with certainty; in a two-adult household, each adult has a fifty–fifty chance of selection, etc.). The resulting sample then under-represents adults in larger households. In analysing adults' risks of crime, the sample is weighted to correct for this imbalance.

Details of incidents revealed by the screener questions were collected in *victim forms*, which provide the basis for classifying incidents. Most victim forms corresponded to one incident, though some covered so-called 'series' incidents, which are discussed later. In 1992, there was a limit of five victim forms. All respondents completed one or other of two versions of a *follow-up* questionnaire, the first containing questions principally about attitudes to sentencing and crime prevention, the second questions about contacts with and attitudes to the police. Personal details were collected from all respondents.[5]

The two main measures of crime risks produced by the BCS are *prevalence* rates and *incidence* rates. Prevalence rates give the number of victims per head of population, regardless of how many incidents each victim may have experienced. Incidence rates (as generally used in this chapter) give the number of incidents per head of population. Because some victims will have experienced more than one incident, incidence rates will always exceed (or at least equal) prevalence rates. (Another measure of crime risk related more specifically to multiple victimization is crime *concentration*: the number of incidents per victim; see, for example, Barr and Pease 1991 for a fuller description.)

THE COVERAGE OF THE BCS

The BCSs – and other victim surveys – are typically limited both in terms of the types of *people* they represent, and the types of *crime* they cover.

The BCS sample

The BCS does not cover all types of potential 'victims' in England and Wales. Some groups are excluded from the scope of the survey, and others will be under-represented in the final sample. These groups may well differ from the sampled population in terms of their victimization experiences, though there has been little quantification of the degree to which this is so.

Sample frame coverage and representativeness

For national studies of individuals and households, there are two frames from which samples may be drawn: the electoral register (ER) and the small user postcode address file (PAF).[6] The former is, essentially, a listing of *individuals* (registered electors); it is largely dependent on self-registration, is only revised every year and dates quickly as it is compiled some months prior to publication. By contrast, the PAF is a listing of *households* (postal delivery points or letterboxes) receiving less than a certain volume of mail. It may exclude some residential households: for example, a self-employed person operating from home who receives a large volume of business mail there.

---

[5] Those aged 16–19 were also given a self-completion questionnaire relating to self-reported offending and drug misuse. Those aged 20–59 were given a self-completion questionnaire covering drug misuse only.

[6] It may also be possible to use council tax registers in the future.

However, the PAF is more comprehensive than the ER, as it is compiled independently of households, and is updated more frequently (every six months).[7]

Until 1988, the BCS used ER samples, switching in 1992 to a PAF sample. Work on the ER (Todd and Butcher 1982) found that it under-represented groups such as the young, movers, and the unemployed, who may be at particularly high risk of crime, and concerns about this had increased with the advent of the community charge. It was thought the change in sampling frame would increase survey levels of crime, as the PAF sample would better cover those high-risk groups that previous ER samples had under-represented. A methodological exercise to test this showed that while the switch in sampling frame did account for an upward shift in crime levels, the impact on rates overall was fairly small.

Business and other corporate bodies

Victim surveys are in general confined to private individuals and their property, and therefore exclude crimes against businesses or institutions (such as local authorities or schools) which are better examined in separate studies.[8] This is partly because neither the (small user) PAF nor the ER cover businesses or institutions to an acceptable degree. But, also, devising an instrument which could cover all types of crime is problematic, and many crimes against businesses or institutions (e.g. shoplifting, vandalism in a school, or credit card fraud against a shop) do not have an 'individual' victim.[9]

Institutional populations

Most surveys, the BCS not excepted, do not cover individuals in institutions (such as hostels, prisons, and residential halls) or the homeless. It is accepted that their victimization experiences could differ, but the complexities of sampling institutional populations make their inclusion in the BCS unfeasible.

Children and teenagers

The 'core' sample of the BCS applies a minimum age of 16 for respondents, and most other surveys have adopted a similar threshold. This is generally considered to be the most acceptable age limit for covering details of household crime, and it avoids seeking parental consent for interviewing children younger than 16, which can add another layer of potential non-response. A further consideration is that a questionnaire used for adults may be unsuitable for use with children. (In the 1992 BCS, children aged 12–15 in responding households *were* partly covered by the use of a separate self-completion

---

[7] The PAF contains a higher proportion of ineligible addresses or 'deadwood' than the ER. The higher the level of 'deadwood', the greater fieldwork costs, as for a given size of *achieved* sample more addresses have to be *issued* to interviewers.

[8] Some of the problems in conducting surveys of business crime are analogous to those of individuals (e.g. identifying who has the necessary information). However, in business crime, it is sometimes difficult to define the *unit* of analysis. For example, is an incident of shoplifting in a supermarket against that particular shop or against the chain to which the shop belongs? The types of crimes experienced by different sectors (e.g. retail and manufacturing) will also vary substantially.

[9] Some commercial or institutional crimes will come up in the course of a victim survey (e.g. the theft of an individual's building equipment, or the owner of a small shop reporting a break-in); these should be excluded in resulting estimates.

questionnaire. A different set of questions on their victimization experiences was devised, thereby precluding any close comparisons with adult crime levels.)

Non-response

It is an inherent feature of social surveys that some households and individuals will be selected for the sample but, for various reasons, will not take part. In the 1992 BCS, around a quarter of the eligible sample (i.e. after 'deadwood' addresses like empty houses or wholly business premises had been excluded) were not interviewed. Table 12.1 shows the reasons for non-response, as recorded by the interviewer. The *main* reason for non-response was a *refusal* of some sort (70 per cent of all non-response); these were mostly direct refusals by the selected respondent, or a refusal to give information about the household needed to select one adult respondent from a household at random. A third of non-response was due to *non-contact* of selected households or individuals.

The level of non-response differs for various groups, and the 1992 BCS can document where the main omissions are since it collected information on area and accommodation characteristics for the whole *issued* sample (Table 12.2). In general, where non-response is higher, proportionately more is made up of non-contacts as opposed to

Table 12.1. Distribution of contacts: 1992 BCS

	All eligible sample %	All non-contacts %
Interview (full or partial)	77	–
All refusal	16	70
Personal refusal by selected adult	8	32
Refusal about numbers of adults in household	4	17
Proxy refusal (on behalf of selected adult)	2	9
Complete refusal of household information	2	7
Broken appointment, no recontact	1	4
Refusal to Head Office	<1	<1
All non-contact	4	18
Contact with household, none with selected adult	3	13
No contact with household	1	6
Other	3	12
Selected adult senile/incapacitated	1	5
Selected adult away/in hospital	1	4
Selected adult had inadequate English	<1	1
Selected adult ill	<1	1
Other	<1	1

Source: 1992 BCS eligible sample (unweighted data).

Table 12.2. Non-response by area characteristics: 1992 BCS

ACORN[a] group	Rate of non-response	% of all non-response		
		Refusal	Non-contact	Other non-response
High risk	30	61	26	13
Medium risk	22	70	18	11
Low risk	22	73	15	12
Inner city	28	65	24	11
Metropolitan	23	75	13	12
Urban	23	69	17	14
Mixed	20	75	14	12
Rural	18	68	21	12
Flats, maisonettes	29	59	28	13
Houses	20	74	14	12
Houses in area:				
mainly/very bad	25	64	23	13
mainly fair	24	67	21	12
mainly good	20	73	14	12
Comparison of respondents' property to others in area:				
worse	33	64	21	16
the same	22	71	17	12
better	16	71	17	12
All	23	70	18	12

[a] ACORN was developed by CACI on the basis of cluster analysis of some 40 variables from the 1981 census including age, class, tenure, dwelling type and car ownership. On the basis of this, each enumeration district in the country (comprising 150 households on average) has been assigned an ACORN code. BCS respondents' census enumeration districts are identified via their postcode. It is important to remember that ACORN categories are not actual areas; rather, they refer to the *type* of area in which groups of individual respondents live. On the basis of analysis of crime risks by ACORN group for the 1984, 1988 and 1992 surveys, the following groups were distinguished:

• *High crime risk* – ACORN groups G (council estates – category III), H (mixed inner city metropolitan areas) and I (high status non-family areas).

• *Medium crime risk* – ACORN groups D (older terraced housing), E (council estates – category I) and F (council estates – category II).

• *Low crime risk* – ACORN groups A (agricultural areas), B (modern family housing, higher incomes), C (older housing of intermediate status), J (affluent suburban housing) and K (better-off retirement areas).

Source: 1992 eligible sample (unweighted).

refusals. Respondents in more urban areas, i.e. those associated with higher levels of crime, are less likely to be interviewed, as are those living in flats. Levels of refusal and non-contact for those living in properties in a worse condition than others in the area are nearly double those for residents in properties in a better condition than others in the area. (The condition of the property was assessed, from the outside, by the interviewer.) Differential non-response means that the interviewed sample will not match the population profile exactly. However, for the attributes in Table 12.2, any under- or over-representation was fairly limited.

While no other individual or household information is directly collected for non-respondents, some population information is available from the census (or national surveys such as the Labour Force Survey). For example, comparisons done for the 1992 BCS indicated that the achieved sample slightly over-represented home-owners at the expense of council tenants, and those in employment at the expense of students. (These differences may not of course be due entirely to non-response.) Representation on the basis of standard region, age of respondent, and ethnic origin was generally good.

The coverage of crime in the BCS

There are a number of limits to the scope of crimes covered. Because of sample exclusions already mentioned, there will be a loss of crimes against organizations (e.g. fraud, shoplifting, fare evasion, commercial burglary, and robbery). Survey offences must also have an identifiable victim who can report them to the interviewer. Homicide is therefore excluded, for obvious reasons. Also excluded are a range of 'victimless' offences (such as drug and alcohol misuse, some public order offences, and consensual sex offences) and crime where people may not be aware of having been victimized, as in an assortment of frauds. (For a fuller discussion of the comparability of police and survey statistics, see the later section 'Comparisons with police statistics'.)

The BCS aims to collect details about offences more or less comparable with legal categories. The survey, and the police, apply legal definitions in classifying and counting crimes; they do not simply accept respondents' definitions of incidents, or indeed necessarily count them at all. In the BCS, any incident that is technically a crime is screened for (the exact techniques and wording of questions used are dealt with below.) On the basis of the victim form information, incidents may be excluded from the final count of survey crime when evidence of crime is lacking, for example, a case where 'suspected burglars' are seen outside a property but never on its premises and there is no sign of a break-in. Otherwise, no threshold of severity is applied. While this means that some incidents initially recorded in the interview are excluded from resulting estimates, it seeks to avoid the more serious (and unquantifiable) problem of eligible incidents not being mentioned. Thus, the survey applies what might be called a *nominal* definition of crime: a count of incidents which according to the letter of the law could be punished, regardless, perhaps, of the value of doing so, and regardless also of whether a lay person would really see the incident as 'crime' as such. The police, in contrast, can be seen as using an *operational* definition of crime: a count of incidents reported by victims which (1) could be punished by a court; (2) are felt to merit the attention of the criminal justice system; and (3) meet organizational demands for reasonable evidence.

Other surveys, e.g. many local ones, the Australian national survey, and the International Crime Survey (van Dijk and Mayhew 1993), leave the task of defining crime to respondents. They use legal or quasi-legal terms in asking screening questions about whether respondents have been 'burgled' for instance, and apply no checks on respondents' definitions. They yield a count of crime, therefore, as defined by the sampled population. Additionally, local surveys in particular are broadening the range of 'crimes' asked about to include incidents of nuisance, malice, and 'low-level' harassment. The rationale for this is that although the majority of such incidents will technically not be prosecutable, some incidents will be considered 'criminal' or troublesome by respondents: this may be more of a consideration in areas such as sexual or racial harassment.

In 'screening' incidents of victimization in the BCS, questions are couched in everyday language rather than using legal terms: For example, the 'burglary' screener reads 'in the last ... months, has anyone got into your home without permission, in order to steal?'. However, the focus on 'crime' in the interview will be evident to the respondent, and their definitions of 'legal crimes' may still play a part in their decision to recall incidents to interviewers. As a corollary of this, incidents which do not fit the 'victim and offender' template assumed by survey designers may not be counted by the respondent as relevant. Take, for example, the case where an 'offender' attacks a respondent 'victim', but in the course of the fight the former is badly hurt, while the latter is uninjured; this may well not be counted by the respondent as relevant.

To sum up so far, then, the BCS cannot claim to provide a measure of the 'true level' of crime in the country. It excludes crimes against businesses or institutions, victimless crimes, homicide, incidents against the very young (aged under 16), and against the homeless or those in institutions. The survey is also likely to under-represent certain groups which, technically, it should cover: e.g. the unemployed, movers, and those in areas with higher risks of crime. In general, poorer coverage is associated with higher crime risk. For those offences that are covered, therefore, estimates of crime levels may – if anything – be understated. That said, on a range of demographic factors for which the sample can be compared to population data, the BCS sample generally represents the population reasonably well.

The BCS definition of 'crime' is dictated by what *can* be prosecuted, and this may not always coincide with a respondent's ideas of what should be. With the exception of threats, the main results of the BCS do not cover 'low-level' incidents which are not strictly illegal, but which may have similar effects to 'crimes'. However, in some areas of study there could well be arguments for including these in a study of 'victimization', and the BCS has itself examined these types of incident on a 'one-off' basis: e.g. verbal abuse at work (Mayhew *et al.* 1989).

SAMPLING AND NON-SAMPLING ERRORS

The information collected in the course of a victim survey will be subject to various sources of error. Some of the main sources of error are discussed below.

Sampling error

A sample aims to be a small-scale representation of the population from which it is drawn. Measures based on this sample will be imprecise, because only a sub-set of the population has been surveyed. Sampling error is a measure of the range of estimates that could have been produced by the particular survey design (if it was used repeatedly).

Since the BCS uses a stratified multi-stage sample, sampling error estimates take account of both simple random sample standard errors as well as complex standard errors – the 'design factor' (or 'deft') being the ratio of the second to the first. Table 12.3 gives 'defts' and 95 per cent confidence intervals for some victimization (incidence) rates as calculated for the 1992 BCS.

Table 12.3. Design factors and 95 per cent confidence intervals: 1992 BCS

Offence	Incidence rate per 10 000 1991	±95% confidence interval	'Deft'[a]
Burglary	678	±90	1.26
Theft from vehicle	1 192	±104	1.15
Theft of vehicle	257	±37	1.09
Vandalism	1 356	±119	1.10
Wounding	154	±46	1.15
Robbery	45	±20	1.17

Notes:
[a] See the text for a definition of the 'deft'.
  Rates for the first four offences are number of incidents per 10 000 households; those for wounding and robbery are number of incidents per 10 000 adults.
Source: 1992 BCS sample. Rates are based on weighted data.

The smaller the level of sampling error relative to the magnitude of the estimate, the sounder the measurement of crime risks. Calculation of sampling error depends, for one, on the size of the sample. The less common an event is, the larger the sample needed to measure it with a given precision. Over the course of a year, experience of crime is rare. For instance, in 1991, only 5.3 per cent of households had been burgled, and 1.0 per cent of adults had been the victim of wounding. The need to estimate risks of particular *offences* for particular groups (e.g. women or the elderly) puts further strain on the 10 000 sample size of the BCS. For this reason, the sample size will increase to 15 000 in 1994.[10]

Sampling error also depends on the degree to which survey design improves the representativeness of the sample, and the nature of the variable under consideration. Crime is unevenly distributed. For instance, in particular types of neighbourhoods, risks of burglary are over twice the average, while young men are about three and a half times more likely than average to have been assaulted in the last year (Mayhew

---

[10] The large sample required makes the BCS costly to mount. Some of the set-up costs are offset by the inclusion of other topics of Home Office interest which would otherwise need separate studies.

et al. 1993). Clustering (e.g. only interviewing within pre-selected areas) tends to increase sampling error. Individuals in a given area will have similar crime experiences to others in their area, not necessarily to the population at large. The areas selected may have unusually high or low crime risks, not typical of the general population. This variation between areas means that the error in measuring crime risks is higher for the complex sample design than for a simple random sample of the same size (shown by 'deft's greater than 1 in Table 12.3). In terms of sample design, the degree to which atypical areas can affect sample estimates is controlled by the *size* and *number* of the final areas taken, and the number of *interviews* conducted within each area. The choice of these three factors will reflect a trade-off between fieldwork considerations and issues of risk measurement. However, survey designs which yield smaller sampling errors are often more costly and take longer to administer. Broadly speaking, techniques which improve the representativeness of the sample reduce sampling error. The sample design must therefore be that which yields an acceptable level of error with manageable costs and procedures.

Response errors

Victims of crime may generally be relied on to give information to interviewers if asked about incidents that the police may not know about, but they may nonetheless give *inaccurate* responses about their own experiences, for a variety of reasons:

1. They might forget about an incident, particularly more trivial ones.

2. They might not know about an incident. For example, respondents may not know (much) about household crimes which primarily involved others in the household.

3. They might remember an incident, but place it inaccurately in time. Incidents could be remembered as happening earlier than they actually did (*backward telescoping*) or later than they in fact did (*forward telescoping*).

4. They might deliberately conceal incidents from an interviewer, or falsify some. Victims of sexual assault or domestic violence may not wish to discuss such incidents with the interviewer. Others may not mention incidents to shorten the interview.

5. They might misunderstand a question. Respondents might be giving accurate responses to the wrong question.

The main way of reducing response errors is through questionnaire design (taken up later). Measurement of the level and seriousness of response error is difficult, and usually requires separate methodological exercises. Clearly, forgetting (1), not knowing (2), and concealment (4) will suppress estimates of crime. Telescoping (3) will threaten risk estimates when it causes incidents in a relevant recall period to be omitted thus reducing estimates, although it may inflate estimates when incidents are erroneously drawn into a recall period (both forms of *external* telescoping). Methodological work (see, for example, Skogan 1981) shows that the net effect of the response biases work, on balance, to *under-count* survey-defined offences, but there will be differential losses across crime categories. In checks where respondents have been asked about offences *known* to have been reported to the police, more trivial crimes (e.g. minor thefts, vandalism, and some assaults) are the ones less likely to be recalled in interview. More serious incidents are disproportionately likely to be captured, and indeed may even be over-counted because more salient events tend to be pulled forward in time (forward telescoping). Overall, memory loss seems to exclude more incidents than 'forward telescoping' includes.

Interviewer and company effects

The respondent is not the only person involved in an interview, and different interviewers might themselves elicit different accounts from the same respondent, because, for instance, they prompt more or less, or appear more or less open to certain responses. Interviewers will also differ in their procedures depending on the training programme of the company they work for.

Table 12.4 looks at incidence rates for the two companies who carried out the 1992 BCS. Sampling areas were allocated randomly between the companies. Interviewers came from the field forces of each company, so that they had undergone separate training programmes; survey briefings were also conducted separately. There was in fact no statistically sound evidence of a 'company effect'; nor was there any suggestion that one company systematically elicited more victimizations than the other. However, 'company effects' may have been smoothed out as the two companies worked jointly on the survey. Whether they undermine comparisons of those sweeps of the survey conducted by other survey companies (or by different personnel with the same company) remains essentially unknown.

To sum up again, then, the point estimates produced by the BCS are often taken to be *exact*, rather than as the 'best guess' available from the survey. It is wise to look at

Table 12.4. Incidence rates, by survey company

Offence	Company A	Company B	Company B/Company A
Burglary	665	691	1.04
Vandalism	1 398	1 315	0.94
Vehicle thefts[a] (owners)	2 409	2 673	1.11
Theft from vehicle (owners)	1 555	1 645	1.06
Bicycle theft (owners)	625	682	1.09
Other household theft	944	883	0.94
Assault	555	618	1.11
Robbery/theft from the person	153	153	1.00
Other personal theft	433	425	0.98

Notes:
[a] Including attempted vehicle thefts.
Differences in incidence rates were tested for statistical significance. None were significant at the 5 per cent or 10 per cent level (two-tailed).
Source: 1992 BCS (weighted data).

them in conjunction with their associated confidence interval, i.e. the range which, with a specified degree of confidence, contains the 'true' estimate. This confidence interval reflects *sampling* error, though it is a moot point whether *non-sampling* response error, or even 'company effects' are a bigger threat to the reliability of the data.

QUESTIONNAIRE AND CODING ISSUES

The BCS and other victim surveys have learnt valuable lessons about measuring victimization and this section now turns fairly briefly to some of these.

Eliciting incidents

The first hurdle is getting respondents to mention victimizations initially. The BCS casts a wide net for incidents with a set of victimization 'screening' questions. These serve to give respondents as many 'prompts' as possible; examples of possible locations are also given to help jog the memory. Victim forms are completed *after* the full set of screening questions (as respondents may 'learn' to say 'no' if every 'yes' is followed by a long set of questions). The separate screener and victim form approach was adopted by the American NCVS (Dodge and Turner 1981). Some local surveys have compromised on this technique, following up 'yes' responses to screening questions with a much shorter list of questions about the incident. There has been no methodological check (to the author's knowledge) of the effect of this on victimization level estimates in this country.

The more screening prompts there are, the more incidents respondents will remember. For instance, since 1982, there has been a general 'assault' screening question in the BCS, intended to cover incidents committed by strangers and people known to the victim; in 1992, an additional screener question specifically prompted for assaults by other household members (although they were not followed up by a victim form). About 320 people mentioned incidents at the general 'assault' screener, of whom 14 also mentioned incidents at the household assaults screener. A further 19 people who had not mentioned incidents at the general screener did so at the household assaults screener. Obviously, screening questions cannot be added endlessly without overburdening respondents, but the fact remains that the number of crimes counted in surveys will depend on the number of prompts for them.

Following up incidents

The vast majority of respondents report no incidents or only one during the previous year, although a few people experience a high number of incidents. To limit the response burden on multiple victims, there is a limit of five on the number of victim forms that can be given (the limit having been four in previous years). In the 1992 BCS, about 4000 people mentioned incidents at the screener questions and so were eligible for victim forms. About 600 had to answer three or more victim forms, of which roughly 100 had to complete five forms.

Recall periods for offences

It is usual to confine the measurement of crime to a fixed and recent 'recall' period. This is both to reduce memory loss and to avoid the problem of evidencing different levels of risk simply because of different periods of exposure (e.g. when asked about 'life-time' victimization, older respondents obviously have more to report). The BCS asks about experiences since the beginning of the previous year. Interviewing is done between January and April, so the recall period is on average about 13–14 months. (In order to produce calendar year estimates, incidents which occurred since the beginning of the year of interview are excluded from analysis.) A recall period of a year is the usual compromise in victim surveys, though the NCVS uses a six-month recall period after tests showing its superiority for risk estimates within a particular calendar year (see, for example, Turner 1981). A period of a year is short enough for respondents not to forget incidents, but long enough to prevent unacceptable levels of external telescoping. It also ensures that more victims will be picked up than with shorter recall periods. (The shorter the recall period, the 'rarer' victimization will be, which brings up those problems discussed earlier in the section on sampling error.)

The BCS sets salient boundaries to the recall period to reduce external telescoping i.e. 'since the 1st January 19...' rather than 'in the last twelve months'. Marking boundaries with *events* may be even more effective. The 1992 BCS asked 12–15 year olds about their victimization experiences 'since the beginning of the summer holidays'. The London survey (Sparks *et al.* 1977) asked respondents about the timing of events such as holidays and birthdays and then related the timing of victimizations to these events. In surveys which incorporate respondent panels (i.e. interviewing the same respondent more than once), such as the NCVS, the previous interview can be used as a starting point for the recall period (and information from this interview used to eliminate double-counting).

Classifying offences

Essentially, there is a choice between accepting the respondent's definition of offences, or collecting other information about the incident to check this or allow a separate classification procedure. As already mentioned, the BCS classifies incidents after the interview on the basis of the detailed information collected in the victim forms. To classify offences, coders look both at a general (open-ended) description of the incident and the responses to pre-coded questions (coding sheets are drawn up for broad offence types containing a list of pre-coded questions to be checked). Close attention is paid to legal criteria in classification and procedures deliberately mirror those followed by the police. Classification on the basis of the more detailed victim form information will also reduce problems of double-counting that may occur within the set of screener questions.

There is a general – though not perfect – correspondence between the final offence code allocated to a victim form and the screener question at which it was elicited. Table 12.5 shows how victim forms arising from three different 'screener' questions were classified. The screeners corresponded to:

Table 12.5. Classification of victim forms (as based on victim form information): 1992 BCS

Screener questions					
Household vandalism	%	Theft of personal property	%	Assault	%
Household vandalism	71.9	Theft of personal property	79.9	Assault	93.2
Attempted thefts[a] no loss incidents	7.5	Vehicle crime	8.6	Robbery	1.6
Vehicle crime	5.7	Theft of household property/burglary	1.9	Threats	1.0
Completed thefts[a]	4.4	Theft from the person	1.3	Household vandalism	0.8
Threats	0.2	Assault	0.3	Burglary	0.8
Insufficient evidence[b]	9.3	Insufficient evidence[b]	1.6	Insufficient evidence[b]	0.3
Out of scope[c]	1.1	Out of scope[c]	6.6	Out of scope[c]	1.4

Notes:
[a] 'Thefts' here comprise burglary, outhouse burglary, and other household and personal theft (excluding theft from the person).
[b] Denotes cases where it is unclear whether offence was criminal or not (e.g. it was possible that loss or damage were accidental in an incident). For household vandalism, this includes cases of *attempted* criminal damage.
[c] Denotes cases which were not covered by the survey (e.g. personal offences against somebody other than the respondent).
Source: 1992 BCS (unweighted data).

(1) a 'household vandalism' question asking whether anyone 'deliberately deface[d] or [did] damage to your house/flat or to anything outside it that belonged to someone in your household?' (previous questions asked specifically about thefts and damage to vehicles);

(2) a 'theft of personal property' screener question which asked whether 'anything of yours [has] been stolen, from a cloakroom, an office...or anywhere else you left it?' (previous questions asked specifically about thefts, and attempted thefts, of items which the respondent had with them, thefts of household property, and thefts from vehicles);

(3) an 'assault' question, which asked whether anyone had 'deliberately hit you with their fists or with a weapon of any sort or kicked you or used force or violence in any other way?'.

Most incidents were classified according to the initial classification suggested by the screener question. However, nearly three out of ten incidents arising from the household vandalism screeners were classified elsewhere, principally in the categories of attempted thefts (mostly attempted outhouse burglaries), vehicle crime (mostly vehicle vandalism), and completed thefts (mostly theft outside the dwelling). In a tenth of cases, there was not enough evidence that an actual crime had been committed. About two out of ten screener 'thefts of personal property' were classified elsewhere, mostly under vehicle crime (the majority being thefts from cars). A relatively high proportion were outside the scope of the survey (these may have involved thefts of property belonging to others in the household).

While some offences are straightforward to code (e.g. a theft of a vehicle from a public car park), others are not. The division between some offences can hinge on detailed criteria (e.g. a theft from a garage with an adjoining door to the house is classed as burglary in a dwelling following police conventions in deciding what a 'dwelling' is; a theft from a non-connected garage is classed under other types of theft). Some offences are potentially classifiable in more than one way: for example, a smashed quarterlight could be evidence of either vehicle vandalism or attempted theft. In some incidents, more than one offence may have been committed (e.g. someone being assaulted in the course of a burglary): following police practice, the BCS allows only one offence code per incident, adopting rules for prioritizing them. Given the plethora of rules for offence classification, classification by a dedicated team of coders (as opposed to respondent or interviewer coding) is most desirable to ensure *consistency* in offence classification.

The BCS questionnaire, then, with its structure of screening questions and victim forms aims to maximize the number of incidents that respondents remember while not over-burdening them. Fieldwork dates are fixed in each sweep to occur at the beginning of the year to give respondents a recall period of just over a year, with a salient starting point to reduce the effects of external telescoping. It is possible that including more prompts and screener questions may elicit more incidents, but there are limits in terms of respondent burden.

The method of classifying offences gives priority to the most 'serious' offence committed at the time, and by using more detailed information about what occurred during the incident allows a tighter legal classification of offences to match police definitions.

ANALYSING THE BCS

Counting crimes

The notion of being able to *count* crimes assumes they are discrete incidents, distinguishable by the respondent. This may not always be the case: for instance an individual may have been threatened repeatedly, and in responding to the survey may have difficulty in establishing how many times this occurred. The BCS defines incidents which are 'very similar...where the *same thing* was done under the *same circumstances* and probably by the *same people*' as *series* incidents. One victim form is completed for the whole series, with detailed questions being asked of the last incident that has occurred. This eases respondent burden and prevents victim forms being 'used up' on very similar incidents.

Incidence rates as quoted in the main BCS publications are based on victim form information. The rates so calculated have two limits on them: first, a maximum number of five victim forms (four, prior to 1992); and, second, a maximum number of five incidents from any victim form referring to a series. The maximum number of incidents that can be experienced by a household or individual is therefore 25 (i.e. five victim forms multiplied by five incidents per victim form). The limit of five incidents in a series was an attempt to impose a more realistic approach to counting series incidents, bearing in mind the need to approximate likely police counting procedures. It also limits the extent to which an individual respondent can sway sample-based estimates of the distribution of risk.

Table 12.6 shows how varying the two limits affects estimates of risks. The *omission* of a fifth victim form generally makes only a small difference to offence rates: mainly in the range of 1–2 per cent. The impact of *adding* a sixth victim form would be even slighter, given the distribution of victimization.

Household offences are generally more affected by the omission of a fifth victim form than personal offences (Table 12.6), although the effect is not large. This is because incidents elicited at the screener questions qualify for victim forms in a pre-specified order (i.e. in the reverse order to the screener question they were mentioned at). The limit of five victim forms will have a greater effect on offences covered earlier in the set of screening questions. The order of the screener questions is: vehicle crime, bicycle theft, burglary and other household theft and vandalism, robbery and theft from the person, other theft of personal property, assaults, threats, and sexual offences. Thus, rarer, personal offences are asked about at the end of the full set.

Doubling the limit of offences *per* victim form can substantially affect those offences of which a high proportion are series, particularly assaults (Table 12.6). These estimates, though, are more unstable as a relatively small number of respondents contribute a high number of incidents. (For example, in the case of assault, one

Table 12.6. Effect on incidence rates of variations in assumptions of (1) the maximum number of victim forms and (2) the maximum number of incidents per victim form

	Incidence rates per 10 000				
	Standard BCS assumptions[a]	Variation I[b]		Variation II[c]	
Burglary	678	668	−1.5%	691	+1.9%
Vandalism	1356	1328	−2.1%	1428	+5.3%
All vehicle thefts[d] (owners)	2541	2472	−2.8%	2562	+0.8%
Bicycle theft (owners)	653	640	−2.0%	656	+0.5%
Other household theft	913	901	−1.3%	943	+3.3%
Assault	586	580	−1.0%	685	+16.8%
Robbery/theft from the person	153	145	−5.2%	154	+0.7%
Other personal theft	429	427	−0.5%	463	+7.9%

Notes:
[a] Standard 1992 BCS assumptions: limit of five victims forms, maximum of five incidents per victim form.
[b] Variation I: limit of four victim forms, maximum five incidents per victim form.
[c] Variation II: limit of five victim forms, maximum of ten incidents per victim form
[d] Includes attempted thefts of and from vehicles.
Source: 1992 BCS (weighted data).

respondent contributed about 5 per cent of the incidents making up the higher rate of 685 per 10 000 adults. Omitting this individual gives a rate of 653 per 10 000.)

The presence of a very small number of individuals who experience a string of very similar victimizations will distort risk patterns for the population in general. Looking at *prevalence* rates rather than *incidence* rates avoids some of the problems and may be preferable for some purposes.

Measurement across time

One use of repeated victim surveys is to look at trends in crime that are independent of trends in reporting to the police (which obviously affect the police-recorded figures). The BCS, having been carried out intermittently since 1982 and now on a biennial footing, provides 'snapshots' of crime at particular points, rather than seamless patterns over time. Ideally, a survey to measure change over time would incorporate some type of 'panel' – interviewing the same respondents over more than one sweep, or sampling from the same areas. This would reduce the level of error with which the trend is measured.

With regard to the BCS, a central question is: do changes in BCS levels of crime solely reflect 'real' changes in crime, and if not, what else can be involved? The BCS may not be immune to changes in the level of reporting incidents to the interviewer. This might occur if there are changes in public sensibility about crime. These may be influenced by changes in 'official' definitions (certain actions may become proscribed by the law, like marital rape) or there may be moves to regard certain criminal incidents more seriously (e.g. domestic violence). For example, survey estimates for the number of incidents of domestic violence against women increased between 1981 and 1991, in contrast to most other forms of violence (Mayhew *et al.* 1993); it is a moot point how far the survey increase reflects real increases, or changes in how willing women are to tell interviewers about such incidents.

There is also the possibility that rises and falls in the level of crime themselves affect the way people regard crime. Arguably, when crime is rare, incidents may be more salient and memorable; when crime is high, respondents may forget more trivial incidents. If this is the case, then we might expect the general level of seriousness of survey incidents to rise in general. This can be tested since, in 1984 and 1992, victims were asked to rate how seriously they thought what had happened to them was, using a 'seriousness scale' where zero represented a very minor crime like theft of milk bottles, and 20 represented murder (Table 12.7). On the basis of these scores, the BCS has seen some increase in the seriousness of incidents. In itself this might indicate either an increasing tendency to forget more trivial incidents *or* to view crime more seriously. The former explanation gets some support from the fact that there were small shifts upwards in other more 'objective' measures of seriousness (Table 12.7).

Obviously, changes in the survey or questionnaire wording may also induce spurious changes in the level of risk. Much effort is taken with the BCS to ensure that the survey remains the same. However, some improvements suggest themselves with

Table 12.7. Seriousness of offences: 1984 and 1992 BCS

	1984	1992
Assaults		
Mean seriousness score	6.1	7.6
% weapon used	19	21
% respondent had broken bones	2	7
% respondent/household member spent night in hospital	2	2
Burglary		
Mean seriousness score	7.1	8.6
% burglary with entry	57	63
% damage (other than damage to get in)	17	20
% violence/threats used by offender	1	3

Source: 1984 and 1992 BCS (weighted data).

experience and in consequence these have invalidated comparisons across sweeps for sexual offences (1982/1984) and theft from the person (1984/1988).[11]

Comparisons with police statistics

Much interest focuses on the 'dark figure' of crime. Offences are not counted in police figures either because they have not been *reported*, or because they have not been *recorded* by the police. However, comparison of the BCS and police figures is not straightforward for a variety of reasons.

Sufficiently reliable comparisons are only possible for a sub-set of BCS offences: residential burglary (including attempts), theft of and from vehicles (including attempts), bicycle theft, criminal damage, wounding, robbery and theft from the person. Additionally, adjustments must be made to the comparable police categories to reflect their (wider) coverage.[12] The main adjustments are to exclude crimes against commercial property and vehicles, and personal crimes against those aged under 16.

---

[11] Between 1982 and 1984, the wording of the sexual screener was altered from asking women whether they had been 'sexually attacked, assaulted or interfered with' to 'sexually interfered with, assaulted or attacked, either by someone you knew or by a stranger'. The rate for sexual offences doubled between the two sweeps (although the higher level is still considered to be a substantial under-estimate). Between the 1984 and 1988 sweeps, there was an artificial decrease of 39 per cent in the rate of theft from the person, due to a change in coding criteria. Since 1988, the questionnaire has asked: 'was [what was stolen] in your personal possession, for example, were you holding or carrying what was stolen?' and this question is checked when classifying offences as 'theft from the person'. Before 1988, the range of offences classed under 'theft from the person' was much wider. In 1994, the BCS switched to computer assisted personal interviewing (CAPI) from the traditional paper-and-pencil methods. Some changes are inevitable, to take advantage of the benefits which CAPI allows. There are general benefits of, for example, customized wording of questions and more complex routing and specific benefits for the BCS such as the automated selection of incidents for victim forms.

[12] Police categories generally cover a wider set of offences than their BCS equivalent, the main exception being bicycle theft. If a bicycle is recovered soon after a theft, the incident may be 'no-crimed'. 'No-crimed' incidents do not appear in police statistics, but for comparison with the BCS figures official police figures are adjusted to take account of them. Police figures for robbery and theft from the person are also inflated for comparison with the BCS, by including offences recorded by the British Transport Police.

(Statistical officers from all 43 police forces were asked to give the (estimated) extent of these adjustments and adjustments made on the basis of their returns.) Overall, the comparable sub-set makes up rather more than half of notifiable offences recorded by the police, and about three-fifths of BCS incidents. Excluded are common assault (not a notifiable offence) and other household and personal thefts, which are recorded under various 'theft' categories.

A comparison of police and survey figures allows estimation of the reporting and recording rates for comparable offence categories; and these have shown the same patterns by offence type across the years. The rates should be regarded as 'best guess' estimates only, because of (sampling and non-sampling) error in the survey measures, and the possibility of mismatches in police and BCS classifications. (While the BCS coding procedures follow the same rules as those of the police, these rules are by no means hard and fast. It is possible therefore that some BCS incidents will have been recorded under a different police category to the one indicated by the survey classification.) Those offences that are less often reported to the police will generally be those which the victim regards as too trivial or not amenable to police action. However the survey count of *unreported* crime is not simply a count of incidents 'not worth worrying about': a good number of unreported incidents are judged to be serious (see, for example, Mayhew *et al.* 1993, p. 27). Table 2.2 (p. 12) and Table 4.1 (p. 49) give a summary of some of the findings of the BCS.

On balance, certainly, surveys count a broader set of incidents than police statistics, and indeed they need to if they are in the business of trying to detects shifts in reporting and recording practices over time.

To sum up, offence rates as calculated in the BCS are limited by certain assumptions, some reflecting questionnaire design decisions, such as the number of victim forms completed. The limit set on the number of incidents counted *per* victim form may have a greater impact than that on the number *of* victim forms for some offences, although rates may become unstable if the limit is increased. This may affect measurement of trends across time. While the measurement of BCS trends is relatively safe from artificial shifts induced by changes in methodology, changes in survey levels of crime over time may still reflect things other than genuine shifts in the rate of crime. However, for those crimes it measures, BCS figures still provide a better trend measure than police statistics, and certainly the only quantification of changes in reporting and recording. As more rounds of the survey have been done, increasing use has been made of its ability to illustrate how far trends in police figures are the result of such changes.

END NOTE

This chapter has concentrated mainly on the counting of BCS crime categories which are more or less comparable to legal ones. However, the BCS can be used to look at alternative classifications of 'victimization'. For one, it can collect information on victimization on the boundaries of, or outside, the area of legal intervention (e.g. threats). In addition, the detailed information collected about victimizations for classification purposes allows the construction of crime classifications which do not necessarily reflect legal categories, but which are nonetheless of interest to the public and policy-makers. Past BCS analysis has, for example, looked at sub-categories of violence, such as domestic assaults or sporting violence, and crime in and around the home. The BCS also has the potential to track backwards types of crime which may emerge in the future as categories of interest (for example, 'carjacking' incidents).

REFERENCES

Barr, R. and Pease, K. (1991). A place for every crime and every crime in its place. In *The Distribution of Crime* (ed. D. Herbert, D. Evans, and N. Fyfe). Gower, Aldershot.

Crawford, A., Jones, T., Woodhouse, T., and Young, J. (1990). *The Second Islington Crime Survey*. Centre for Criminology, Middlesex Polytechnic, London.

Dodge, R. W. and Turner, A. G. (1981). Methodological foundations for establishing a national survey of victimisation. In *The National Crime Survey: Working Papers*. Volume I: *Current and Historical Perspectives*. US Department of Justice, Bureau of Justice Statistics, Washington DC.

Farrington, D. P. and Dowds, E. A. (1985). Disentangling criminal behaviour and police reaction. In *Reaction to Crime: the Public, the Police, Courts and Prisons* (ed. D. P. Farrington and J. Gunn). John Wiley, Chichester.

Hales, J. (1993). *1992 British Crime Survey Technical Report*. Social and Community Planning Research, London.

Jones, T., MacLean, B., and Young, J. (1986). *The Islington Crime Survey*. Aldershot, Gower.

Mayhew, P., Elliott, D., and Dowds, L. (1989). *The 1988 British Crime Survey*. Home Office Research Study No. 111. Home Office Research and Planning Unit, London.

Mayhew, P., Aye Maung, N., and Mirlees-Black, C. (1993). *The 1992 British Crime Survey*. Home Office Research Study No. 132. Home Office Research and Planning Unit, London.

Skogan, W. G. (1981). *Issues in the Measurement of Victimisation*. US Department of Justice, Bureau of Justice Statistics, Washington DC.

Sparks, R. F., Genn, H., and Dodd, D. J. (1977). *Surveying Victims*. John Wiley, London.

Todd, J. and Butcher, B. (1982). *Electoral Registration in 1981*. Office of Populations Censuses and Surveys, HMSO, London.

Turner, A. G. (1981). The San Jose recall study. In *The National Crime Survey: Working Papers*. Volume I: *Current and Historical Perspectives*. US Department of Justice, Bureau of Justice Statistics, Washington, DC.

Van Dijk, J. and Mayhew, P. (1993). *Criminal Victimisation in the Industrialised World: Key Findings of the 1989 and 1992 International Crime Survey*. Directorate of Crime Prevention, Ministry of Justice, The Hague, Netherlands

Index

Index compiled by Ann Barham